THE FRENCH REVOLUTION IN THEORY

Reinventing Critical Theory

Series Editors:
Gabriel Rockhill, Associate Professor of Philosophy, Villanova University
Jennifer Ponce de León, Assistant Professor of English, University of Pennsylvania

The *Reinventing Critical Theory* series publishes cutting edge work that seeks to reinvent critical social theory for the 21st century. It serves as a platform for new research in critical philosophy that examines the political, social, historical, anthropological, psychological, technological, religious, aesthetic and/or economic dynamics shaping the contemporary situation. Books in the series provide alternative accounts and points of view regarding the development of critical social theory, put critical theory in dialogue with other intellectual traditions around the world and/or advance new, radical forms of pluralist critical theory that contest the current hegemonic order.

Commercium: Critical Theory from a Cosmopolitan Point of View
   Brian Milstein
Resistance and Decolonization
   Amílcar Cabral—Translated by Dan Wood
Critical Theories of Crisis in Europe: From Weimar to the Euro
   Edited by Poul F. Kjaer and Niklas Olsen
Politics of Divination: Neoliberal Endgame and the Religion of Contingency
   Joshua Ramey
Comparative Metaphysics: Ontology After Anthropology
   Pierre Charbonnier, Gildas Salmon and Peter Skafish
The Invention of the Visible: The Image in Light of the Arts
   Patrick Vauday—Translated by Jared Bly
Metaphors of Invention and Dissension
   Rajeshwari S. Vallury
Technology, Modernity and Democracy
   Edited by Eduardo Beira and Andrew Feenberg
A Critique of Sovereignty
   Daniel Loick—Translated by Amanda DeMarco
Democracy and Relativism: A Debate
   Cornelius Castoriadis—Translated by John V. Garner
Democracy in Spite of the Demos: From Arendt to the Frankfurt School
   Larry Alan Busk
The Politics of Bodies: Philosophical Emancipation With and Beyond Rancière
   Laura Quintana
Domination and Emancipation: For a Revival of Social Critique
   Luc Boltanski and Nancy Fraser—Edited by Daniel Benson
Zero-Point Hubris: Science, Race, and Enlightenment
   Santiago Castro-Gómez—Translated by George Ciccariello-Maher and Don T. Deere
The French Revolution in Theory
   Sophie Wahnich—Translated by Owen Glyn-Williams

THE FRENCH REVOLUTION IN THEORY

SOPHIE WAHNICH
Translated by Owen Glyn-Williams

ROWMAN & LITTLEFIELD
Lanham • Boulder • New York • London

Published by Rowman & Littlefield
An imprint of The Rowman & Littlefield Publishing Group, Inc.
4501 Forbes Boulevard, Suite 200, Lanham, Maryland 20706
www.rowman.com

86-90 Paul Street, London EC2A 4NE

English translation copyright © 2022 by The Rowman & Littlefield Publishing Group, Inc.

Originally published in French as *La Révolution française n'est pas un mythe*
Copyright © Klincksieck, Paris 2017

All rights reserved. No part of this book may be reproduced in any form or by any electronic or mechanical means, including information storage and retrieval systems, without written permission from the publisher, except by a reviewer who may quote passages in a review.

British Library Cataloguing in Publication Information Available

Library of Congress Control Number: 2021944957

ISBN 978-1-78661-617-3 (cloth) | ISBN 978-1-78661-619-7 (epub) | ISBN 978-78661-618-0 (paperback)

For Régine

CONTENTS

Introduction: The French Revolution Is Not a Myth: Satre, Lévi-Strauss, Foucault, Lacan, and Us   1

Part I: The French Revolution as an Object for Sartre   11

1. How Did the French Revolution Become an Object for Sartre?   13
2. Working with Historical Details against the Fetishization of the Real   25
3. No Longer Dissolving the Real Actors of the French Revolution   41
4. Restoring the Role of the Sacred   53
5. Apocalypse and Fraternity-Terror   63
6. The Question of Dialectical Time, or the Inanity of the Notion of the Rearguard   75

Part II: Rebuking Sartre and His Final Humanist Object: The French Revolution under Scrutiny   97

7. Three Humanities in One: European, Colonized, Savage   103
8. Finishing a Book, Concluding a Discussion   119
9. Michel Foucault and the French Revolution: A Misunderstanding?   133
10. The French Revolution: Between the Archaeology of Knowledge, Discursive Formations, and Social Formations   147

11	On the "Iranian Revolution": Retrieving the Missed Object, with Foucault and Despite Foucault	*163*
12	"The French Revolution as Matrix of Totalitarianism": The Enigma of a Bizarre Statement	*177*
13	Sade and the Ethical Fold of the French Revolution	*193*
Conclusion: Clearing Some Foggy Patches		*211*

INTRODUCTION

The French Revolution Is Not a Myth: Sartre, Lévi-Strauss, Foucault, Lacan, and Us

> "For contemporary man to fully play the role of historical agent, he must believe in the myth of the French Revolution."[1]

We have to admit that this belief of the "historical agent" has been inactive for a long time. The French Revolution, as revolutionary and as French, is a repressed historical moment, reduced to amusing signage displaying the edge of a guillotine, Phrygian caps, and three national colors that are either an object of suspicion or overinvestment. It is thus folklorized, instrumentalized, and deactivated as a fulcrum for exigent political and theoretical reflection. Nevertheless, when Claude Lévi-Strauss writes this phrase, which appears in his 1962 *The Savage Mind* in polemical response to Sartre's *Critique of Dialectical Reason*,[2] they are both responsive to political and theoretical exigency, and each knows his French Revolution with an impressive degree of precision.

VALUE OF MYTH, VALUE OF TRUTH

This investigation aims first to understand, over fifty years later, the past and present stakes of the debate between Lévi-Strauss and Sartre over the French Revolution. The French revolutionary sequence does indeed occupy a large place in the *Critique of Dialectical Reason* and its preparatory

---

1 Claude Lévi-Strauss, *The Savage Mind* (London: Weidenfeld and Nicolson, 1966).
2 Jean-Paul Sartre, *Critique of Dialectical Reason* (London: Verso, 2004).

prolegomena. However, I also seek to understand, for my generation, the stakes of its forgetting: forgetting the *Critique of Dialectical Reason*, its vertiginous undertaking, and the avalanche of responses it provoked, an avalanche that no doubt contributed to its foreclosure.

Neither Sartre nor Lévi-Strauss, at least consciously, guided my historical work on the French Revolution, which began around the time of the bicentenary. I did not encounter them until recently, thanks to a work on Sartre and the history of the French Revolution.[3] I humbly admit that up until that moment, I had not been aware that Sartre was so intensely interested in it.

Nevertheless, this polemic was not entirely unfamiliar territory for me. Without a doubt, it continued to inhabit the debate of the bicentenary years (1985–1995). This debate pitted the so-called Jacobin (so as to avoid being called Marxist or communist) history of the Sorbonne against the "Critical" history of the EHESS,[4] which, ever since the publication of Francois Furet's and Denis Richet's respective volumes on the French Revolution in 1965 and 1966, fought against Marxist historiography, and Albert Soboul in particular. The bicentenary debate, which determined studies of the French Revolution and their dissemination through universities, schools, and society in general in France and beyond, opposed two historiographical currents rooted in the debates of the 1960s.

The "Jacobins" were assumed to uphold what Claude Lévi-Strauss calls "the myth of the French Revolution," that is, a narrative that allows a social group to ascribe meaning to its actions. The self-proclaimed "critical" historians of the EHESS presented themselves, with much condescension, as the critical judge of this myth and the presumed practitioners of the "true" science of history.

This "critical" position was informed by the Sartre–Lévi-Strauss polemic. Hence, François Furet's famous "revolutionary catechism," published in 1971 in response to the Marxist historiographical critique of his work with Denis Richet and reprinted in *Interpreting the French Revolution* in 1978, set the stage. He effectively paraphrased Lévi-Strauss in his criticism of the position of the Marxist historiographical current: "If the historian continues to believe (in the political stakes of his work) it is because he has to: imaginary participation in political struggles is as comforting to the

---

3 First (2008), Miguel Abensour upon the publication of *La Longue Patience du peuple, 1792, naissance de la République* (Paris: Payot, 2008). He asked me why I had not been referencing Sartre. He then pointed to Lévi-Strauss's response to Sartre as a gateway. Michel Kail later asked me to reflect on the manuscripts published in the *Revue des études sartriennes* for a conference (2009). These two instigations were foundational to this work.

4 *École des* hautes études en sciences sociales.

scholastic as it is illusory. It delivers maximum psychological satisfaction with minimum disturbance."⁵ Furet continued to speak of "the exercise of a residual shamanic function." But what did Lévi-Strauss say after qualifying the French Revolution as a myth? "This truth [of myth] is a matter of context, and if we place ourselves outside it—as the man of science is bound to do—what appeared as an experienced truth first becomes confused and finally disappears altogether."⁶

In order to distance themselves from the situation, the "critical" historians drew more from the historiography of the French Revolution than from the event itself. To a certain extent, they reconstructed what Lévi-Strauss calls the "historian" as one "who strives to reconstruct the picture of vanished societies as they were at the points which for them corresponded to the present."⁷ But for Furet and those in his orbit, it meant reconstituting the stages of development of a historiography.

In the 1980s, this division of places and methods for "doing the history of the French Revolution" had become caricatural and exaggerated, itself contingent and rooted in the situation. Of course, scientific and critical distanciation was not absent from the Sorbonne approach because Marxism was itself already critical, engaged in debates between differing currents including the Althusserian current, which struggled with this mythical function without renouncing political commitment. Conversely, a mythical function was evident in the work being done at the EHESS, but this myth took the shape of putative scientific neutrality deployed in defense of an anti-totalitarianism buttressed by the Solzhenitsyn event (1974) and the liberal conceptions of the "second left." The argument from "true science" became the myth that allowed to pass as true what was in fact a thoroughly political position defended with great ardor: a liberalism that drew its strength from the anti-communism of the moment.

This is why the time has evidently come to interrogate anew both the value of myth and the value of truth in today's historical work. This also involves working as a quasi-ethnological historian to make sense of how we got from Lévi-Strauss's claim in the 1960s that "[t]he so-called men of the Left still cling to a period of contemporary history which bestowed the blessing of a congruence between practical imperatives and schemes of interpretation,"⁸ to today's leftist who frequently rejects the revolutionary period as obsolete and reduces it to the invention of the parliamentary

---

5 François Furet, "Le catéchisme révolutionnaire," *Annales* ESC, no. 2 (1971): 256.
6 Lévi-Strauss, *The Savage Mind*, 254
7 Ibid., 256.
8 Ibid., 254.

system, economic liberalism, and colonialism. Lévi-Strauss was thus lucid in claiming that "[p]erhaps this golden age of historical consciousness has already passed." Yet he strikes me as much less lucid in his adoption of the mere passage of time as an explanatory mode: "That this eventuality can at any rate be envisaged proves that what we have here is only a contingent context like the fortuitous 'focusing' of an optical instrument when its object-glass and eye-piece move in relation to each other. We are still 'in focus' so far as the French Revolution is concerned, but so we should have been in relation to the Fronde had we lived earlier."[9] The frequent rejection of the French Revolution by some on the left, and its reevaluation by some on the right would seem to me to owe little to the passage of time, but much to a specific set of efficacious arguments, as scientific as they are political. Moreover, I venture to say, this prediction may be turned around with new developments.

Certainly, "we" no longer know where we stand on the French Revolution. But could we know, and under what conditions? To what extent can reading Sartre's *Critique of Dialectical Reason* open paths, or at least allow them to be reflected?

These fifty years enable us to observe, not an ineluctable estrangement from knowledge of the French Revolution, but robust variation in relation to it according to what Lévi-Strauss calls the contingency of the situation. "We" will attempt to stake out a position vis-à-vis the French Revolution when the situation demands it.[10] Relatively recent events gathered under the banner of the "Arab Spring," for instance, led to a recirculation, sometimes with many doubts, of the concept of revolution,[11] a concept which has decreased in value since the Cambodian disaster, among other tragic events associated with the concept. Jean-Claude Milner's *Re-Reading the Revolution*[12] attests to a renewed interest, and it is not alone. Prior to these events, some more faint signs had already indicated a renewal of interest in

---

9 Ibid.
10 Thus, the large-scale work carried out on the first abolition of slavery on 16 Pluviôse Year II, in a social and political context where it was a question of having the slave trade recognized as a crime against humanity. We have indicated in the book titled *Les Émotions, la Révolution française et le present* (Paris: CNRS, 2009), how the development of this focal point could intuitively be part of the work of the historian of the French Revolution.
11 Comparisons and analyses flourished; let us point out for the record the dossier coordinated by Guillaume Mazeau and Jeanne Moisan on the site of the *République des livres*, the book published under the aegis of the CVUH and the IHRF titled *Pourquoi faire la Révolution?* The section of the journal *Socio* coordinated by Boris Pétric and Pénélope Larzillière titled *Révolutions, Contstations, Indignations* (Éditions de l'EHESS, 2013).
12 Jean-Claude Millner, *Relire la révolution* (Lagrasse, Verdier, 2016).

this particular historical object.[13] A variety of contemporary social actors[14] appear to sense the necessity of seizing the sharp edges of an event which for them, despite everything, remains tied to a foundational and emancipatory imaginary. In their case, the either intense or faint interest in the object would reflect more of a moving adjustment than a natural estrangement. It would articulate this mythical function that one could more simply call the social function of historical consciousness, and a discourse of "the man of science".

And yet, if it is possible in this way to affirm the French Revolution as a contemporary political object, and thus reject the ensemble of discourses which portray it as decidedly unfashionable, if not wholly expired in light of a changed world, we must also recognize that since the 1960s it has become and remains, for a part of the political left, a source of ambivalence.

Doubtless, Lévi-Strauss's critique of Sartre introduces a modality of this ambivalence, in the form of an epistemological reflection on historical knowledge as scientific or mythical. In essence, Lévi-Strauss claims that "it does not follow that [. . . mythical] meaning, just because it is the richest (and so most suited to inspire practical action), should be the truest."[15] The quest for the "truth" was thus made incongruent with the quest for meaning, and it became imperative to know if history should produce meaning or genuinely scientific knowledges.

In fact, the object "French Revolution" appears at the heart of the upheaval around historical knowledge, which, like the Revolution itself, appears today as at once antiquated and impossible to establish scientifically, impossible to purify of its mythical dimension. Some ask, what is the point of history? While others reaffirm that—faced with the crises of the present—the need to grasp history is greater than ever, even if it comes from a place of belief.

---

13 In the introduction to our cowritten book, *Histoire d'un trésor perdu, transmettre la Révolution française*, we invoke *Les Onze* by Pierre Michon (2009), Sylvain Creuzevault's show *Notre terreur*, performed in 2009 and 2010, but before the bicentenary, one could also mention the work of Claude Simon, *Les Géorgiques*.

14 Hence the theater once again takes hold of texts that reflect the event in an explicitly past/present relationship. In spring 2014, Irène Bonnaud made her conservatory students work on Büchner's *Danton*, the Aubervilliers theater programmed Holderlin's *Hyperion* for the 2014-2015 season. The fall of 2005 saw the appearance of three theatrical performances on the French Revolution in Paris: one under the direction of Marcel Bozonnet titled *Soulèvement(s)*; one at the Amandiers in Nanterre under the direction of Joël Pommerat etitled *Ça ira, fin de Louis*; the other under the direction of Anne Montfort titled *Révolution(s)*, in a collaboration between a Portuguese author, a German author and a French director. But knowledge of the French Revolution is also pursued by a number of civic and even political associations.

15 Lévi-Strauss, *The Savage Mind*, 254.

It is this ambivalence and rejection, against the backdrop of the dismissal of history as useful for life, and the rejection of the salience of the French Revolution that I wish to address in this examination.

THE STRANGE BICENTENARY BATTLE

Is "wish" the right word? Does that not imply aspiring to understand that which escapes you, traveling a circular route with new and unexpected encounters, encounters which give the impression that something is becoming clear? Let us clarify, therefore, the statements that functioned as leitmotivs throughout the bicentenary years. When François Furet claimed that "the French Revolution is finished," his detractors and adversaries responded: "The Revolution is not a cold object." Once the French Revolution became, again according to Furet, the "matrix of totalitarianism," challenges to this peculiar statement were scarcely heard.

Following the lively debates of the bicentenary years, interpretive routines maintained their presence in *basso continuo*. But they were difficult to understand and decipher for those who, entering the profession, were at a remove from the luster of their origins. For my generation, the battle of the bicentenary unfolded in a patch of fog.

The idea that political divides were playing out, as is usual with the French Revolution,[16] does not suffice as an explanation of the configuration. It is expected that the division of positions on the French Revolution pit a counterrevolutionary right against a left inheritance of the Revolution. Throughout the 1980s, there was certainly a virulent right wing, which, shoulder to shoulder with Pierre Chaunu and Ronald Sécher, invented the notion of "Franco-French genocide" and extended the assimilation of the French Revolution and quasi-Nazi totalitarianism. More striking still, however, are the dividing lines among those on the left. Michel Foucault, during the Iranian revolution and counterrevolution, was allied with François Furet, the only historian of the French Revolution whom he declared respectable, because "critical." Yet Foucault embodies rebellion and Furet, a certain establishment. If the question of how to do the history of the French Revolution—with what archives and what questions—is primarily a matter of knowing which historian can claim the mantle of producer of "critical knowledge" and escape the commemorative and trite view of

---

16 *Contra* Jean-Clément Martin, "À propos du 'génocide vendéen.' Du recours à la légitimité de l'historien," *Sociétés contemporaines* 39, no. 1 (2000): 23–38.

history, this can only be a kind of stopgap for an age that seems to no longer know what to make of its revolutionary history.

If the notion of "critical" history is in fact the disputed concept, and has been unduly appropriated by some, those who claim its mantle against the communists, Jacobins, and Marxists are referred to by the latter as "revisionists." The word "revisionist," which emerged from Albert Soboul's 1974 response to François Furet, is ill chosen. History should always be revisited and therefore revised, and "revisionist" is primarily associated with denial of the Nazi extermination of the Jews. At the same time, tying the French Revolution to Stalinist totalitarianism in this way is to fabricate semantic regimes of equivalence between objects and practices that cannot be rendered synonymous.

Nevertheless, while the statement "the revolution is finished" was in part tied to the Sartre–Lévi-Strauss debate, the claim that the French Revolution is the matrix of totalitarianisms does not seem to me to have emerged out of that debate. The effort to make Nazism and Stalinism equivalent under the guise of totalitarianism occurred downstream of another construction of equivalence—another relativization, if you will—which renders quasi-interchangeable the enjoyment (*jouissance*) of doing good and the enjoyment of doing evil. "Kant with Sade," Lacan tells us, in the same intellectual milieu as the debate between Sartre and Lévi-Strauss. What was he saying in stating "Kant with Sade"? This will have to be addressed.

But in fact, for other subsequent psychoanalysts, the Revolution shares with totalitarian societies the cultivation of the unitary social link, which is to say a link that derives from the desire for "One," for faultless unity realized through a death drive, any alterity having become dangerous. This unitary link compresses the mind and annuls the space for play, which is necessary for democratic invention. For Jacques André[17] the Revolution is "fratricide." For Jacques Derrida,[18] it is "*parégicide.*"[19] In all cases, it is cruel and as a result is undifferentiated from all cruel political situations. Certainly, the Terror is also one of the focal points of Sartre's *Critique of Dialectical Reason* because the "pledged group," as a group that is formed to some extent by fraternity, solidifies and produces this Terror. Here too there are knots to observe, to understand. In fact, psychoanalysis, like Marxism, was a central concern for Sartre, who saw it as an interrupted theoretical site:

---

17 Jacques André, *La Révolution fratricide. Essai de psychanalyse du lien social* (Paris: PUF, 1993).

18 Jacques Derrida, "Psychoanalysis Searches the States of Its Soul: The Impossible Beyond of a Sovereign Cruelty," in *Without Alibi*, ed. and trans. Peggy Kamuf (Stanford: Stanford University Press, 2002).

19 Jacques Derrida's neologism.

"After a spectacular beginning, psychoanalysis has stood still."[20] Its Lacanian revival could not have left him indifferent.

In the end, however, the rejection of the Revolution as a matrix of totalitarianism was only made in terms of a necessary utopia.[21]

From 1948, the anti-totalitarians of the left effectively claimed that only utopian experience could put an end to the totalitarian experience. Yet Miguel Abensour—recalling the words of Edgar Quinet, "the French Revolution brought back faith in the impossible"—has never stopped asserting that the experience of the French Revolution forms a part of these unfulfilled and necessary utopias.[22] This response, which was based on the German Marxist tradition, had trouble clearing a path. "Utopia" under the Marxist and communist conception marks a flight from effective material and social reality, and the Sorbonne was generally not amenable to it. The most radical historians, who without claiming to be left anti-totalitarians, criticized the portrayal of the French Revolution as bourgeois and placed special emphasis on theories of natural right and right to existence that crossed all the social groups of the revolutionary period, were often dismissed for their supposed "utopianism."[23] But it is not only here that the opposition between the left anti-totalitarians and communists was anchored. It was also based on the place assigned to the concept of progress. Where the anti-totalitarians of the left criticize this notion by asserting the discontinuity of historical time and even its possible bankruptcy, the communist historians (and those rooted in communism) often claim progress as their credo. They assert that whatever is not situated on this temporal line comes from mere "anticipations." What was thought out during the French Revolution in advance will happen in its time of "progress". The line of time, therefore, does not at all look the same—broken, interrupted, discontinuous, forming complex rings and folds for some. For others, continuous and ineluctable, tending toward a better world.

In any case, the bicentenary had opened with the need to honor the great event and manage the legacy of the revolutionary period. It unfolded by undermining, more and more with the passing of each day, the aim of the transmission.

---

20 Jean-Paul Sartre, *Search for a Method* (New York: Vintage, 1968), 28.
21 See the preface to Miguel Abensour and Anne Kupiec, eds., *Œuvres complètes de Saint-Just* (Paris: Gallimard, 2004).
22 Miguel Abensour, *Utopiques 1: Le procès des maîtres rêveurs, Utopiques 2: L'homme est un animal utopique* (Paris: Sens et Tonka, 2013).
23 As occurred with Guy Robert Ikni or Florence Gauthier.

EPISTEMOLOGICAL ANAMNESIS

By accepting the invitation extended to me twenty years later immerse myself in the intellectual debates of the 1960s—political, philosophical, historiographical, and epistemological debates—it appeared possible to rediscover what had disappeared in the 1980s at a kind of crossroads.

In no way do I claim to be able to substitute for the philosophers and specialists I encounter here: Jean-Paul Sartre, Claude Lévi-Strauss, Michel Foucault, Jacques Lacan. Engaging as a historian of the French Revolution in the debates that profoundly transformed my field and my object of study, I want to show how these debates were formed and unraveled and in fact produced ambivalences and doubts concerning the very value of the event of the "French Revolution." These debates disseminated traces, constellations of agreements and disagreements on the value of the French Revolution and how to examine it.

Moreover, there will be no claim to exhaustiveness in this work. Rather, it will seek to make the most of a few encounters and clarifications[24] so as to better understand how the intellectual history of the French Revolution transformed throughout the 1960s and 1970s: to understand the effects of this transformation on theories of history, politics, and revolution starting with the bicentenary and following it in its aftereffects. And I seek to understand these effects in order to propose, for us today, a way (or ways) to recapture these threads. As a result, this work will have been for me a kind of epistemological anamnesis.

If we are attempting a critique of the ideas at work in the debates of the 1960s and 1970s, and the 1980s and 1990s, it is essential that we do not content ourselves with this critical posture, rather seek to understand how, today, this legacy can be turned to our advantage: on the one hand, for our renewed interest in revolutions and their emancipatory stakes, and on the other—similarly to the left anti-totalitarians—to find weapons against the repetition of what horrifies us in our faltering democracies.

---

24 With this aim in mind, only texts referenced in the footnotes have been consulted and worked on.

I

THE FRENCH REVOLUTION AS AN OBJECT FOR SARTRE

1

HOW DID THE FRENCH REVOLUTION BECOME AN OBJECT FOR SARTRE?

During the 1980s, a university course on the French Revolution could leave you completely ignorant of Sartre's reflection on the revolutionary period.[1] Yet there were numerous Marxist teachers of the history of the French Revolution. But they were more often situated in the shadow of this historical object. Manifestly, this Marxism had not absorbed the Sartrean critique of a particular impoverishing use of Marxist categories in the study of history. Beyond what can be reduced to quarrels within the field of Marxism, this missed encounter has deep roots in the French historiographical tradition. Between the field of historical studies and the study of philosophy, a manufactured barrier has held strong. Not that philosophy was really absent when it came to the French Revolution, inasmuch as the proximity of Enlightenment philosophy made Mably, Locke, Rousseau, Kant, Fichte, and many others not only admissible but also sources forming a part of the archive. But the interest of twentieth-century philosophers in work on an eighteenth-century historical object had long appeared more difficult to legitimize, as if reading philosophy as a historian made one suspected of yielding to a useless and cumbersome philosophy of history. On the question of poaching categories and breaching presumed boundaries separating modes of thought, the philosophers recoiled in turn. But can we focus merely on segments of Sartre's work without betraying him? And if they are segments, historians renew their questioning: Can we put Sartrean categories to work without committing the crime of anachronism?

It is nonetheless possible, within this dual constraint, to acknowledge a fact: the French Revolution was very much an object of Sartre's reflection, an object therefore caught up in a philosophical conception that is indeed

---

[1] This was true of me until Miguel Abensour questioned me on the subject.

anachronistic and interpretive, and caught up in an extremely lively intellectual and political debate with major consequences for the imaginaries that would come to surround this object.

EXITING WAR, ENTERING THE COLD WAR

Histories of the French Revolution have all been marked by the historical and political conditions of their writing. But in reverse, philosophers think by reading historians rather historical sources, and the ways of conceptualizing the history of the French Revolution are therefore dependent on these historical conditions and available historiographies. There are thus close connections between historical, political, philosophical, and historiographical conditions for the production of a thought on the French Revolution.

The particular historical period of the postwar years to the 1960s informed Sartre's theoretical pursuits, his view of the French Revolution, and his political engagement.

The experience of the war effectively gave rise—almost everywhere and particularly in France and its colonial empire —to a desire for social and political justice, demands for individual and collective freedom, and the reconciliation of Revolution and democracy. The intellectual world of the left was rethinking the concept of commitment (*engagement*) in light of the war. Jean-Paul Sartre then occupies a decisive place, imploring us not to dissociate the individual and collective stakes of the struggle. He and Merleau-Ponty assert this in *Les Temps Modernes*. The individual cannot be free alone, but individual freedom should not, as a result, be neglected. He also expresses this view in his *What Is Literature?*, published in 1947 in the periodicals of several parties, and again under the title *Situations II*, with Gallimard in 1948. He thus states:

> We must at the same time teach one group that the reign of ends cannot be realized without revolution and the other group that revolution is conceivable only if it prepares the reign of ends. It is this perpetual tension—if we can keep it up—which will realize the unity of our public. In short, we must militate, in our writings, in favour of the freedom of the person *and* the socialist revolution. It has often been claimed that they are not reconcilable. It is our job to show tirelessly that they imply each other.[2]

---

2 Jean-Paul Sartre, *What Is Literature and Other Essays*, Cambridge, MA: Harvard UP, 1988, 223.

To show that this reconciliation is possible, Sartre chooses to make of the object "French Revolution" a sort of laboratory-situation. The Revolution could indeed be a fulcrum for rethinking the foundations of democracy and reinscribing the collective subject of Freedom in History. Doubtless, the colonial situation (from 1945 on) and the Cold War hampered the power of its exemplarity, diminishing the inherited principles of the French Revolution. Yet far from being obliged to renounce the necessity of revolution, for him, this particular historical situation rendered this necessity more poignant. Each of us knows well that during the war and at its end, the French Revolution was at once an anti-Vichyist and communist point of reference. We must therefore examine it up close so as neither to be the pawn of the communists nor to abandon this event, which, according to Sartre, reconciles individual freedom with the work and realization of collective freedom.

In one and the same movement, Sartre worked on the *Critique of Dialectical Reason* and tested his thought in the primary materials and sources of the French Revolution. He felt the need to return to the archive, or at least to sources on the revolutionary *initium* of May–June 1789, and to what he already considered the revolutionary aporia: the Terror, which he analyzes through the figure of Joseph Le Bon. Indeed, he begins by writing a screenplay in the 1950s on this character from the Terror.

But Sartre's testing of his thought is not limited to the archive or to artistic creation as a specific praxis. It consists of a continual back-and-forth between theory, the archive, and the political moment that provides empirical reserves for his notion of "praxis." This work aims at political action and, in Sartre's terms, the need for History to "give itself its own Enlightenment."[3]

In fact, the political positions that punctuate the work that unfolded from the end of the war to the 1960s obey a particularly tumultuous sequence. The revolutionary investments of the years between 1945 and 1947 took place in an assessment of the war, but the situation was transformed in 1947 by the exit of Communist ministers from the government of France. Then, in 1956, the subduing of Hungary by Stalin's tanks had a startling effect on many communists and fellow travelers.

Thus, when Sartre seeks to overcome what he calls the "Marxist vulgate" by refocusing on the precise facts from the revolutionary moment and seeking, through the minutiae of historical analysis, to produce another way of looking at the French Revolution, the stakes of his work and its relation

---

3 "se donner ses propres Lumières."

to the present shift. The first task is to enlighten oneself within the communist and revolutionary world, and subsequently to enlighten oneself in the face of the Stalinist side of communism. Hence, in seeking to produce other analytic categories for apprehending the revolutionary event, Sartre is in fact inscribed in a political and historiographical conjuncture in which he finds himself caught between his anti-Marxist right side and his Marxist left side.

THE FRENCH REVOLUTION ALREADY EXPOSED TO CRITICISM

In general, eminent Anglo-Saxon historians refused the fetishized categories of "Bourgeoisie" or "Feudalism," which, according to them, obstruct a true understanding of the revolutionary event. On the side of Marxist historians, an international constellation[4] of them worked on popular movements, revolutionary crowds, political militants, and on the social structures of the eighteenth century, in the name of a research itinerary defined in large part by Georges Lefebvre and Renest Labrousse and deploying the aformentioned categories.

The most important among the detractors of French revolutionary history is American historian Alfred Cobban, who taught at the University of London. On March 6, 1954, he delivered a public lecture—heard by the ambassador of France, among others—titled "The Myth of the French Revolution," which indulged a loose conflation of the event as such and its historical narrativization. The Anglo-Saxon critique denies the active potential of the French Revolution and turns its heroic story into a fable. For Cobban, the reign of Louis XVI was a period of reforms that the Revolution did little more than continue. According to him, feudalism no longer existed in the eighteenth century, with mere fragments remaining of the political system based on the landed gentry and seigneurial levies. He asserts that, far from being bourgeois or capitalist, the Revolution is first and foremost an aristocratic revolt carried out by royal officers living as nobles, who did not seek to establish capitalism but to gain power and position in the royal court.

In a 1956 article titled "The Myth of the French Revolution," published in *Annales historiques de la Révolution française*, George Lefebvre

---

4 Richard Cobb and George Rudé (UK), Johachiro Takahashi (Japan), Walter Markov (GDR), Käre Tonnesson (Norway), Galante Garrone and Armando Saitta (Italy), Victor Daline (USSR), and Albert Soboul (France) are the major Marxist figures from international congresses. They published their work from 1958–1961, thus contemporaneously with the drafting of Sartre's *Critique* and his archival work.

responds to Cobban. He replies scientifically, demonstrating that feudal rights had not disappeared, and that the *seigneur* still owned the "reserve" and ceded the rest of the land for ground rent and levies. What the men and women of the eighteenth century called "feudalism" was all these rights and a series of privileges: financial exemptions, property transfer taxes, police rights and honorary rights, hunting, fishing, and dovecote privileges, and so on. While Lefebvre accepted some of the advances in social history indicating that the bourgeoisie was composite, he also reaffirmed that the French Revolution opened the way for capitalism by proclaiming economic freedom and sacralizing property. All the while refusing simplistic argumentation, he concludes on a political note, evoking the Sorelian myth of the general strike as projection toward the future, and suggesting that the French Revolution remains a similarly mobilizing myth. If the notion of myth is ambiguous in Cobban, referring mainly to the banal idea of narratives which merely obscure historical truth, Lefebvre's evocation of Sorel opens the path for a more anthropological interpretation of the concept.[5]

By appropriating the historical object "French Revolution," Sartre wishes to oppose this double perspective on myth: that which denies Marxist historiography and sows doubt as to the status of the event as a rupture, and the one which claims that effective politics may need myths. For Sartre, it is a matter of producing knowledge in order to act, but not, for all that, a knowledge that disregards the truth. Dialectical reason must accommodate both the exigency of truth and the urgency of action. The aim of the *Critique of Dialectical Reason* is to provide an idea (*pensée*) of the dialectic of situations which is simultaneously a dialectic of the past and the present, and thus of knowledge and praxis, a dialectic of the freedom of subjects and the constraints that weigh on their actions, a dialectic of the most lucid possible praxis. From within this dialectic of reason in action, he asserts that history is always at once the history of a situation and the History of humanity as a whole, that every event carries this History of humanity.

---

5 *Archives Ina* (http://www.ina.fr/video/I06290910): "Myths are the stories that people tell themselves or hear told and that they consider as having no author, [. . .] stories incorporated into the collective inheritance by having been repeated and transformed through these successive repetitions, and by means of which every society tries to understand how it is made, the relation of its members with the outside world, and the position of man in the universe as a whole. So these are stories that tend to be grounded in what happened at the beginning of time, the reason things are the way they are. [. . .] The peculiarity of myth [. . .] is to give a global interpretation, in other words, to locate in a single matrix, [. . .] the reason why [. . .] the sun is at a good distance, [. . .] incest is forbidden, [. . .] and a whole range of intermediate problems [. . .], it is a type of explanation which tries to make all the problems which can arise for man contribute to a single model of explanation."

The objective is extremely ambitious: totalization as History, and History as the Truth of Man. As such, History for Sartre can be understood both as a political anthropology and as an analysis of the effects of a living philosophy-world, namely that of Marxism reinvented. Before publishing the *Critique* in 1960, Sartre had elaborated the methodological stakes of this ambition in his *Search for a Method*. In the latter, he criticizes what he calls "vulgar Marxism." The French Revolution thence becomes a Sartrean preoccupation because it was first a Marxist preoccupation. However, to criticize Marxism, Sartre feels compelled to return to his flagship objects. Yet this text, *Search for a Method*, not only explains objects and methods, but it also describes a subjective trajectory, a way of posing oneself in the world, that of Sartre and a part of his generation.

NAÎTRE ENFIN À UN MARXISME MORIBOND

Search for a Method is often presented as a work which is occasioned by specific circumstances, and it was in fact written at the request of a Polish journal. Published in 1957, it was reissued in 1960 as a synthetic foreword to the *Critique*. Nevertheless, responding to a request can also coincide with the right opportunity to give form to a thought, a position. In this text, Sartre questions his own trajectory, from his student years in the 1920s to the man shaped by the postwar era.

He recalls that when his generation was counseled to read Marx while studying at university, it was in order to be able to refute Marxism. In 1925, even communist students were very careful not to risk their grades by exhibiting dialectical reasoning. Not even Hegel held his rightful philosophical place in the university curriculum. It is nonetheless in this context that Sartre claims to have read *Capital* and *The German Ideology*, to have felt as if he understood everything, and only realized long after that he did not have the lived experience of the world which would allow him to truly understand this philosophy: "It took the whole bloody history of this half century to make us grasp the reality of the class struggle and to situate us in a split society. It was the war which shattered the worn structures of our thought. War, Occupation, Resistance, the years which followed . . . we finally understood that the concrete is history and dialectical action."[6] To understand, he said, "is to change, to go beyond oneself."[7]

---

6 Jean-Paul Sartre, *Search for a Method* (New York: Vintage, 1968), 20.
7 Ibid., 18.

Nevertheless, the evidence of having become a Marxist does not lie in a free subjective position. Sartre claims to have been drawn toward this philosophy "as the moon draws the tides."[8] That which he will call "practico-inert" is already king vis-à-vis the illusion of freedom. And the "practico-inert," here, is the power of attraction of Marxism as an effective philosophy-world in the context of the war and the postwar period.

From the outset in this text, and through his own life experience, Sartre seeks to understand how people forge their lives—given the practical human desire to govern over matter and transform it into "worked matter"—while restricted by this very worked matter, which nevertheless determines them.

Sartre considers ideas —like things —as worked matter. They are both domains of the practico-inert. Marxism, as a force of attraction, belongs to the domain of worked matter. Marxism as a force of attraction belongs in this register of worked matter. Thus, the method and the project of the *Critique of Dialectical Reason*, as an attempt at a living reappropriation of Marxism, are presented from the outset as necessitating biographical reflexivity. It is the movement between a text and a lived experience of the world that makes it possible to change oneself, and thereby in Sartre's words to become a man, this being who is "characterized above all by his going beyond a situation, and by what he succeeds in making of what he has been made."[9] Changing one's place in the world and the changing the world do not mean being under the illusion of a perfectly free will. The individual is "made" by the practico-inert, and operates with this given. No synthetic knowledge can be preconstructed, it can only come from experience and a lived history. Understanding one's history and the history made by humans is therefore a matter of experience. In either case, no one is free because no knows the history they are making. Nobody knows this because nobody can know the constraints of the practico-inert which governs us and upsets the objective of our actions.

But before explaining that the world, as it was, had produced this change in him, transforming the student shaped by Aristotelian training into a man of his time—that is to say, a Marxist—Sartre had also explained that he viewed Marxism as a veritable philosophy, distinct from ideology.

This philosophy, which he calls a "philosophy-world," is "a totalization of knowledge, a method, a regulative Idea, an offensive weapon, and a community of language, this 'vision of the world' is also an instrument

---

8 Ibid., 21.
9 Ibid., 91.

which ferments rotten societies, this particular conception of a man or of a group of men becomes the culture and sometimes the nature of a whole class."[10] He adds that a philosophy becomes "the humus of every particular thought and the horizon of all culture."[11] This is why, with respect to certain philosophies, "there is no going beyond [them] so long as man has not gone beyond the historical moment which they express."[12] This is the meaning of Sartre's assertion that Marxism is "the one philosophy of our time which we cannot go beyond."[13] As long as the conditions that engendered it have not been surpassed, as long as "the yoke of scarcity" has not been overcome, Marxism will remain the philosophy-world. And it is because of this friction of the world, and the tragic feeling engendered by its lived contradictions, that one becomes a Marxist, more so than the reading of Marxist texts or even one's decisions. It is therefore in this undecidable back-and-forth between the world and philosophy that makes a philosophy a philosophy-world. "By its *actual* presence, a philosophy transforms the structures of knowledge, stimulates ideas: even when it defines the practical perspectives of an exploited class, it polarizes the culture of the ruling classes and changes it."[14]

His praise of Marxism is thus connected to a very specific conception of philosophy: "born from the movement of society, it is itself a movement."[15] Hence, "a philosophy remains efficacious so long as the *praxis* which has engendered it, which supports it, and is clarified by it, is still alive."[16] Philosophy is not supported by itself alone. It is sustained by relations with the world that, at first, it merely translates and formalizes, and if its adequacy is strong, it becomes-world (*devient monde*): product *of* the world, effective force *on* the world.

Now, as much as it remains unsurpassable, for Sartre, because the yoke of scarcity has not been surpassed, it is this movement itself which Marxism appears to have lost. Sartre evokes a Marxism which is "arrested," no longer nourishes, and can no longer learn anything. In his view, a separation of theory and praxis has destroyed the force of Marxism, because "concrete thought must be born from praxis and must turn back upon it in order to clarify it."[17] It is this movement that is no longer unfolding, depriving

---

10 Ibid., 6–7. Translation altered.
11 Ibid., 7.
12 Ibid.
13 Ibid., xxxiv.
14 Ibid., 17.
15 Ibid.
16 Ibid., 5–6.
17 Ibid., 22.

Marxism of its vital and heuristic character, its capacity to bind itself to the analysis of concrete situations, or what Sartre calls "singular totalities."

The "free becoming of the truth with all its discussions and all the conflicts it involves" has been replaced by a scholasticism of totality which has dispensed with detail, forcing meaning onto certain events and retaining only "unchangeable, fetishized 'synthetic notions.'"[18] The production of Marxist knowledge consisted of clearing a path in the unknown, which made the truth appear through repeated trial and error, which required the production of categories and concepts that in turn require examining the world so as to understand it without relying on a pre-constituted total theory.

On the one hand, empirical investigation of the world seems futile if the ambition of future theoretical production no longer guides inquiry. But if we only have recourse to a theory which precedes observation, Knowledge (*Savoir*) is frozen.

In such a situation where Marxism has become an idealism detached from the concrete, even material experience can be denied. As Sartre ironically says, "Budapest's subway was real in Rakosi's head. If Budapest's subsoil did not allow him to construct the subway, this was because the subsoil was counter-revolutionary."[19]

Sartre's way of going over with a fine-tooth comb the different ways that 1950s Marxists analyzed the world was read as an attack on the communist party, largely because he had, in fact, broken with the PCF (Parti Communiste Français) after the entry of Soviet tanks in Hungary. However, his criticism is not aimed solely at one political entity but at a manner of reflecting, analyzing, thinking, and reducing the world to fetishized categories. It is all Marxists, and not just those in the PCF, who are seen to be lacking dialectical competence. This is why he also refuses the Trotskyist interpretation of the invasion of Hungary, which they described as "Soviet aggression against the democracy of the Workers' Committees." Sartre explains that these "Committees" did not yet exist at the time of the first Soviet aggression. They only emerge in their infancy during the resistance. What does this falsification of history consist of? "[T]hey reject the equivocal givens of experience," which "could only lead one astray,"[20] in favor of two simultaneous operations: "conceptualization and passage to the limit."[21] Which concepts? Soviet aggression becomes "Soviet bureaucracy,"

---

18 Ibid., 27
19 Ibid., 23.
20 Ibid., 24.
21 Ibid.

the committees, "direct democracy." For Sartre, these are "general singularities," which have become fetishized when discourse endows them with real powers. What therefore disappears is the precise analysis of the situation. Certainly, such analysis is insufficient on its own. But it enables the "synthetic-interpretive reconstruction," which is the proper terrain of the dialectical relation between theory and the analysis of concrete experience. According to Sartre, this operation became a "simple ceremony." "The heuristic principle—'to search for the whole in its parts'—has become the terrorist practice of liquidating the particularity."[22] "Discarding detail," "forcing meanings," "distorting facts," "inventing them so as to ultimately achieve eternal knowledge": all operations which dismay the Jean-Paul Sartre who is committed to factual truth. By becoming, in Lukács's terms, a "voluntaristic idealism," this Marxism no longer had any connection with historical and dialectical materialism.

THE ALLIANCE OF MARXISM AND EXISTENTIALISM

This is how Sartrean existentialism, because of its attention to concrete things, becomes a philosophy allied with a living Marxism. "Existentialism, like Marxism, addresses itself to experience in order to discover there concrete syntheses."[23] But these syntheses should never become frozen. They are conceived within a moving, dialectical totalization which is nothing else but History. Hence Sartre calls History "philosophy-becoming-the-world."[24] Truth is never given once and for all. It is in motion because it is thought confronted by experience, itself in motion. Thus, for Sartre, History is "a never-ceasing movement of totalization."[25] This is why each generation can speak of "History," because "Particular facts . . . are neither true nor false so long as they are not related, through the mediation of various partial totalities, to the totalization in process."[26] Which is why there is no history other than contemporary history. Knowledge is always in motion in its ceaseless effort at totalization, which is never a pre-given, frozen totality, but on the contrary, a totality which is undone and recomposed to the rhythm of the moving situation in the face of which the effort to think it unfolds. "Totalization" is therefore a practice of theoretical reflection in

---

22 Ibid., 28.
23 Ibid., 30.
24 Ibid.
25 Ibid., 170.
26 Ibid., 30–31.

action. It leans on praxis and the experience of facts. In this ceaseless process that is the very effort of thought to know and to understand, uncertainty reigns. And yet thought constantly aims to reduce this uncertainty through the effort to be *of* this world, rather than the world of Platonic ideas.

Within this handful of brilliant and precise pages, Sartre thus shows that his effort to hold Marxism and Existentialism together does not arise from a desire for theoretical prowess, but rather consists of a search for the means of exiting a hopeless situation. How could one not despair of a philosophy which is dead and yet unsurpassable? "[A]fter liquidating the categories of our bourgeois thought, [Marxism] abruptly left us stranded."[27]

It is in historical detail—that of yesterday and that of today—rather than readymade categories, that Sartre affirms the possibility of retrieving the lived world. And this lived world is what Existentialism brings to Marxism and what enables it to come alive again. From the third page, Sartre invokes the French Revolution to explain his point of view.

THE FRENCH REVOLUTION AS LABORATORY-SITUATION

The French Revolution now literally inhabits the Sartrean text, beginning with *Search for a Method*, where it appears to function as an obvious and telling example. Next, in *Critique of Dialectical Reason*, it is an object of study, a genuine laboratory for the analysis of the group, of the oath, of fraternity, sovereignty, fear, and terror, and no longer simply the object of a discussion with Marxist historians. But even before assuming its place in the *Critique of Dialectical Reason*, the French Revolution is analyzed, original materials in hand, in two manuscripts: "Mai–juin 1789," and "Liberté-Égalité." These works of a philosopher-historian, which remained unfinished as such, nevertheless remain highly instructive, revealing how this historical laboratory allowed Sartre to put his concepts and method to the practical test. The manuscripts are now accessible,[28] and analyzing them enables us to better understand the back-and-forth between the detailed analysis of the lived-fact and the theoretical text on practice.

The editing and republishing of these writings sheds light on how Sartre thought of the revolutionary moment with his own tools. But they can also, in my view, help historians of the revolutionary period to better

---

27 Ibid., 21.
28 "*Sartre inédit avec les manuscrits 'Mai–juin 1789' et 'Liberté-Égalité,*'" under the direction of Jean Bourgault and Vincent de Coorebyter, *Études sartriennes* no. 12 (2008).

understand how their subject was perceived within the intellectual, historiographical, and political debates of the 1960s. In these texts, the principal categories of the *Critique of Dialectical Reason* are put to work, allowing us—armed with patience and courage—to enter the vast conceptual jungle of the *Critique,* inhabited by the revolutionary ring. They encourage us to apprehend for today the French Revolution as Sartrean object in a dialectic of situations: that of the moment Sartre is seized by it, the one in which he is criticized, and our current moment, in which we can revisit the French Revolution as an object of Sartrean reflection.

There are thus several ways, and on different occasions, that the French Revolution becomes a preoccupation of Sartre's. On the whole, they constitute an assertion—against Alfred Cobban and even Georges Lefebvre, against fetishized Marxist discourse—that the French Revolution is not a myth but a very real event carried out by real people rather than allegories. They assert that writing the history of this event necessitates seeking to understand it in the back-and-forth of the archive, revealing the most concrete details to a theory that always remains to be readjusted in light of these details, these particularities, these singular experiences that nonetheless continue to speak to us.

When Sartre looks to the French Revolution, informed by postwar revolutionary necessity, he asks himself questions which were already those of the revolutionaries of 1789–1794. How does a society reach the point of wresting itself from its inertia? How can an emancipatory rupture be effectuated both individually and collectively? How is this rupture rendered irreversible? Finally, what is the place of violence in this wresting movement and revolutionary consolidation? These are the questions that lead him to look to the past and present of history, or in Sartre's terms, to knowledge and praxis. It seems to me that these remain the questions which make the study of the French Revolution necessary —for both knowledge and praxis —since the revolutionary question and the counterrevolutionary question are again contemporary.

2

WORKING WITH HISTORICAL DETAILS AGAINST THE FETISHIZATION OF THE REAL

The French Revolution appears with force in *Search for a Method* as Sartre approaches the problem of mediations. He is searching for a new method for History as true knowledge (*connaissance*). Because his goal is to revive Marxism, his historical analysis aims at escaping conceptual fixity and reintroducing movement by focusing on historical details. His criticism of what he calls vulgar Marxism consists in demonstrating that Marxist historical thought contents itself with situating historical objects without actually analyzing them. Instead, it imposes *a priori* concepts which are not drawn from experience. Hence the famous "conceptual fetishes," dead and deathly because immutable. The work of Marxist historians appealed to in the *Critique of Dialectical Reason* is therefore presented as largely disqualified—hence why Sartre leans on the Revolution itself, reading voraciously and analyzing certain available documents himself. As a result, he does not approach interpretations of it as simply a philosopher, but as a historian-historiographer. More precisely, his historiographical intervention is of critical importance to the larger philosophical argument. The disciplinary distinction is shattered at the moment that the discipline of "history," history as people's lives in the present and history as "philosophy-becoming-the-world," are both intermeshed. In this criticism of vulgar Marxism, the question of ideology is decisive.

THINKING EMANCIPATION, REFLECTING IDEOLOGY

Even before tackling the historiographical debate, which becomes the basis of an epistemological debate, Sartre bases his reflection on a French Revolution that functions as a site that must be visited if one seeks to address the question of emancipation. This is why the first "philosophy-world" described in *Search for a Method* is the one which allows us to understand the revolutionaries' manner of thinking and acting: Cartesianism. In the eighteenth century, this philosophy had, according to Sartre, become a tool of collective emancipation that not only inspired philosophers, but permeated all of society and especially the Third Estate. And not only the bourgeoisie but also the working-class milieus (*milieux populaires*) that Sartre describes as having been "infiltrated" by this philosophy. The use of "universal Reason" means, he argues, that "the immediate response of the oppressed to oppression will be *critical*."[1] This critical response, common to the bourgeoisie and the lower classes, is on the one hand, conducive to collective emancipation and, on the other, to concealing social contradictions under a common language. Language is at once a lever and a lock, the preeminent site where contradictions are tied and untied. Revolutionary languages are therefore contradictory and complex, and it is this complexity that makes them a very particular practico-inert. Language is thus not simply mediation, but that which allows us to both extricate ourselves from and be trapped by the repetition of history.

For Sartre, language raises the question of the efficacy of ideology, within each of us and in "every endeavor of spirit"—within what he calls a cultural system. A cultural system, he says, is "an alienated man who wants to go beyond his alienation and who gets entangled in alienated words; it is an achievement of awareness which finds itself deviated by its own instruments [. . .] It is at the same time a struggle of thought against its social instruments, an effort to direct them, to empty them of their superfluity, to compel them to express only the thought itself. [. . .] [T]he idea must be considered to be both the objectification of the concrete man and his alienation."[2] As a result, time must be spent apprehending the subjective meanings of the words used by a thinker, rather than merely situating them, because what matters is understanding how words divert and are displaced, and how contradictions in thought express the contradictions and struggles of contemporary ideologies. Sartre takes the example of the Marquis de Sade: "Sade's thought is *neither* that of an aristocrat nor that of a bourgeois; it is the lived hope of a noble, outlawed by his class, who has found no means of expressing himself except through the dominant concepts of the rising class, and who made use of these concepts by perverting them and by distorting himself through them."[3] The language of

---

[1] Jean-Paul Sartre, *Search for a Method* (New York: Vintage, 1968), 6.
[2] Ibid., 115.
[3] Ibid., 116.

the Enlightenment is not entirely suited to what Sade seeks to articulate, but it nevertheless allows him to say that he does not represent his class but rather those who are fighting against it, even if they do not have the same ultimate aims. By alienating this language for his particular ends, by diverting it, Sade is able to escape the aristocracy, to disalienate himself. He is able to move—hence why it is worth having an analytical ear for the use of words. The singular movement of history—individual or collective—passes through their use.

For Sartre, "the instruments of praxis" are always shifting in relation to the effort at disalienation. "History is cunning" because it is made in part behind the backs of the speaker (*l'énonciateur*), who has their subjective intentions displaced by a cultural system. From his actions spring an objective situation which has no connection to his intentions. Individuals are always caught in unique conflicts, which cannot be reduced "to the universality of a class ideology."[4] For all that, the ensemble of individuals does not constitute what Luckács—against whom Sartre fights hard—calls a "carnival of subjectivities" because each subjectivity is of its time. From the outset, the individual appears as a singular universal who at once embodies the universality of class and the singularity of a cultural appropriation of ideology.

For Sartre, "It must be understood that whatever an ideological project may be in appearance, its ultimate goal is to change the basic situation by becoming aware of its contradictions."[5] This ideological project is born of "a particular conflict which expresses the universality of class and condition, it aims at surpassing it in order to reveal it, to reveal it to make it manifest to all, to manifest it in order to resolve it."[6] But between the emergence of conflict and this resolution, there are mediations which can either help it advance or create obstacles. Most often, though, they do both at once, as is the case with language.

Thus, in my view, the dissociation of individual and group is not possible for Sartre. The individual who attempts this "coming to consciousness" (*prise de conscience*), that is to say, allows themselves be gripped and articulated by the contradictions that inhabit them, enables these contradictions to be dialecticized (*dialectiser*) and hence surpassed. Subjectivities are therefore not individualities but entities through whom the collective speaks even in their individual effort to make this speech at once unique and universal, even while trapped in the glue of language.

---

4 Ibid., 115.
5 Ibid., 112.
6 Ibid.

Mediations and discursivity are therefore a node in which asymmetrical antonyms proliferate: emancipation/alienation, subjective individuality/individuality as incarnation of a social class, ideology as intentional mystification/ideology as the power of the unintended. Language is not neutral and simply at our disposal. As the Althusserian historians of the 1970s would say, language is not transparent. Insofar as the latter cultivate discourse analysis as a political tool—a theory and methodology for ideological and political analyses[7]—they are quite close to what Sartre claims here.

SARTRE AS CRITIC OF DANIEL GUÉRIN AND THE CONCEPT OF THE BOURGEOIS REVOLUTION

Sartre tests the theoretical stakes of his claims by carefully critiquing Daniel Guérin's book, *Class Struggle in the First French Republic*.[8] In Sartre's view, "Despite all the mistakes (due to Guérin's wish to force history), it remains one of the few enriching contributions that contemporary Marxists have made to the study of history."[9] In spite of its redeeming qualities, and the extent to which Guérin can be distinguished from classical communists, he is nevertheless vilified for his outrageous oversimplification. Against Guérin's desire to reduce politics to the social, Sartre vigorously defends the analysis of political praxis. "[I]t would be a poor Machiavellian who would reduce the ideology of 1792 to the role of a simple cover-up for bourgeois imperialism."[10] When Sartre discusses Guérin's interpretation of the French revolutionaries' entry into war in 1792—activating the Anglo-French commercial rivalry—he demonstrates that the operation and function of warmongering language cannot be reduced to social and economic reductionism or "economism." Sartre is very familiar with this moment in 1792,[11] and for him, the entry into the war springs from Girondin political

---

7 I am of course thinking of Régine Robin's masterful and foundational thesis, *La Société française en 1789, Semur-en-Auxois* (Paris: Plon, 1970), of her great book *Histoire et Linguistique* (Paris: Armand Colin, 1973), but also to the work of the *l'équipe de Saint-Cloud*, who produced the *Dictionnaire des usages sociopolitiques du français pendant la Révolution française*, under the direction of the Althusserian Jacques Guilhaumou.
8 Daniel Guérin, *Class Struggle in the First French Republic* (London: Pluto Press, 1977).
9 Jean-Paul Sartre, *Search for a Method* (New York: Vintage, 1968), 37.
10 Ibid., 43.
11 It does not seem possible to me that the only moments that interested Sartre were 1789 and the Terror, *contra* Claude Mazauric, *Études sartriennes* no. 14 (2010), and in Mazauric, Claude. "Sartre et l'histoire de La Révolution Française." *Études Sartriennes*, no. 14 (2010): 99–123. Sartre knew the entire French Revolution well, and is capable of taking critical positions on an impressive number of objects of revolutionary history. He was really interested in detail, as one can be interested in the daily details of their own time.

praxis, that is to say, "their wish to submit the populace whom they despised to the enlightened elite of the bourgeoisie (that is, to confer upon the bourgeoisie the role of enlightened despot)."[12] The operative terms are those of a "verbal radicalism," a "practical opportunism," which led Brissot to plunge France into war through a naïve Machiavellianism: "We have need of great treasons."[13] Sartre recalls the facts leading up to this: "The king's flight, the massacre of the Republicans at the Champ-de-Mars, the shift to the Right on the part of the moribund Constituent Assembly and the revision of the constitution, the uncertainty of the masses, who were disgusted with monarchy and intimidated by repression, the massive abstention on the part of the Parisian bourgeoisie (10,000 voters as compared with 80,000 for the municipal elections)."[14] All of this, he argues, speaks in favor of a political interpretation of the war, rather than an exclusively social and economic interpretation, which would be insufficient for understanding the historical movement of the revolution. We must therefore reject, Sartre tells us, "apriorism" and "economism," and not forget that politics "*by itself* had a social and economic meaning, since the bourgeoisie was struggling against the bonds of an ancient feudalism."[15] The transformation of economic structures, he maintains, cannot be considered the intended goal of the warmongers in their 1792 call to arms. Only a detailed understanding of the (admittedly complex) motivations of individual and group actors allows for the comprehension of revolutionary history. And during the revolutionary period, these motivations are first of all political, even if the structures are both political and economic. "[I]f one totalizes too quickly, if one transforms—without evidence—signification into intention, and result into an objective deliberately aimed at, then the real is lost."[16] When Sartre asserts that "we must at all cost guard against replacing real, perfectly defined groups (*la Gironde*) by insufficiently determined collectivities (the bourgeoisie),"[17] it is the very notion of "bourgeois Revolution" which is ultimately being criticized. He therefore affirms, in this very movement, that this criticism applies not just to right-wing figures like Cobban, but consists of a rejection of all attempts to pass off theoretical knowledge as an analysis of the situation, especially when one claims to be analyzing ideology.

Sartre shows that genuinely Marxist work requires holding together not just the intentional and unintentional, clear ideas and ideology, but also the

---

12 Ibid., 39.
13 Brissot, quoted in Ibid., 41.
14 Ibid., 40.
15 Ibid., 41.
16 Ibid., 45.
17 Ibid.

imaginary and the real. His emphasis on "the truth of imaginary praxis" leads him to assert that Roman clothes, for example, is a truth of the imaginary that produces a doublet of real and objective action *and* imaginary praxis that envelops the real action and which, as a result, diverts it and alters it in reality. It is subjectively that these multiple displacements occur. Sartre thus concludes that the *Brissotins* "believed they were juggling with the Revolution for their own advantage; in fact, they made it more radical and democratic."[18]

"LIBERTÉ-ÉGALITÉ," MANUSCRIPT ON THE GENESIS OF BOURGEOIS IDEOLOGY[19]

Sartre began this work on ideology, or more specifically "bourgeois ideology," in a series of notes. Because Stalin is mentioned as alive, they are dated by the editor as having been written prior to 1953, and later more precisely placed in 1951, nine years before the publication of the *Critique*. These unfinished notes, titled "Liberté-Égalité" and subtitled "Manuscript on the Genesis of Bourgeois Ideology," were published in 2008. It may seem vain to want to find Sartre in extracts from notes and occasional remarks and comments written in history books (most, but not all of them, Marxist). In no way should we claim that it is possible to place these notes, this archive of Sartre's work, on the same terrain as texts like the *Critique*, as dense as it is. In my view, these notes must be analyzed as prolegomena which allow us to measure the distance between the Marxist vulgate (to which, at the time, Sartre belonged), and his work properly speaking, especially the *Critique*.

In the volume *Études sartriennes* on *Sartre, History, and Historians*, published in 2010, the manuscript is analyzed by experts either of the French Revolution or of Sartre. On the one hand Claude Mazauric, the Soboulian orthodox Marxist historian of the Communist Party, emphasizes a more Marxist Sartre than the one offered by the usual representations. On the other, the Sartrean philosopher Vincent de Coorebyter pulls Sartre toward a non-Marxist conception of ideology. Both of them essentialize a moment of Sartre's work, even if it means not seeing what is said in these notes, overlooking that which would correct them in the movement of Sartre's thought. For my part, I simply wish to see in these notes but a moment of work which allows us to evaluate the decisions which inhabit *Search for a Method* and the *Critique* itself. It seems to me important to grasp what Sartre

---

18 Ibid., 45. This is well demonstrated in Jean Renoir's *The Marseillaise*.
19 Manuscript published in the previously mentioned volume of *Études sartriennes*, published in 2008.

seeks to highlight by accentuating what he terms "bourgeois ideology" in 1789, and to compare his work in the 1950s and its traces in the *Critique*. But this on its own is not enough. We must also attempt to confront these notes with a contemporary analysis of this putative ideology, embodied discursively for Sartre in the Declaration of the Rights of Man and the Citizen and its earlier drafts. Of course, the Declaration exceeds the category of "fetishized" bourgeois ideology.

Sartre appears in these notes to have had difficulty understanding the text of the Declaration of rights, which he takes as an emblem of the contradictions of bourgeois ideology during the revolutionary period, and even more difficulty, in my view, with Sieyès's *Exposition raisonée*. He describes this text as absurd on several occasions and misses the central notion of "reciprocity of right" (*réciprocité du droit*).

OF WHAT FREEDOM DOES THE FRENCH REVOLUTION SPEAK?

Before arriving at the analysis of these two texts, Sartre opens his remarks with an analysis of the conceptions of freedom and equality available in 1789. On the one hand, he quite surprisingly opposes freedom and equality as if he were seized by the Cold War context and its dominant discursive formation, in which communist equality is paid for by the loss of freedom. On the other hand, he opposes positive and negative freedom in the vocabulary of Isaiah Berlin's *Two Concepts of Liberty*, which does not appear until 1958 but which European intellectuals are already familiar with. Sartre thus speaks of the positive freedom of the nobility, who are according to him "structurally free" or "free by virtue of being noble," since they make active commitments by pledge, honor, potlatch. Freedom, says Sartre, is this "power," and it is identified with privileges. He contrasts the demands for equality by the Third Estate with the positive freedom of the nobility that is articulated through the social hierarchy of those who have power versus those who lack power and over whom it is exercised. Citing Barère in 1788, he asserts that the Third Estate did not demand freedom, and it would have come to terms with absolutism so long as it led to equality of nobles and non-nobles before the despot.[20] He then asserts that the Third Estate's conception of freedom—when it rises from its own

---

[20] This effectively denies any reciprocal freedom, identified (as in Machiavelli) with the safety of all, or becomes "equaliberty" as a result of this reciprocity, in the terms formed by Étienne Balibar around the time of the bicentenary. See chapter 12 below.

midst—is at once "abstract and universal and negative."[21] However, this negative conception of freedom as absence of obstacles in no way allows Sartre to understand the question of the reciprocity of right (*droit*), which is limitation of the freedom of some by that of others and a singular mode of regulation at the heart of popular, republican government.[22]

If absolutism cannot effectively allow for this reciprocal freedom, constitutional monarchy, which restricts the monarch to an executive function, can. Equality is then the simple reciprocity of freedom, which is at once power and reciprocal limitation, and is thus always essentially positive. If your freedom is without limits, and mine is, too, your freedom augments mine. If my freedom has limits, and yours does, too, this is conducive to promoting the regulation of legitimate limits, which allow us to live in a common space without hampering the development of human potentialities.

By missing this notion of the reciprocity of freedom, Sartre fails to notice an ideal place to unearth and make legible the contradictions of the 1789–1794 moment, whether the contradictions of slavery or of unlimited economic freedom. He thus considers the statement "all men are owners of their person, or none are" as empty. Yet it stems from this reciprocity of freedom and right. The statement is shorthand for the following: "If a man is denied ownership of his person, all are reciprocally injured, and as a result, there is no more freedom, either individual or collective." Or, in the terms of article 34 of the 1793 Declaration, which are very explicit on this point: "There is oppression against the social body when a single one of its members is oppressed; there is oppression against each member when the social body is oppressed."

But for Sartre, since there are in reality at this time slaves and free men, the statement should have been expressed in the form of an imperative (*devoir être*). He fails to see that, because the statement is in the present, it produces a norm. A norm in the making, to be sure, but one that can be abstracted from the contingency of the moment to function as a point of reference for slaves on plantations seeking freedom. If the text of the Declaration is ideological yet emancipatory, it is precisely because it is using a trapped language to bring about another world. But in 1950, the question of this ensnared language is not one of the lines of inquiry in Sartre's notes. So, when Sartre dwells on the words "nature" and "right," he senses that

---

21 Sartre inédit avec les manuscrits "Mai-juin 1789" et "Liberté-Égalité", sous la direction de Jean Bourgault et Vincent de Coorebyter, Études sartriennes, n° 12, 2008.

22 In this regard, see Ernst Bloch, *Natural Law and Human Dignity* (Cambridge, MA: MIT, 1996) (originally published in 1961), and in its wake, the work of Florence Gauthier, *Triomphe et mort due droit naturel en Révolution, 1789, 1795, 1802* (Paris: PUF, 1992).

they are effectively *trapped*, but he focuses not so much on the nature of this trap as on what these words evoke philosophically. He cites Spinoza, who renders them mutually exclusive, but refuses to enter the crucible of a new freedom identified with reciprocity and which guarantees physical and economic non-domination and the absence of slavery.

Sartre, then, declares that "since fact can never justify right, the following paragraph is absurd."[23] He cites the well-known passage from Sieyès: "Nature makes some weak and some strong, but it does not follow that there may be inequality of rights." But "rights to what?" asks Sartre, unable to consider that individual freedom arises from a protective right, which is not a "right to," but an affirmation of equality in all effective rights, current or future.

Thus, the reflection on ideology and language presented in *Search for a Method* constitutes an important revision of his work in this text, which appears to remain captured by the very vulgar Marxism that, by the time of the *Critique*, he relentlessly criticizes.

SARTRE TRAPPED BY THE VULGATE

This vulgate is economistic, something that Sartre denounces in 1960 even in Guérin. He thus jumps to the assertion that one should write: "Every man consumes everything he needs, or nobody consumes, which means a socialist reform of property."[24] He may very well jump the gun in his proposal that everything is reducible to the question of scarcity, which, though undeniably fundamental to the Marxist philosophical worldview in *The Critique of Dialectical Reason*, prevents him in this instance from envisaging the possibility that there can be more or less political equality as such, and therefore the capacity of acting on the progressive development of this scarcity through the redistribution of consumer riches and goods. Finally, when Sieyès claims that the social order follows from and complements the natural order, Sartre declares that this is absurd, since "the natural order is violence." Here again he neglects the very important debate on the imagination of nature, not as violence but as the source of human independence, as was argued for example by Saint-Just.[25] The latter in particular, in his

---

23 *Études sartriennes*, 2008, 172.
24 Ibid., 173.
25 In particular, in the text *De la Nature*, Saint-Just, *Œuvres complètes*, ed. Miguel Abensour and Anne Kupiec (Paris: Gallimard, 2004). Even if, as Claude Mazauric claims, Sartre had read Albert Ollivier's biography of Saint-Just, this is not apparent in the text.

book *De la nature*, formulates natural individual independence on the one hand, and collective political freedom instituted in opposition to the enemy or adversary on the other. According to Saint-Just, it is precisely independence, denatured and distorted by history, which transformed man into a violent "savage." Hence, this violence is not natural but historical. Saint-Just is studied by Dionys Mascolo.[26] who introduces his *Œuvres* in 1946,[27] and by Deleuze in his reflection on institutions,[28] a work of which Sartre appears to have been unaware.

By refusing to see another conception of nature and of right (*droit*), a nature which would not be violence and a right which would not be an expression of this violence[29] but given as a condition of humanity, Sartre seems to me to be misapprehending his object. If humanity is conceived by the revolutionary men of 1789 as natural, and its denaturing as historical, then humanization is envisaged as the juridical reconquest of humanity precisely in order to protect it from the oppressive violence of its denaturing. Right would then be a form of emancipatory—rather than merely mystifying—praxis. In this respect, Sartre appears unaware of social right such as it appears in the work of Gurvitch[30] before and after the Second World War, nourishing the reflections of French constituents in 1945–1946. Yet, beyond the fact that Gurvitch defends an idea of right that flows from society and which is therefore not oppressive, he promulgates a complex conception of society which resonates with the theses defended in the *Critique of Dialectical Reason*. In essence, for Gurvitch, social life is marked by a dynamic of permanent change, initiated by the proliferating play of unresolvable conflicts, that is to say, permanent conflicts which cannot be indexed to a single, central conflict such as the struggle over the distribution of goods. For Gurvitch, this conflictuality of the social epistemologically

---

26 Denys Mascolo had only a brief stint in the Community Party from 1946–1949, and a polemic with Sartre in 1953 in the work titled *Le Communisme: Revolution et communication, ou la dialectique des valeurs et des besoins* (Paris: Gallimard, 1953).

27 *Présentation des Œuvres de Saint-Just*, Cité Universelle Press, 1946.

28 Gilles Deleuze, *Instincts et institutions* (Paris: Hachette, 1955(, 35. In the introduction to this collection of documents, Deleuze accounts for Saint-Just in the following terms: Contrary to the theories of the law which place the positive outside of the social (natural rights), and the social in the negative (contractual limitation), the theory of the institution puts the negative outside the social (needs), to present society as essentially positive, inventive (original means of satisfaction). Such a theory would finally give us political criteria: tyranny is a regime in which there are many laws and few institutions, democracy a regime in which there are very few laws but many institutions. Oppression shows itself when the laws bear directly on people, and not on prior institutions that protect them.

29 On this point, Sartre is closer to Carl Schmitt than to the revolutionary ideology of right.

30 Georges Gurvitch, *L'Idée du droit social*, (Paris: Recueil Sirey, 1932); Gurvitch, *La Déclaration des droits sociaux* (Paris: Vrin, 1946).

supposes a "dialectical empiricism," which is alone able to account for the "perpetual struggles" and "irresolvable antinomies" that define the social.

As a result, what appears to be in the background of these notes is a classical opposition between formal and real rights which cannot respond to what is already of the order of opposable rights in the Declaration, rights which are neither formal nor real but natural and normative—a recourse for bringing about a reality which conforms to justice, depending on the ability of agents to mobilize it. The work of Ernst Bloch comes as a response to this Marxist tradition, which is weak in the face of right.[31] In *Natural Law and Human Dignity*, first published in 1961,[32] Bloch argues that the supposed bourgeois Revolution is more than simply bourgeois precisely because it bears this Declaration of rights, which "one must know how to actively inherit." According to Bloch, socialist mistrust of natural law is sometimes salutary but often nonsensical, and he recalls that if Marx criticizes the bourgeois content of the "rights of man," he also shows the latent content that makes them contemporary and effective against all dictatorship. Socialism must enable the realization of the potentialities opened by the Citizen, rather than work toward a supposed objective right.

When the question of protecting the weak from the strong arises, Sartre points to an ambiguity. Does Sieyès have physical force in mind, or other forces such as economic force? Based on the positive law of 1791, Sartre claims that Sieyès's statement is contradictory with the right to use and abuse one's property, established particularly in the laws passed by the *constituents* consecrating economic liberalism, such as the famous Le Chapelier laws. Sartre then asserts that "right is this tautology: everyone has the right to own what they have. The rich, their riches, the poor, their poverty."[33] He concludes that "right guarantees the property of the bourgeoisie against the nobility and against the poor." Sartre ends up identifying the rights of the individual with economic liberalism, pertaining only to the possessing individual who uses and abuses their property, and as such opposes government, corporations, and the traditional powers of the king, which he considers as contradictory. Yet he never hypothesizes that there may actually be two conceptions of freedom coexisting and openly conflicting during the revolutionary period: the freedom to dispose of one's property as one sees fit, and freedom as reciprocal limitation. As a result, he goes as far as calling the Sieyès of the Declaration "false and filthy," because "freedom can go further and forbid itself." "We go to socialism or

---

31 "faible face au droit."
32 Ernst Bloch, *Natural Right and Human Dignity* (Boston: MIT, 1987).
33 *Études sartriennes*, 2008, 173.

Nietzscheanism and fascism from Sieyès."[34] Sartre therefore does not envision the liberal political critique of economic liberalism. He believes this text bears witness to an arrested thought, to its non-dialectical dimension. He thus flouts its potentiality for precisely the radical revolutionary praxis that produced the revolutionary movement of 1789–1794.

Ultimately, when Sartre analyzes the question of the nation, he declares that the very notion of the nation, like that of right, produces a mystification, that "national sovereignty remains a myth."[35] According to Sartre, the legitimation obtained does not concern the nation and its constituent power, but the power of the representatives vis-à-vis royal power. This is what he calls "mystification."[36] But when the nation intervenes—not its representation but its active power—on October 4 and 5, 1789, to ratify the August decrees, the Declaration of rights and the abolition of privileges, he describes the actors of these days not as the synthetic metonymy of the "whole," but in terms of the "active minority that resolve the conflict through violence."[37] What he misses, then, is the right to resistance against oppression, which makes it possible to distinguish between oppressive and liberatory violence, and to consider that the real remedy in the face oppression is indeed the sovereign nation *understood as those parties acting on the basis of the natural right of resistance* and not as their electoral representation. The Declaration of rights is precisely what gives this nation—even if it is represented—not only real legitimacy but also the right to act and to resist by insurrection, which goes well beyond its representation. Here again the resources for revolutionary praxis are considerable, and yet are overlooked by Sartre.

To be sure, he ultimately affirms, through the reading of Jacques Godechot, that "the idea exceeds contingency."[38] He notes that the Declaration of the Rights of Man and Citizen leads to the Republic, universal suffrage, the abolition of slavery, and the right to rebel. But he considers that if the figure of universal man had been produced in opposition to the particularisms of the Ancien Régime, these particularisms return under the name of "realism" among the bourgeoisie. He concludes with the Thermidorian perspective: "Freedom for the property owner in the form of right-freedom (*droit-la-liberté*), for the poor in the form of duty."[39]

---

34 Ibid., 175.
35 Ibid., 184.
36 Ibid., 182.
37 Ibid., 184.
38 Ibid., 187.
39 Ibid., 192.

In 1950, Albert Soboul's *1789, Year I of Freedom* (1939) was reprinted by Éditions Sociales. Is Soboul, without being named, one of the Marxist historians that Sartre castigates in the *Critique of Dialectical Reason*? It is difficult to say, but it is a fact that in his manuscript, Sartre explicitly refers to Soboul and not to Georges Lefebvre.[40] But he also reads the radical socialist Paul Bastid on Sieyès and Jacques Godechot on the institutions of the revolution. If he is mistaken, it is not necessarily owing to his readings of classical Marxists, but rather to his conception of ideology as masking the real, and of the ideology of 1789 as bourgeois rather than universalist.

SARTRE BEFORE THE "'CRITIQUE'"

The Sartre which appears in these notes on the genesis of ideology is at odds with what we analyzed in *Search for a Method*. One thus finds it difficult to follow Vincent de Coorebyter in his article "Liberté-Égalité, une genèse non marxiste de l'idéologie bourgeoise."[41] In it, he claims that these handwritten pages bear witness to a non-Marxist interpretation of bourgeois ideology because Sartre recognizes the political power of national sovereignty and its capacity to make natural law a tool in the fight against monarchy—an egalitarian tool which it believes in even if it does not entirely follow through with its consequences.

Even if here, in these notes, ideology is not simply mystifying from end to end, it is nonetheless on this mystifying aspect that he mainly insists, without highlighting the power of the ideology of the Third Estate contained in the Declaration and the preparatory texts that preceded it. If there is sincerity in the doctrine of freedom, it seems to me that Sartre does not emphasize it at this time. The doctrine itself is strong, according to Sartre, but those who activate it bring it to a halt and mystify it in a desire to hide the object "right" from those who might seize it. This is why the manuscript appears, on the contrary, caught in the precise error Sartre criticizes in *Search for a Method*, where he declares that the ideology of the Girondins cannot be reduced to their class position or to mere mystification. Here it is a question of the ideology of Sieyès and the *constituents*.

In fact, he does repeat these analyses in the *Critique* or in the form of smaller residual statements. When he works on totalities in fusion, he evokes the "sovereign and by extension totalising nation" as a group which

---

40 Ibid., 189.
41 Vincent de Coorebyter, "'Liberté-Égalité': une genèse non marxiste de l'idéologie bourgeoise," *Études sartriennes* no. 14, *Sartre, l'histoire et les historiens*, 2010, 27–54.

"produces itself as its own idea."[42] He then claims that representative assemblies are *"parasites of the electoral body as a practico-inert thing,"* and "the origin of the contradictions which split the ideology of the Constituent Assembly and, particularly, of its theoretician Sieyes."[43] These statements are like abutment, because it is no longer a question of asserting that ideology is an intentionally mystifying product, but rather the site of a tearing apart. This ideology is no longer described as bourgeois but as "of the Constituent," and its contradictions are not related to a manufactured deception but to the agency of the practico-inert, which gives force to representation instead of recognizing the sovereign power (*puissance*) of the people. In my view, it is a completely different discourse.

In the *Critique*, Sartre returns to the Sieyès moment a second time, and indicates to what extent Sieyès does not play a mystifying role in the spring of 1789. He thus writes:

> Sieyes' question about the Third Estate, which was nothing (and therefore a pure multiplicity of inertia, since it existed as nothing) but could be everything (that is to say—as certain people then thought, including Sieyes himself, by an abstraction from which, as a liberal bourgeois, he soon recovered—the nation, as a totality perpetually reshaping itself, the nation as permanent revolution) shows clearly how *through the troubles of 1788-9 and the groups which formed* sporadically (which up to that time were called riots) the bourgeois even more than the worker in the cities (though work was really done by the workers) glimpsed the transition from an ossified, cold world to an Apocalypse. This Apocalypse terrified them; [. . .] But it was France as the Apocalypse that they discovered through the storming of the Bastille. And through this people's battle, they learnt not only what the inert words of this speech suggested to them: its 'power,' the contradictory 'necessity' of governing both through it and against it etc.; they sensed that History itself *was revealing new realities*.[44]

Once again, notes in a drawer and a published text should not have the same exegetical status. Here, the glue of inert words appears again, and there is no further discussion of which words should have been used by the Constituents; no phantasmagoria, either, because social and political contradictions are at the very heart of the matter, with the "reality of workers' work" as what remains invisible in accordance with Marxist theory. Nor

---

42 Jean-Paul Sartre, *Critique of Dialectical Reason* (London: Verso, 2004), 363.
43 Ibid.
44 Ibid., 383.

is there discussion of the great fear, the dread that the revolutionary event produced in the very bourgeoisie who were actors in the 1789 moment. And for all that, the event and its early theoretical indicators are not treated as an *illusio* but rather as the excesses of invention, the profusion of the new, including for those terrified members of the bourgeoisie.

It is not a matter, therefore, of taking interest in Sieyès alone but in a Sieyès who appears to embody this apocalyptic moment, which he brings about and which scares him because at precisely this moment of History, Sieyès produces statements that make situation speak.

When we look at both the text published in 1960 and the recently published notes, it is possible to determine the path taken by Sartre between 1951 and 1960, and to reveal a thought at work and in motion. In "Liberté-Égalité." Sartre gives his readers (and even the actors of 1789!), a lecture on Marxism. In 1960, he proposes a complex intelligibility of the contradictions and inventions that led to what he calls the "Apocalypse." He neither rejects social categorizations nor takes refuge in positivist concepts which would level the events themselves, far from it. The bourgeoisie he describes comes alive and is not reduced to mere cynicism, they are a thinking and acting bourgeoisie, which in turn accounts for their fear. And the Nation, finally, is revolutionary; it is the permanent Revolution, a ferment. Sartre thus refers to "a more radical and deeper novelty" than the groups that were then constituted: "free *praxis* becoming through society as a whole and through the conflicts of antagonistic groups the *developing statute* of all the social structures of inertia."[45] Thus, the non-fetishization of reality affords him access to it, and the revolutionary laboratory allows him to explain the relevant way of producing knowledges (*des savoirs*) worthy of the name.

The French Revolution allows Sartre to be confronted by History in such a way as to test his theoretical elaboration, as well the possibility of emancipation, the possibility of this free praxis, which, he shows us, occurred at least once in History. "For our purposes," he writes, "this is enough: its real, dialectical existence and its emergence from the liquidation of petrified forms are sufficient reasons for taking such a *historical reality* as our starting point."[46]

The Revolution, then, is an object of political analysis common to diverse interlocutors in the 1944–1960 conjuncture, and this makes it possible to avoid discussing method on a purely theoretical plain, and to avoid

---

45 Ibid.
46 Ibid.

invalidating the method of vulgar Marxism without first demonstrating its extreme negligence, and indeed testing this negligence.

In the *Critique of Dialectical Reason* and then in *Search for a Method*, one cannot help but be struck by Sartre's desire to enter these famous "details" along with all these discussions of revolutionary historiography. What is the role of Robespierre, first warmonger and then cautious? That of Cambon, owner of national goods and responsible for the decree of December 15, 1792, on the possibility of exercising coercive action in Belgium? Can we really consider, as the Marxists do, that the Girondins and the Montagnards are simply two wealthy parts of the bourgeoisie, one maritime, the other landowner? Are these not social categories that are invented precisely where individualities play such an important role and where wealth is ultimately minimal? All of these details are there to show us that the historical narrative can appear true and yet simply be a methodical falsification. "Why are we dissatisfied? Why do we react against Guérin's brilliant, false demonstrations? Because Marxism ought to study real men in depth, not dissolve them in a bath of sulphuric acid."[47]

Sartre carries out this in-depth study in the 1950s—in the manuscript for "Mai–Juin 1789"—in a way that is more successful and leaves much deeper traces in the *Critique*, if not in terms of the subject matter addressed then at least in its operative categories.

---

47 Sartre, *Search for a Method*, 43–44.

3

NO LONGER DISSOLVING THE REAL ACTORS OF THE FRENCH REVOLUTION

In the unfinished manuscript "Mai–Juin 1789," Sartre seeks to grasp how real people actually make history by searching for the historical details that produce reversals, logical contradictions, aporias which cannot be subsumed *a priori* by a pre-constructed totalization but which, on the contrary, require understanding to some degree the lived experience of history and the entanglement of historical actors in the practico-inert.[1]

We are, then, at the heart of Sartre's methodology: starting from the immediately lived and rising toward structures, seeking to render the play of these historical structures intelligible. He named this the "progressive-regressive movement," which deploys the methodology *par excellence* of the historian in that it considers the description of the facts as but one step in an effort which aims to clarify that which is not immediately visible.[2] Sartre borrows this method from Henri Lefebvre, which he will employ repeatedly.

Sartre undertakes painstaking, meticulous work so as to understand May–June, 1789, as a decisive moment which transforms a tradition, that of the Estates-General, into a revolutionary invention, the National Constituent Assembly. This event, most often presented in history books as a "juridical revolution" initiated under the guise of a "joint verification of powers,"[3] is often evaded. This narrative portrays it as if it had been a mere formality

---

1 Recall the definition we tried to give in the previous chapter. This *practico-inert* is that which, in the will to govern matter and the practice of turning it into "worked matter," falls back on us as this very worked matter comes to govern us. Ideas are considered in the same way as things—as worked matter—so they are also in the domain of this practico-inert. Humans are not free, because they do not know the history they are making, and they do not know it because they do not know how the practico-inert they create will come around to frustrate and displace the objectives of human actions.
2 This method is adopted first by Marc Bloch and then by Nicole Loraux.
3 *"vérification des pouvoirs en commun."*

and the important things only started with the storming of the Bastille—as if, in the apparently narrow scope of the May–June debates, there was only evidence of institutional reforms and not a real revolution. In the historiography of the statement "juridical revolution," the "juridical" aspect ended up effacing the "revolutionary" aspect. Sartre restores the latter by demonstrating how difficult it was to bring about, in opposition to the orders of the Ancien Régime, a national common made up of individuals united in a shared project. He then shows that the question of the vote-by-head (*vote par tête*),[4] left suspended by the king, is the site of this revolutionary battle. This vote-by-head has less to do with the nature of the assembly insofar as it is *national*, given that the king speaks of "the national assembly that I have convened,"[5] but rather insofar as it affects the nature of the nation in question. For Sartre, the political contradiction is posed like this: "Originally, there are two conceptions involved. The hierarchichal nation and the Nation united as equals. And the third cannot appeal to the latter against a nobility that has accepted the former. The proof is that in the discussion between the commissioners on May 25th, the Third Estate uses arguments that appeal to Tradition and not to the rational principle of the sovereign nation."[6] It is certainly no small thing to indicate in this analysis that the Revolution does not invent the nation but transforms its content: whereas the nation had existed but in a hierarchical organization, it is a question of bringing about a nation of equal individuals. Sartre shows that the negotiation involves great political finesse, as the initial challenge will be for reason to "accommodate" tradition as a kind of precedence, and then to substitute reason for tradition—"Take reason as the arbiter." Cartesianism, which is to say the philosophy-world of this historical moment, thus comes into play. It is affirmed in the request made to the nobles to reject all tradition and replace it with reason. "We ask (the nobles) to replace nobility (conferred by tradition) with citizenship (conferred by reason). In short, originally and before any deliberation, the nobles are asked to destroy the aristocracy."[7]

But this destruction is not necessarily thought of in this way by the actors involved, including those who ultimately brought it about without meaning to—without knowing it—by ardently demanding the vote-by-head. The idea of the vote-by-head is in this respect a practico-inert, and Sartre demonstrates this by analyzing the event's protagonists, very real

---

4 As opposed to the vote-by-order.
5 *Sartre inédit avec les manuscrits*, "Mai–Juin 1789" and "Liberté-Égalité," *Études sartriennes*, no. 12 (2008): 22.
6 Ibid., 23.
7 Ibid., 25.

figures who are at once free and alienated: Malouet, Mounier, Mirabeau, Le Chapelier, all of whom demand the vote-by-head with a united will, but for reasons and with methods that were not necessarily envisaged in advance. A revolutionary event can be achieved by the convergence of actions emanating from both reactionary and revolutionary actors. It asserts itself with a necessity which could be called a totalization in progress but does not necessarily have a "totalizer." The event has protagonists, but it does not unfold through the mastery of a grand strategy which implements a plan of action.

In any case, what seems to interest Sartre is the way in which the political experience of each of these protagonists governs their position in the event, positions which constitute variations on the theme of the reunion of the three orders in a single National Assembly. He therefore proposes to analyze this juridical revolution insofar as it produces, starting from disjointed Estates, a unity. In this analytical work, his theories organize the analysis in the same vocabulary that allows for description.

ANALYSIS OF THE REAL ACTORS OF MAY–JUNE 1789: EFFECTIVE BLINDNESS

Let us begin with the case of Mounier, deputy for Dauphiné: "Mounier wants the union of the three orders and achieved this union in a province: the Dauphiné."[8] He wanted the parliamentary deputies to be elected through vote-by-head and as a result have the imperative mandate to vote by head at the Estates General as well. In the Dauphiné, this is done through the agreement of the privileged against the king, in the name of the powers of *Parlement*. This is, for Sartre, Mounier's "experiment."

When Mounier arrives at Versailles,

> 1) He carries out an experiment, he believes: he proves through action that the unity of the three orders is possible. 2) His presence at Versailles and his mandate as a deputy are the proof that it is possible and is indeed the very product of this possibility. He was elected by nobles and members of the bourgeoisie. In a certain sense, the essence of his mandate and the very substance of his status as a parliamentary deputy embraces the unity of the three orders. He himself is this unity, it anoints him, and he is possessed by it [. . .] This abstract essence based on an equally abstract transcendent unity is concretized in the binding mandate to

---

8 *Sartre inédit avec les manuscrits*, 41.

demand the vote-by-head. [. . .] It is therefore bound by an *essence*. It is the indissoluble *past* in the present. Not a flexible enterprise, a project vaguely sketching the future, but an abstract norm in the form of *duty*, which turns the state of separated orders into a state of disorder, a chaos where nobles and clergy are already *guilty parties*. He is a judge, and has within him the juridical imperative in whose name he judges them. This is why his Roman flexibility here becomes *intransigence*.[9]

Through this figure, we find the notions of "incarnation" and "totality of envelopment," which are developed in the *Critique of Dialectical Reason*. The totality of envelopment is the manner in which this figure embodies the whole of the assembly, the three orders, through his experience of "performing" the situation. Elected by electors from all three orders, he embodies the three orders and champions their unity. However, Sartre does not describe this incarnation in terms of free will, but as "possession." In fact, Mounier does not really decide anything.

We thus encounter the practico-inert of experiences and ideas that shape the present. What strikes me as remarkable about Sartre's approach is that he identifies that part of subjective engagement which is unknown even to the actors, and becomes the inventive part of history, the unintentional of the intended. Mounier radicalizes a position of moderate jurist, without his knowledge. The work of the historian consists neither in treating actions as the product of clear intentions, as if ideas could simply be applied, nor in identifying unconscious investments and impulses such as is done by psychoanalysts. Neither does it consist of reading social trajectories as ineluctable determinations and preestablished potentialities of action. Borrowing Sartre's expression, it is a question of analyzing, within the situation, how the *ruse* of history places all its ingredients in its dialectical crucible at a distance from the efficiency of clear thought.

Mounier, a jurist ennobled by his office, represented the liberal nobles and the bourgeois who aspired to nobility but not the totality of Dauphiné society. He claims his position is moderate, but within the situation that he poorly analyzes, thinking only of reproducing what he already knows, it becomes of a position of great radicality.

Here Sartre shows how this historical figure is both a free subject and a constrained historical subject, a bourgeois who wants to feel that he is a noble. He considers Mounier's effort as one of internalizing this nobility in the form of imperatives more than the assumption of the universal reality of being a citizen. Protect the nobles even from themselves by convincing

---

9 Ibid., 45–47 (author's emphasis added).

them to unite with the other orders. Nevertheless, it is this double determination that engenders the historical movement, which in this instance is emancipatory, because without being "political," Mounier in fact contributes greatly to the advent of the National Assembly. That is to say, he does so without understanding that the situation cannot be resolved peacefully. Nevertheless, Mounier is described by his contemporaries as being engaged in an intransigent but zealous struggle, always ready to seek conciliation outside the Assembly as he continues to admire the nobility and wants to arbitrate as a judge. As a result, Sartre tells us, Mounier "splits"[10] the Assembly by simultaneously belonging to the three orders while being perceived by the Third Estate as "fleeing" toward the other two orders.

On this issue of conciliation, the figure of Malouet—close to Meunier in terms of social determination—stands out. Essentially, the absence of any possible conciliation is what concerns him. In case of failure, Malouet recommends that the king again ask the voters of the bailiwicks to choose between the vote-by-head and the establishment of two chambers, a higher chamber for the clergy and the nobility, and a lower chamber for the Third Estate. His skepticism toward the union of the three orders stems from the fact that it can only be based on the "experience" of freedom that belongs to the privileged. Commissioners of the Third must ask them to freely choose, out of generosity, to unite with them, because such is the quality of the greats. Mounier thinks that such an action would lead to the Third constituting a separate State, and he is against it, but Malouet wants this constitution, believing that it would bring the orders together without imposing anything on them. He is on the side of Tradition while wishing for the vote-by-head. For Sartre, he wants to "set an example. Proving the two orders wrong through the observation of discipline and obedience to customs and the law."[11] To this extent, for Sartre, Malouet is governed by his disposition "of high bourgeois functionary who abhors resistance and who, respecting hierarchies, assumes his place with dignity."[12] For Sartre, this is the only technocratic position: inefficient in the event, essentially seeking the implicit support of the king vis-à-vis the nobility, as he had been able to do in his preceding conflicts with the archbishop of Aix or the marshal of Castries. The practico-inert can render a position inefficient. For Sartre, "Malouet produces anxiety at the heart of the assembly."[13] He is a pessimistic and defeatist official, and to defend itself against him, the

---

10 Ibid., 53
11 Ibid., 30.
12 Ibid.
13 Ibid., 35.

assembly repudiates him with "boos." In fact, Malouet is the "Other" of the project of the Assembly. In his *Mémoires*, he senses that he is regarded as a quasi traitor because of this otherness. He is viewed "as an obstinate aristocrat." In this respect, Sartre's analysis allows us to rediscover the very meaning of the categories of "traitor" and "aristocrat," which I ultimately describe as equivalent to the "political foreigner" (*étranger politique*) in *L'Impossible Citoyen*.[14] For the Assembly, Malouet is the embodiment of a figure who is a stranger to himself. Yet this type of figure also creates the dynamics of revolution. Sartre hopes to show that it is paradoxically the position of inertia which, in this context, is the most political.

APPARENT INERTIA AS A POLITICAL CHOICE

Sartre then takes the example of Le Chapelier, the Breton parliamentary deputy who arrives at the Assembly with the strength of experience in Brittany. Both Bretons and the Dauphinois want to repeat what happened before, but what took place radically separates them from the nobility because the latter pushed the situation to the point of violence by betraying the parliamentary alliance between nobles and non-nobles.

Le Chapalier was a lawyer, from a good but non-noble family. He embodies, for Sartre, "disappointment" with the nobility, even "resentment and bitterness."[15] At any rate, the demonstrations of 1789 led to the physical confrontation between the nobility and the Breton youth that resulted in deaths on the side of the Third Estate. It opened the eyes of those who, in the past, thought they could form an alliance against absolutism. The division is thus already consumed by violence. The Bretons are intransigent toward the nobles and introduce, according to contemporaries, a "climate of violence in the Assembly." The violence in question is a passive violence: that of the strike, the refusal to do anything until satisfaction has been obtained. This tactic was tested at Rennes. The strike in the provincial states had led to the intervention of the king, recourse to popular arbitration, and ultimately to the victory of the people without a single direct decision having been made. It was a matter, therefore, of doing nothing, observing the defection of the privileged orders, and then declaring oneself the sole representatives in the absence of others and placing oneself under the protection of the Parisian people.

---

14 Sophie Wahnich, *L'Impossible Citoyen, l'étranger du discours révolutionnaire, de 1789 à thermidor* (Paris: Albin Michel, 1997) (paperback edition, 2010).

15 *Sartre inédit avec les manuscrits*, 61.

It is therefore a question of tactics, and for them to be effective, some had to be visible and others invisible; visible is the inertia of the Assembly, invisible is the creation of a *"club breton,"* which, as an active minority, prepares the strategy and its rhythm. It is a matter of thinking about the temporality of the event in this way, of letting it "mature." Among those associated with *club breton* are liberal nobles like the Mirabeaus, Lameth, La Fayette, Duport, but also Grégoire and Sieyès. All are conscious of this tactic of inertia and understand that it is a question of knowing when to end it.

So, what Sartre says is that the most political actors are not exempt from the experiences of the past continuing into the present as practico-inert, but they are not totally possessed by the practico-inert either. They are active in the present and attentive to its possible tipping points. Far from letting the past act alone, they are attuned to the necessity of seizing the *kairos*, the right moment to act. Thus for Mirabeau, quoted by Sartre, "soon it will be time to put limits on this inaction, not through vain and illusory conciliation, but by becoming more and more aware (for the communes) of their strength and dignity, that they expect nothing except what they themselves bring. If their patient tolerance is ineffective, everything will soon give way to this generous resolution and France will owe them her glory, the Constitution, her freedom."[16] The first letter from Mirabeau to his constituents dates from May 7, which indicates an awareness that the necessary inertia and suspense had to last to be effective; this commits each real actor to confronting this act of waiting, which, for Sartre, becomes the political gesture of the moment.

To convey the reality of this tactic and the men involved in it, it is therefore not enough to say where it comes from or who carries it out. You must enter what Sartre calls the biographical details to understand how each individual lives this waiting. These individuals find support in precedent and the practico-inert, as passive resistance is indeed part of the repertoire of actions inherited from the parliaments. The latter made the king wait before registering his edicts, up until the point of clashes in the courts. Doing nothing is thus legal. If it is (implicitly) recognized that the powers of the representatives of a national assembly must be jointly verified, it is legal not to verify them separately. We do not do anything because we cannot do anything. It leaves everyone alone.

But this waiting takes on another meaning for those who invest it with the possibility of a future explosion: the Bretons. Inertia—waiting—is lived as the coming *coup de force*. It is more than a weapon; it is a *coup de force*.

---

16 Ibid., 64.

Yet as Sartre explains, it only has this function because the nobles play this game against the Third Estate. If they agreed to jointly verify their common powers, the weapon would be defused.

So there is not only the reality of those who lucidly make history and those who do so with a lack of understanding, but also those who refuse to do so, and in this very refusal, create new fronts of struggle, new tipping points. Sartre challenges us to understand the nobility and its contextual motivations for refusing to engage the situation, which is also "political."

The political event is therefore a ring where we must both study each opponent and, above all, observe the form taken by this fight as its decisive blows are delivered. To this end, Sartre suggests that the historian never renounce the synthetic point of view, another term for the dialectic: synthesis of the unaware and the intentional, of the indissoluble past within the present and the present inhabited by the future, of conflicting positions—not in order to reduce them to an overarching perspective, but in order to understand how contradictions are active and complex.

To enter the reality of the nobles is to recognize their desire to thwart a trap. If they recognize that they are representatives of the nation and not of their estate, they must accept voting by head and not voting by order. But if this were their reason for opposing it, it would be political. So once again, Sartre shows how the nobility are possessed by ideology, and that this aristocratic ideology makes it *de facto* non-political.

He then explains that for the nobles, it is impossible to think of themselves as representatives of the nation because then they would represent people that they consider inferior. Election is "a mystical transfer of powers which takes place between people with the same potential, the same Mana."[17] "Blood elects blood." Evidently then, the nobility will refuse to jointly verify powers and will thus be considered as failing by the Third Estate when it decides to take the violent leap of asserting that the Third embodies the whole of the nation and that the absent nobles are always wrong.

This, however, is only the point of view of the politicians who are aware of this tactic. Others are dragging their feet in order to get the king's arbitration, to make him give way as the parliaments had often made him do.

Sartre completes his demonstration by recalling that the bourgeois, too, are caught up in an ideology and not just a specific experience. For Sartre, this ideology is that of natural law, which makes everyone each other's equal—not hierarchized beings, but equals due to the presence in each of us of the whole of reason: "The presence in each of us of the

---

17 Ibid., 70.

juridical entity 'man.'" So everyone has the right, says Sartre, to determine the general will. Moreover, the notion of social utility allows the bourgeoisie to feel legitimate. Because they are active and owners, they not only have an equal interest in running the country, but they also consider themselves superior to the idle (nobles), and to the landless workers who depend on them.

The fact remains that if conditions converge in this way, the event itself depends on the capacity to produce something decisive and irreversible: a qualitative leap, which is generative of a new situation.

A HISTORIOGRAPHICAL PHILOSOPHY OF THE "LEAP"

Sartre enters into a host of very detailed analyses in an attempt to understand how, with such different actors, this juridical revolution actually comes about, a revolution which in fact invents the sovereignty of the non-hierarchical Nation. In this sense, he chooses the perfect object to test the method. There are scattered actors who embody partial totalizations, and the analysis of history aims to understand how they bring about a political totalization. But he also chooses the perfect object to show that history is always becoming and not written in advance thanks to a theory. In this respect, it is not a text that, strictly speaking, provides new knowledge in terms of the archive, but rather a new way of looking at history and of staging it, of weaving it. Sartre shows that the May–June 1789 moment is constantly surrounded by uncertainties, frailties, paradoxes, illogicalities, sleights of hand. To make it an object that enlightens readers in the present, it is thus necessary to treat this historical moment as replete with contradictions which cannot be summarized as the bourgeoisie versus feudalism. The contradictions are manifold and sometimes unpredictable. In a complex way, they traverse individuals who are at once unique in their experiences and members of a group in their ideology. So it is the improbable arrangement of these contradictions, and these individuals that play a determining role in the rich picture, that Sartre sketches of these days of waiting, which makes it possible to depict the tipping point as an impossible point requiring what he calls a "leap." It is the ability to prepare for that leap that is, for Sartre, the political capacity. Only the most lucid, the most aware of the different contradictions at work, possess this capacity and are political—they are to some extent, partially free. The others are only toys of the practico-inert. However, whether one is an actor or agent of the situation, the situation is constantly changing and requires the arrangement (*agencement*) of these famous partial totalizations, which are synthesized in the successful leap. The uncertainty derives from the shifting and yet not ineffable political game that is unfolding. Nothing is ever won in advance, Sartre seems to say, and this is why the real actors really matter for the possibility of thinking emancipation. Here it is about the emancipation of the Nation through the possibility of having equal and individual representatives where the Nation had only existed in hierarchical form. The idea was of course already there, but what is at play in terms of political praxis is decisive. The idea is not enough; you need active actors and agents. But if ideology is philosophy-world, politics is praxis and requires this ability to observe the swarming of the present of history at the moment when a tipping point is possible but not given; it must be imagined and made to come about.

In *Search for a Method* Sartre claims that

> it is the *very ambiguity* of the event which often confers upon it its historical efficacy. This is sufficient for us to affirm its specificity. For we do not wish to regard it as the simple unreal signification of molecular[18] bumps and jolts—neither as their specific resultant nor as a schematic symbol of more profound movements. We view it rather as the moving, temporary unity of antagonistic groups which modifies them to the extent that they transform it. As such, the event has its unique characteristics: its date, its speed, its structures, etc. The study of these factors allows us to make history rational, even at the level of the concrete.[19]

Thus, the inquiry into the actors/agents of May–June 1789 is a political sociology of the situation in action, undoubtedly prior to the drafting of *Search for a Method*. There is no point in knowing where individuals come from if we do not seek to know how they act according to their sociological coordinates. There is no immediate sociologism, or, more exactly, the actions are never completely determined by these sociological coordinates. But this indeterminacy is not the restoration of a free subject the affirmation that History always invents with and without freedom. Belonging to the same social class, individuals can act in very different, even diametrically opposed ways, because the subjective and conscious historical experience is very different. One can be possessed in a different way by identical sociological coordinates. Or one can be similarly possessed and conduct distinct emancipatory efforts. The historian's task is of course made more complex, and its alliance with sociology modified, by the need to bring in a

---

18 Ten years later in *Anti-Oedipus*, Deleuze and Guattari use this same vocabulary, without doubt belonging to a shared discursive formation.
19 Jean-Paul Sartre, *Search for a Method* (New York: Vintage, 1968), 129.

contingency which is not indeterminate but one of the manifest possibilities of this determination which remains open.

To a certain extent, then, the event ultimately escapes the actors. They can work for it, but success or failure depends not only on them but also on that unpredictable movement which is irreducible to anticipation.

One has to shed some light, act on what is seen, all while knowing it can fail. But to neglect the details, contenting oneself with vulgar Marxist socioeconomic theory, is to move forward blindfolded and without the means to truly act in "politics."

Thus, to explain this political sleight of hand, making the people with the missing part of the nobles and the bishops, in such a climate of uncertainty and even of risk, Sartre studies a point which is obscured by Marxist historians even today: the role of the "sacred" in what unfolds.

4

RESTORING THE ROLE OF THE SACRED

The question of the sacred is not a Marxist question, and as such the two unfinished manuscripts distance themselves from Marxism by approaching it—each in their own way—in an original manner.[1] I was struck by the analytical power that combines concepts from Existentialism, Marxism, and dialectical reason to demonstrate the role of the sacred, which still today is refused by Marxist historians of the French Revolution. By taking the historical materials and situations he analyzes seriously, Sartre describes an unrecognized Revolution, which is still most often obscured by classical historiography. To make it exist, he takes into account the articulation of the concrete, the material—for example a room, bodies—and the symbolic, an oath. The ensemble produces what he calls "emotional energy," which is linked in Sartre with the notion of "magic." To this extent, the sacred exists more in the register of emotion that Sartre analyzes, beginning in 1938,[2] precisely in terms of magic. "Emotion may be called a sudden fall of consciousness into magic; or, if you will, emotion arises when the world of the utilizable vanishes abruptly and the world of magic appears in its place."[3]

According to Sartre, "the category of 'magic' governs the interpsychic relations between men in society [. . .] The magical, as Alain says, is 'the mind crawling among things'; that is, an irrational synthesis of spontaneity and passivity. It is an inert activity, a consciousness rendered passive."[4] It is because the activity in the assembly of the Estates-General is inertia that something arises from this order of the magical.

---

[1] To this end we credit the interpretation of Vincent de Coorebyter. Sartre is indeed not simply Marxist in the "Liberté-Égalité" manuscript.
[2] Jean-Paul Sartre, *Esquisse d'une théorie des émotions* (Paris: Hermann, 1938).
[3] Ibid., 60–61.
[4] Ibid., 56.

THE POLITICAL SACRED OF THE MATERIAL AND THE SYMBOLIC IN MAI–JUIN 1789

In Sartre's analysis, the materiality of things, what he calls "worked matter," is also an actor in situations, particularly in May–June 1789. The magic is first of all that of things and more specifically of place. The question of the sacred, far from eliminating the material dimension of historical situations, sheds light on the way that materiality is the basis of the sacred.

Thus, as there is no specific room for the *communes*, they occupy the room intended for everyone: the Salles des Menus-Plaisir, or Hall of the Estates,[5] Necker deplores it. In effect, this is what Sartre calls a *"material event,"* heavy with consequences. As of May 6, as the privileged orders are no longer in the common hall, they are "absent," and their absence can be experienced as a "deficiency" (*carence*). Here again it is the experience of materiality that gives the situation meaning for Sartre: "This absence, materialized by the emptiness of certain rows, could not but be experienced as a lack. And first of all by the people and public who frequented the room: they saw the Hall of the Estates with a part of the Estates in it, and suddenly this part of the Estates symbolically became the Totality of the Estates, pierced by absences."[6] "If the Third Estate had had a room, the reunion of the three orders would have required an act. [. . .] It would have been necessary to ask for a room. Instead of the inertia of the deputies being dictated by things, they waited for the other two orders like the benches and the rows awaited them."[7]

Thus, it is indeed the material configuration of the situation[8] that not only makes it possible to give meaning to the strategy of inertia, but even, according to Sartre, who dictates this strategy and who totally depends on it. Now, it is this relationship between materiality and the situation, "the haze and the void of an act of waiting," which leads the Third Estate to be no longer solely the Third Estate.

For Sartre, from then on, "this room is the body of the assembly."[9] He explains that the public then regards this place as sacred, and the Third as the National Assembly: "The Third already considers itself, as an object for the Other, as a National Assembly."[10] In this context, inertia is the act

---

5 Salle des États.
6 *Sartre inédit avec les manuscrits*, "Mai–Juin 1789" and "Liberté-Égalité," *Études sartriennes*, no. 12 (2008): 83.
7 Ibid.
8 Ibid., 84.
9 Ibid., 82.
10 Ibid., 84.

of internalizing this objectivity: the Third Estate becoming "the hall," and then becoming the "National Assembly." The public, the famous "Others," therefore constitute the hall and the deputies of the Third Estate as "waiting by the place that is sacred to all."[11] Sartre concludes with the homothety (*homéothétie*) between the Hall and the expected Society, and it is this homothety that he ultimately names as *sacred* because it produces the exigency of the situation. "The Hall is Society as a reality in the midst of the world and as an exigency. It is sacred."[12] He speaks again of the "spritualization of the concrete container," of the hall which gives "being to meanings." So the sacred is a double movement: "Through matter the idea is materialized to the extent that matter is idealized. A society is first of all the place that contains it."[13]

What Sartre describes resembles what anthropologists call "the place of the political":[14] a place that effectively contains society, similarly to Marc Abélès's Ochollos but where what is at stake emerges from a requirement called for by the place itself. Indeed, the places of politics are also then the places of the sacred in politics. But this sacred does not fall under the theologico-political. As for the specific relation to the public (the Other), which constitutes the deputies as revolutionary actors, the historian Timothy Tackett has since highlighted it. He underscores, on the side of lived emotions, the possibility of finding the courage to be revolutionary amid the acclamation and expectation of the public. However, he does not speak of the sacred, but works on the role played by the emotions that are experienced.[15] Now it is precisely a question of enthusiasm, which presupposes the presence, if not of God, at least of "sacred fire."[16]

---

11 Ibid.
12 Ibid., 85.
13 Ibid.
14 This expression is from Marc Abélès. The "place of the political" associates the notion of anthropological place, dear to Marc Augé, and this notion of politics. Marc Augé reserves the notion of anthropological place for "this concrete and symbolic construction of space [. . .] to which all those to whom it assigns a place, no matter how humble, refer." These places have at least three common characteristics. They are "identitarian, relational, and historical." "The plan of the house, the rules of residence, the districts of the village, the altars, the public places, the division of the soil, each correspond to a set of possibilities, prescriptions and prohibitions whose content is both social and spatial." The anthropological place of the political in the strict sense is present here, since the *Salle des menus plaisirs* is a place of the invention of the deliberative political sociability that intends to carry weight in the making of the National Assembly, and then of the law, and thus gives a prescriptive function to those who occupy it.
15 Timothy Tackett, *Par la volonté du peuple. Comment les députés de 1789 sont devenus révolutionnaires* (Paris: Albin Michel, 1997).
16 On enthusiasm, Pierre Ansart (in "La psychanalyse comme instrument d'analyse des situations idéologiques," *L'homme et la société* 51 (1979): 151–61) works in the lineage of Marx's "Eighteenth Brumaire of Louis Napoléon Bonaparte" along with Freudian psychoanalysis (especially *Civilization and its Discontents*, *Totem and Taboo*, and *Group Psychology and the Analysis of the*

In fact, this materiality of the container makes it possible to highlight what Sartre calls a "synthetic totality that surpasses the actors and awaits them," a surpassing which leads to the famous spiritualization of the political. This surpassing also takes another form, that of a phantom roaming the Assembly. "The majority does not exist, there is in the Assembly a strange and sacred force, without a face, which is called the 'we.'"[17]

Sartre reports that in his memoirs, Grégoire evokes the crucial moment of the vote on the creation and recognition of the National Assembly in these terms: "How can the vote of 12 to 15 people determine the conduct of twelve hundred deputies, he was told it is because the word 'we' has a magical force. [. . .] By saying, among the patriots 'we' agreed on such measures, *we* means four hundred as much as it means 10."[18] For Sartre, this magical character stems from the fact that individuals do not vote out of lucidity but out of obedience to a phantom of the majority. This is why the will of the Assembly is also produced by the imaginary created by "Others," and does so outside of each individual.

So for Sartre, "the will of the Assembly falls outside of each individual. The whole Assembly is transcendent in relation to its members. Pure myth and the representation of the Assembly itself, it is incomplete and open."[19] "It transforms itself from Third order into Totality minus something." We know that Sieyès had already affirmed this strange relation of positive subtraction in *What Is the Third Estate*: "Who is bold enough to maintain that the Third Estate does not contain within itself everything needful to constitute a complete nation? It is like a strong and robust man with one arm still in chains. If the privileged order were removed, the nation would not be something less but something more."[20] The Third, like the room, is the embodiment of the whole of the awaited society of individuals against the society of orders. Even alone, the deputies of the Third embody unity, and it is in this way that they are *sacred*.

Ego). He thus offers Freudian theoretical propositions for those rationally inexplicable moments, those that Sartre calls sacred under cover of "magic" and "the emotions." But Ansart is not attached to the sacred investment of objects. Concerning the link between the sacred investment of objects and psychoanalysis, Michel Poizat's work offers a new perspective, and much more recently, Fethi Benslama, in *Soudain la Revolution* (Paris: Stock, 2011), which returns to these subjective tipping points (*bascules*) tied to concrete investments of words, places, objects. Finally, in his *L'investissement symbolique* (Paris: PUF, 1996), Pierre Lantz proposed an analysis that articulates different sociological and political perspectives which also allow us to understand this "enthusiasm" and "magic."

17 *Sartre inédit avec les manuscrits*, 80.
18 Ibid.
19 Ibid., 81.
20 Abbé Sieyès, *Qu'est-ce que le Tiers État?*, 1788.

SACREDNESS OF TIME

Sartre then evokes a sacred time, one where regeneration comes first from the abolition of past history and then from the event considered as a new birth. What matters to him is to show that the event ultimately arises not only from a lucid tearing down but also from this magical dimension, which is akin to the religious *illusio* and which produces symbolic effects. Now, in the eighteenth century, these magical phenomena are indeed experienced, and at the same time rationalized in terms of tactics or political maneuvers. Tactics and political maneuvers are invested[21] as sacred acts which thereby acquire a mythical dimension. But while he uses this term here, he does not explain its usage. The set of acts that Sartre then analyzes in an attempt to understand the operation of historical causality at work shows that it is impossible to master a situation. He mentions only that "the failure of the conferences" (conferences with the clergy) produces a "negative" ever closer to spirituality,[22] because "an absence cannot act materially."[23]

Sartre is particularly animated by the question of time, and evokes the famous question of the future of the sacred anticipation. According to him, "the future is both transcendent and cut off from the present (waiting passivity), both formidable and hidden as a secret at the heart of the present."[24] This is why the courage to wait is not an empty phrase; uncertainty is the lot of the deputies.

In this context, the act proposed by Sieyès of calling the other members by bailiwick, regardless of the class of citizens or order they belong to, becomes a "sleight of hand." The latter is described by Sartre as "metaphysical" and then as "mystical" because it consists in "making yes with no." Those absent will appear as such, and those who are present will be the National Assembly made up of the majority of the deputies, "the greatest part," which refers to an electoral formula that existed under the Ancien Régime but without the same meaning. Therein lies the leap, the juridical and magical tour de force. It was necessary to create itself as a National Assembly and then to name itself as such, and this was done in three stages: The self-recognition as a "National Assembly" in the words of the king, and as such refusing to have the powers of deputies separately

---

21 On this question of symbolic investment, see Pierre Lantz, *L'Investissement symbolique* (Paris: PUF, 1996).
22 Concerning these spiritual stakes, Foucault, in his analysis of the Iranian Revolution, is ultimately very close to Sartre. See chapter 11 below.
23 *Sartre inédit avec les manuscrits*, 115.
24 Ibid., 93.

verified. Waiting. Stating that it is time to vote without waiting any longer, and voting.

Sartre then quotes Bailly's comments, which summarizes the affair by speaking of an "Abbé Sieyès who has a lot of metaphysics in his mind."[25] Bailly continues:

> Elsewhere it can do harm, here it was necessary. He was the only one who in these new circumstances had a sufficiently clear idea of the powers to trace this progression of summoning, calling, and absence, and who subsequently, by consequence of his principles, could point toward a mode of constitution which guaranteed us our rights without destroying those of the other orders and which, by placing us at the center of activity, established us as sole agents, leaving them absent and in the wrong.[26]

Sartre therefore highlights a sacredness specific to a concretely situated politics, one which does not relate to the theologico-political since it has nothing to do with God but has everything to do with what overflows the expected rationality of the actions taken in the situation. Once again, it is precisely what the actors cannot determine which takes central stage in the crucial event: not only the practico-inert of the past history of each individual, but also worked matter as such, in its very concrete effects on people's lived experience. Empty rows, absent men that "we" say we can finally do without. The transmutation of the Estates-General into National Constituent Assembly is thus not a juridical revolution in the sense that it would consist of an agreement between people of good company who made the decision by discussing and planning the transition from a society of orders to a society of individuals. It is a process in which the forces involved, far from emerging out of rational juridical procedures, arise from out of that which exceeds each and every one. This is why Sartre insists on the fact that things happen "beyond everyone." including when we search for an elusive totality.

The experience of May–June 1789 allows us to appreciate the unpredictable character, the incalculable nature of the revolutionary leap, which, in this respect, assumes this sacred dimension. Sartre's analysis, however, also shows that this leap is not simply of a messianic nature. It is not enough to wait for the magic to occur. It is necessary to attempt actions that bring it about. There must be conditions of possibility which are sometimes

---

25 Mémoire de Bailly, t. I, p. 129–30.
26 Cited by Sartre, *Sartre inédit avec les manuscrits*, 128.

strokes of luck: a hall which is refused, one which is invested with great significance. Sometimes, it is the metaphysical competencies of a specific actor. This way of describing an event in its situational complexity makes it possible both to make each actor responsible for their reflective actions, since all gestures contribute to the success or failure of the transmutation, but also to affirm that the dialectical leap does not arise from an analytical and deductive thought but from a gesture of courage that gives meaning to the happy convergence of rationality and magic. "It consists of a synthetic movement of ideas (dialectical, not deductive and analytical) where Sieyès's motion vanishes in smoke if it does not engender a more immense idea: the constitution of the National Assembly."[27] The notion of right (*droit*) that makes it possible not to have to choose between reason and tradition, however fallacious and inventive, allows the deputies to have the feeling of being in the right and to accept the "leap." If we follow Sartre, an event is the happy convergence of what actors consciously and unwittingly bring about, of what worked matter unexpectedly and magically effectuates, and what happens at the moment of the dialectical leap. The latter emerges at once from magical thinking, making law which is not law but which nevertheless gives the courage to act, and from rational creativity, from thought. As we can see, the responsibility for the failure as well as for the success of such a Revolution does not rest with the actors alone, but they nonetheless cannot at any time shirk their responsibility either. In this way they are wholly free.

CONFLICTS OF SACREDNESS AND THE ROLE OF THE OATH

Sartre distinguishes between three points of sacredness which conflict in the event and beyond it: for the nobility, "blood," for the clergy, "the priesthood," and for the Third Estate, "the sovereign will of the nation." He analyzes the conflicts of May–June 1789 in terms of these conflicts of sacredness. Initially, the sacrality of the Third Estate derived from that of the king, since the Assembly was convened by the king. The only sacred is in this instance effectively theologico-political. But as soon as the king indicates to the Third that he disapproves of it by refusing it access to the Hall of the Estates, this sacredness withdraws. In fact, by constituting the

---

27 Ibid., 129.

Assembly without waiting for a royal order, the Third Estate has already "split"[28] the sacredness of the monarchy and conquered a part of the sovereignty. The Assembly makes decrees, takes decisions. As long as royal disapproval was not expressed, the Assembly could pretend to itself and others that it was acting for the king and his sacredness in bringing about a National Constituent Assembly. In other words, they could appear as an extension of the sacred will of the king. But on the 20th of June, it is as bare subjects who are nevertheless capable of investing themselves with their own sacred dimension that the deputies of the Third Estate act and invent another lived sacredness through the Tennis Court Oath (*le serment Jeu de paume*). The deputy trades his "sacrosanct value as elected official" in the midst of monarchical sovereignty for a sacredness conferred on the Assembly in the name of law, but in an economy of magic. This is why "when they are driven from the room, they [the representatives] attempt to reconstitute this unity by taking the Oath. The Tennis Court Oath is the interiorization and spiritualization of the room as *concrete container*."[29] For Sartre, if history has remembered this episode much more than the constitution of the National Assembly, it is because it attests to the presence of something sacred, and is produced by a "holy word" (*une parole sainte*). When the sacred space of the Hall is prohibited by the king, it is replaced by this word.

According to Sartre, the oath is the "channelling and sublimation of a violent emotion." "Everyone agrees that their heads were gone. The phenomenon consisted of making a short-circuit between the emotion and the act, and of directing the emotional energy into a space where it explodes in a bouquet of fireworks."[30] The Tennis Court Oath is at once incredible and dangerous, since the deputies are outside the law in that they spurn the king's orders. Albert Mathiez refers to a deputy who blew his brains out because he could no longer bear the tension.[31] Sartre shows to what extent this transmutation is tied to the emotions which run through the deputies at the moment of the oath as a consecration of themselves and the Assembly. In a sense, it is the consecration of the political "We," which henceforth acquires consistency.

Sartre speaks again of a "sacred period of *metamorphosis*. [. . .] [The Third] is a sacred and free body whose invention, creation, and unique

---

28 Ibid., 134.
29 Ibid.
30 Ibid., 146.
31 Albert Mathiez, *Les Grandes Journées de la Constituante* (Paris: Les Éditions de la Passion, 1989).

possibility is the Constitution." However, this constitution "in turn 'regenerates' France, that is to say, returns to the Nation to make it an organized body with proper organs and conditioning."[32] Now, worked matter returns in the form of the Constitution itself. The event therefore incites a circulation of sacred objects, places, and people.

To resist monarchical sovereignty, the Assembly places itself under the protection of the people, thus affirming that the sovereignty of the people is more sacred than that of the king. But through the oath, it does so in a symbolic way. It is not a question of opposing the force of the people to the force of the king's bayonets, but rather of opposing right to force. It is essentially natural law which becomes sacred. The Assembly is indeed the famous "*natura naturans*" that is evoked in the manuscript of "Liberté- Égalité" and right (*droit*), the "*natura naturata*" that will take the name of the Constitution. It is in this respect that the Nation "as sacred undifferentiation"[33] is "a *creative* juridical power."[34]

Through the oath it has thus become a free subject that makes demands and that alienates itself from its task of producing the Constitution. The sacred is now in the Assembly, but also in each of its members. The dedication to the cause of the Constitution is then also a dedication to the people, which is itself sacred, and this generosity, Sartre concludes, is nobility conferred on the Third Estate. Honor no longer belongs exclusively to the nobility. It belongs to the function of deputy, whose oath henceforth demands that he obey, but obey only it. "That is to say, to his purest freedom, but to his alienated freedom."[35]

In the "Liberté-Égalité" manuscript, Sartre addresses this question in these terms: "When it comes to limiting a power which is sacred, it must be done by the sacred."[36] For him, the challenge for the Constituent Assembly is one of "constituting itself as a sacred power against monarchic sovereignty." But whereas in the "Mai–Juin 1789" manuscript he ends with a success, here he finishes with a failure: "contradiction in the ideology of 1789: it is the fact that utilitarianism, interest (material nature) prevails over the sacred (natural law) in the sense that we cannot base one on the other."[37] When Sartre attempts to define natural law, he oscillates between two positions. On the one hand, "natural law is conceived as that which is sacred in man" and therefore comes to limit all "sacred power". In this

---

32 Ibid., 147.
33 Ibid.
34 Ibid., 148.
35 Ibid., 153.
36 Ibid., 199.
37 Ibid.

case, it is about recognizing its efficiency in the economy of the sacred where natural law is "the recognition of the sacred in each of us."[38] On the other hand, Sartre considers man as in fact constituted by his struggle against privileges. By that very fact, it cannot be based on natural and sacred law, natural law being no more than an artifact. We have already explained ourselves on this text.[39] It strikes me as quite deficient, in view of the sophisticated analysis of the May–June 1789 moment. On the other hand, in the *Critique of Dialectical Reason*, we can find analyses similar to the "Mai–Juin 1789" manuscript's, particularly when the latter explicates *Apocalypse, fused groups (groupes en fusion)*, and *the pledged group*. The role of the oath in the consolidation of the fused group echoes perfectly and analogically with Sartre's description of May–June 1789, but it then shifts from the creation of the Assembly to the creation of the sovereign Nation.

---

38 Ibid., 200.
39 See Chapter 2.

5

APOCALYPSE AND FRATERNITY-TERROR

The question of the sacred takes a decisive turn in the *Critique of Dialectical Reason*, where Sartre makes "Apocalypse" the moment of the fused group's creative act and the oath, the founding moment of the fusion of this group and the retrieval of freedom through the creation of a robust "we," which simultaneously preserves individual and collective freedom in the "pledged group."

However, this rediscovered freedom comes at a high price because the oath also introduces a relationship of sacred violence which, for Sartre, makes "fraternity," "violence," and "Terror" inseparable. He writes the word "terror" with a capital *T*, so that the notion of "Terror" refers not only to the feeling of fear but also, in the historiography of the French Revolution, to the period of the Terror. The category itself is first invented in an enunciative reversal at the moment of Marat's death: "They want to terrorize us, let us be terrible!"[1] But it acquires its disqualifying scope during the Thermidorian period, in which the notions of "terrorists" and "terrorism" are invented. It quickly becomes a historiographical controversy, and even if this sequence remains a subject of disputes between different historiographical currents, we have most often reserved the term "Terror" for the period of the revolutionary government. Sartre investigates this period with intensity, including in his attempt at a script on the Assembly member Joseph Lebon. But for Sartre, this historical sequence is a dead end and leads him to deploy an extremely pessimistic conception of humanity. If his project remains that of uncovering an anthropology where History is the "Truth of Man," and if the Terror is the Truth of revolutionary history,

---

1 Jacques Guilhaumou, "La terreur à l'ordre du jour (juillet 1793–mars 1794)," in *Dictionnaire des usages socio-politiques (1770–1815)* (Paris: Diffusion Champion, 1987).

the Truth of man is troubling, to say the least, and collective freedom is not simply joyful, as we shall see.

The interview[2] conducted in 1972 between Pierre Verstraeten and Sartre sheds light on this pessimistic dimension of Sartre's theoretical and historiographical work. Sartre states: "I know what I must tear myself away from, but I do not quite know toward what. Or again, what is the least well founded, for me, is optimism: the reality of the future. I have optimism, but I cannot ground it. And really, that is the heart of the matter."[3] Can we ground a revolutionary optimism? When Verstraeten asks him, "Is this not the meaning of becoming conscious of the tearing away (of being) which defines a revolutionary political orientation, in any case an accomplishment carried out in view and for the sake of the assumption of freedom?" Sartre responds that this "becoming conscious" is, for him, called truth: "But these are truths for me! It is not grace that gives me this, that invests me with this belief. Or if you prefer, 'grace' is the truth, the truth for me at least." He concludes by asserting: "Finality is as impossible for freedom as the pure violence of desire."[4] While it is possible to connect the notion of grace-freedom-truth and the notion of the sacred, Sartre's sacred is not that of Bataille,[5] nor is it linked to a faith which would have any connection to theology. As he clearly reaffirms, "I refuse the theological position."[6] If there is faith, it is in the consciousness of truth. The certainty that commits one to radical politics comes from true knowledge (*connaissance*): "It is enough for me to know my reasons for challenging this society."[7] Nevertheless, the sacred that he persisted in recognizing in the history of the French Revolution under the heading of "Apocalypse" and of the "pledged group" were not just the sacralization of known Truth, but indeed a specific regime of truth which allowed him to elucidate what brings about a rupture even when the actors are unaware of the effort they are engaged in.

APOCALYPSE AND FUSED GROUP

Sartre distinguishes between collectives, fused groups, and pledged groups. The first are a series of individuals who act, but as practico-inert. Inert individuals, in the sense of being unfree, constitute a discontinuous series

---

[2] "Je ne suis plus réaliste," reissued in volume 14 of *Études sartriennes*, 3–23.
[3] Ibid., 18.
[4] Ibid., 23.
[5] *Sartre et Bataille, Lignes*, n 1.
[6] "Je ne suis plus réaliste," 19.
[7] Ibid.

dependent on an external situation. No freedom presides. The transition from the collective to the group is a change produced by the need to act together with an objective which is felt as necessity. It produces a change of state like the passage from solid matter to liquid or gas. "From this moment on, there is something which is neither group nor series, but what Malraux, in *Days of Hope*, called the Apocalypse, that is to say, the dissolution of the series in a fused group (*groupe en fusion*)."[8]

Sartre chooses to analyze the storming of the Bastille in order to shed light on this transmutation, which is partially linked to the sacred by the Apocalypse. To this end, he takes up the most conventional sequence in the historiography of the French Revolution and abandons May–June 1789, which does not occupy a central place in the *Critique*. While May–June 1789 provided a foundational empirical laboratory, the storming of the Bastille allows him to stage a new question, that of ubiquity: everywhere at the same time and without necessarily a point of contact, necessity becomes active and common. The site of politics in May–June 1789 was a Hall. On the 14th of July, it is a city. It also helps explain how a population becomes a subject of History.

For Sartre,[9] as long as each Parisian acts on their own account in order to defend themselves from the royal threat, they constitute a mere "collective." "The city was both the place, in its totalized and totalizing configuration (the threat of siege determining it as a milieu) and the population designated in the form of materiality sealed by military action which produced it as a confined crowd."[10] When faced with the gathering of the troops summoned by the king, there is effervescence and common action through imitation, as in a crowd: "People were running in the streets, shouting, forming gatherings, and burning down the gates of the toll houses."[11] Yet Sartre refers to a connection characterized by the "alterity of quasi-reciprocity"[12] between individuals who share the same fate. Collective conduct is not yet a common praxis that rises to an act of freedom, and Sartre evokes the classic term for the description of crowds: "contagion."

---

8 Jean-Paul Sartre, *Critique of Dialectical Reason* (London: Verso, 2004), 357.
9 The description produced by Sartre is not consistent with the event, as it does not take into account the fact that the armies massed in the Champ de Mars are populated by soldiers who refuse to obey orders to shoot the rioters. There is indeed a siege of the Bastille, and of the armies massed around Paris by the king, but not really of the city. There is also no individualized or serialized safeguard, in Sartre's vocabulary, because the bourgeois militia composed of 48,000 men is already prepared on July 12, and the weapons sought at the "Invalides" and the Bastille must serve to arm them. The process described by Sartre therefore has little empirical validity. We will soon see why.
10 Sartre, *Critique of Dialectical Reason*, 353.
11 Ibid.
12 Ibid.

But he quickly asserts that this term is not suitable. Even if fear has led this collective to arm themselves by looting the armories, it is not yet a *group* that arms itself, because each one does so in competition with the others. Fear of massacre can lead members of a collective to kill rather than help each other. And yet for the Parisians, "the weapons themselves, in so far as they had been taken for the sake of opposing concerted action by soldiers, suggested in their very materiality the possibility of concerted resistance."[13] The series is still present here, but dissolves in the decision to produce a militia of forty-eight thousand citizens and to charge the districts with constituting it. It should be noted that the reasoning that animates Sartre's description here takes up the categories which had made it possible to analyze May–June 1789: a contained place which engenders the feeling of commonness, the materiality of worked objects which leads to the transmutation of the series into a group.

But for Sartre, the situation is still filled with contradictions between the interests of the Parisian authorities who do not want the formation of this group, and the crowd that pushes for its realization and which finally does so through a confrontation with these deceptive authorities.

When, extraordinarily, the crowd gains the upper hand—with a view to the "public safety" (*salut public*), as the revolutionaries would say—without a leader dominating and without the action being concerted, then the fused group emerges and attests to a free praxis. "[I]n the Apocalypse, though seriality still exists at least as a process which is about to disappear, and although it always may reappear, synthetic unity is always *here*. Or, to put the same point in another way, throughout a city, at every moment, in each partial process, the part is entirely involved and the movement of the city is fulfilled and signified in it."[14] Ubiquity makes it so that the universal is realized in myriad analogous singular universals. In each singularity resides the common universal. "'By evening [of July 13th],' wrote Montjoye, 'Paris was a new city. Regular cannon shots reminded the people to be on their guard. And added to the noise of the cannon there were bells sounding a continuous alarm. The sixty churches where the residents had gathered were overflowing with people. Everyone there was an orator.' The city was a fused group."[15]

Sartre then describes the storming of the Bastille philosophically and in an extremely complex, almost hallucinatory way, especially for readers who are not philosophers. It is not my intention here to reproduce this

---

13 Ibid., 354.
14 Ibid., 357.
15 Ibid., 357–58.

complexity, but to grasp what actually led Sartre to choose July 14, 1789, as a historical example that makes it possible to understand the economy of creation of the fused group. This choice is rooted in a set of philosophical, historiographical, and historical concerns. "The reason for using the example of the Fourteenth of July is that it shows how a new regroupment dissolves a habitual seriality into the homogeneity of a fused city: the constituted reality had ceased to exist long ago and for a time the violence of the danger and the pressure (what Jaures called a historical fever) overcame social heterogeneities."[16] Thus the notion of the fused group is linked to an imaginary in which history is already affected by a temperature, "hot" or "cold," as in the Marxist historiographical tradition. The history of emancipation assumes an intense heat, a moment of indistinction when individuals are no longer assigned to a given collective and can merge with the event.

Such a fusion, or co-fusion resembles what socials sciences today call "desectorization,"[17] which is the creative moment of a historic event in the social field. Yet Sartre takes special care to explicitly distinguish this phenomenon from the question of coalition in struggles, which he characterizes as "neopositivist," "utilitarian," and "non-dialectical." It is not the fact that nobody can protect themselves without unifying that creates fusion, but rather that the feeling that one's own death has become "a specification of the common danger."[18] In the first case, reason remains analytical; in the second, it consists of dialectical reason. "The truth is not that the campaign of repression linked individual risks to the risks run by everyone. [. . .] [T]his kind of rationalism is not dialectical, and, though Marxists sometimes make use of it, its analytical, utilitarian origins are quite apparent."[19] For Sartre, "This type of group (a homogeneity of fusion) produces itself as its own idea [. . .]: it is (by totalising extension) *the sovereign nation*."[20] So it is not interest at work but the social imagination, or ideology in the emotional dynamics described: fear, effervescence, the feeling of having been betrayed by the authorities, but also sacredness of matter worked into weapons, the city as a site containing the society to come. "At this level, everyone, as a *third party*, became incapable of distinguishing his own safety from that of the Others. This was not an issue of altruism and egoism; such behaviour, in so far as it exists in this very schematic form, constitutes itself on the basis of existing circumstances and it preserves human relations

---

16 Ibid., 362.
17 On this point I go back to Michel Dobry, *Sociologie des crises politiques, la dynamique des mobilisations multisectorielles* (Paris: Presses de sciences politiques, 1986).
18 Sartre, *Critique of Dialectical Reason*, 368.
19 Ibid.
20 Ibid., 363.

which are engraved in the practico-inert field, in transcending them."²¹ This transcending (*dépassment*) is thus not ineffable. It is the role of the historian to describe the field of the practico-inert in order to understand the event. This field is certainly a sign of the inertia of the series, but also in certain circumstances the promise of regeneration not simply of the group, but of "humanity itself."

The word "Apocalypse," foundational to this philosophical reflection, returns regularly to the tip of Sartre's pen. He uses it in *Situations II* to evoke and analyze the Liberation of Paris, and he explains in the *Critique* that if he studies it, it is because "its historical reality is undeniable: in certain circumstances, a group emerges 'hot' (*à chaud*) and acts where previously there were only gatherings and, through this ephemeral, superficial formation, everyone glimpses new, deeper, but *yet to be created* statutes (the Third Estate as a group from the standpoint of the nation, the class as a group in so far as it produces its apparatuses of unification, etc.)."²² The fused group is endowed with a free praxis that creates a new world.

There is no doubt that in the description of the storming of the Bastille, the images of the Liberation of Paris evoked in *Situations II* function as a superimposition and distort the description. Hence in Paris, in the month of August 1944, "the soldiers we met in the streets were young men in short sleeves; their weapons were revolvers, a few guns, a few grenades, some bottles of gasoline; they got drunk in front an enemy covered in iron, feeling the freedom, the lightness of their movements. [. . .] And one could not help but think of what Malraux, in *L'Espoir*, calls the 'exercise of the Apocalypse.' Yes it was the triumph of the Apocalypse [. . .] that is to say a spontaneous organization of revolutionary forces. All of Paris felt during this week in August that man's chances were still intact. The FFI have at all times, behind every barricade and on every road, exercised freedom for themselves and for every Frenchman."²³

Sartre speaks again of the "explosion of freedom," of "rupture with the established order," and of the "invention of effective and spontaneous order." All terms which he could apply to either of these events. In the text on the Liberation, Sartre compares it to the storming of the Bastille, but opposes the men of July 1789, who were unaware of the symbolic meaning and stakes of their action, with the men of August 1944, who are conscious of making history. We know as historians today that the commemoration of the symbolic stakes of the storming of the Bastille did not wait long to

---

21 Ibid., 367–68.
22 Ibid., 382.
23 Jean-Paul Sartre, *Situations II* (Paris: Gallimard, 1948), 189.

take shape, and even that the figure of despotism that was the shadow of the fortress over the Saint-Antoine neighborhood forms a part of what makes it possible to think the "taking of the Bastille."[24] Fifteen years later, in the *Critique*, Sartre knows it, too, and there is another conception of history that he can therefore offer with acuity. We will come to that.

THE PLEDGE AND TERROR

The question of the Oath assumes great significance when it comes to understanding how what Sartre calls a "fused group" can be consolidated into a "pledged group." The fused group is in effect extremely fragile. As soon as the action is taken, it can disappear. Indeed, if it is a synthetic procedure of totalization, it is one that is never complete, which makes it possible to guarantee the freedom of each singularity in the ubiquity (all places are concerned at the same time and in the same way).

> In short, my integration becomes a *task to be done*; in so far as I am designated abstractly in my membership of the group (as one of its members) and in so far as I am really unified by my *praxis* as common *praxis here*, I become a *regulatory third party*, that is to say, my action presents itself as *the same* in the very slight dislocation which derives from the non-realisation of membership; and as it is freedom, this infinitesimal (but impassable) distance produces it as the free reflection here of the common action.[25]

The gap between each of us and one another is not, for Sartre, an obstacle but a condition of the fused group. To this end, he speaks of that which is neither pure transcendence nor pure immanence. Pure immanence would lead to a hyper-organism which would do away with "the innumerable refractions of *the same* operation," and there would be no regulating action: "In other words, the action would be blind, or would become inertia. Pure transcendence, however, would shatter the practical community [. . .]."[26] So as a totalization that remains in progress, the fused group can always come undone and return to the inertia of the series.

In order for the fused group to avoid collapsing, it must consolidate, and Sartre calls this act of consolidation the "pledge": "When freedom

---

24 On this point, see H.-J. Lusenbrink, and R. Reichardt, "La Bastille dans l'imaginaire social de la France à la fin du XVIII e siècle (1774–1789)," *RHMC*, Paris, no. 2 (1983): 196.
25 Sartre, *Critique of Dialectical Reason*, 408.
26 Ibid., 409.

becomes common *praxis* and grounds the permanence of the group by producing its own inertia through itself and in mediated reciprocity, this new statute is called *the pledge (le serment)*."[27] The pledge thus becomes that which is non-dialectical in the process of dialectical freedom, "an inert determination of the future"[28] which "protects" the group "against the threats of the practico-inert."[29] The "pledge-conjuration" of the Tennis Court Oath is again evoked, but as a possible form of this "stabilized freedom."[30] Sartre speaks of a movement that consists of swearing (*jurer*) to make others swear where each one becomes a demand for the freedom of the other in a common gesture. "Let us swear" is thus a slogan decided together. "Yes, in *this dangerous mission* which may save *us*, or save me in the totality, I exist in everyone as his trust and courage."[31]

This notion of rescue evokes, as we have said, the notion of public safety (*salut public*) in relation to the French Revolution, and indeed what Sartre seems to describe stems from this reciprocity of freedom that founds collective responsibility in the very same movement, even if each, as a third-party mediator, retains a responsibility which is also individual in nature. In Sartre's vocabulary—which is also partly the vocabulary of the revolutionaries—if the enemy proposes a separate negotiation, exercises terror, practices torture, it is a question of standing up in the face adversity, of neither fleeing, nor disbanding, nor betraying. We can clearly see that the French Revolution and the Second World War both inhabit the empirical imagination of this theorization of the pledge, just as the storming of the Bastille and the Liberation of Paris inhabited the theorization of the fused group. From this point of view, Sartre is a philosopher who weaves the empirical and the theoretical and thus invites analogies which, in my opinion, have methodological value for the historian in their political contract, but still lack a historicism which would make it possible to ground the scientific contract.

Nevertheless, the reciprocity of the pledge is ambivalent here. It is liberating because it saves everyone's freedom through consolidation in the face of the enemy. But it "limits this freedom from within," and this is what Sartre names "Terror." "The regulatory third party reveals that the diminishing fear of danger is the real threat, and that it must be counteracted by an increasing fear of destroying the group itself."[32] To save the

---
27 Ibid., 419.
28 Ibid., 420.
29 Ibid., 421.
30 Ibid., 419.
31 Ibid., 426.
32 Ibid. 430.

common interest, there must be established "a set of real means (accepted for everyone by all) of establishing in the group a reign of absolute violence over its members."[33] The pledge "simply gives everyone, as a member of the group, the right of life and death over everyone, either as an individual or as a member of a series."[34] "To swear is to say, as a common individual: you must kill me if I secede. And this demand has no other aim than to install Terror within myself as a free defence against the fear of the enemy (at the same time as reassuring me about the third party who will be confirmed by the same Terror)."[35] Sartre also calls this "the origin of Humanity," as "freely sworn faith,"[36] where one is both ready to die and to kill in the name of freedom—hence the revolutionary statement "liberty or death." For Sartre, violence is then free because it is not exercised from without by the enemy, but from within as self-constraint, which constitutes freedom as Terror. Claude Lefort says nothing less a few years later when he affirms that with terror, as with freedom, you have to want it.[37] For Sartre, therefore, it is the human capacity to assume its own violence that also grounds its capacity to found itself as humanity. Violence should not be designated only as a danger, but as a means to avoid ceding on the continued necessity of making humanity. To perfect, if you will, the picture, this Terror-Humanity is also called Terror-Fraternity, because it involves, within the pledged group, the assertion of justice through a violence which is reciprocal and latent, and sometimes actual. The pledge thus creates a kind of brother-in-arms, ready to exercise justice on anyone in the event of betrayal. Fraternity as "*our common being*" is not "*an identical nature.*" Rather, "it is a mediated reciprocity of conditionings: in approaching a third party, I do not recognise my inert essence as manifested in some other instance; instead I recognise my necessary accomplice in the act which removes us from the soil: my brother, whose existence is not other than mine."[38] "We are brothers in so far as, following the creative act of the pledge, we *are our own sons*,[39] our common creation." "[F]raternity is expressed in the group by a set of reciprocal and individual obligations."[40] The fused group has become a group with freely agreed constraints and who produces its institutions of constraint. For

---

33 Ibid. 430–31.
34 Ibid. 431
35 Ibid.
36 Ibid.
37 Claude Lefort, "La Terreur révolutionnaire," *Passé-Présent* 2 (1983): 25.
38 Sartre, *Critique of Dialectical Reason*, 437.
39 Also evoked by Lynn Hunt in *The Family Romance of the French Revolution* (Berkeley: University of California Press, 1992). Also Jacques André in *La Révolution fratricide, essai de psychanalyse du lien social* (Paris: PUF, 1993).
40 Ibid., 437.

Sartre, the Terror is thus jurisdiction—the constrained group produces right (*droit*). Sartre returns once again to the sacred dimension of this bond: "Any pledged group, as a diffuse power of jurisdiction, manifests itself for every third party, and in the totalization performed by the other third party, as a sacred power."[41] Free praxis "recognises the inert limitation in it of its possibilities as an absolute gift and a creation which proceeds from inert freedom as a sacred power."[42] For Sartre, Terror-violence manifests itself in negative forms (liquidation of the different, the suspected, the treacherous) and positive forms (fraternization). To get rid of the negative forms would amount to also renouncing the positive, and to this extent renouncing humanity as a process of humanization through free praxis.

Free praxis or collective freedom thus comes at a terrible cost, that of death which is constantly lurking. It is through a collectively assumed violence that the pledged group protects itself against external violence. It has won its solidity at this price. But this violence in and for everyone can, in its turn, become deadly. If humanity is formed on such a basis, no optimism is possible. Because far from grounding fraternity in the love of a common object, even in the society created by the pledged group, it is grounded on the one hand in a permanent effort, and on the other in mutual suspicion. The inertia of the group, that is, its ability to last, depends on this double movement: I can strive to be free if my brother also strives to be. I cannot save my individual freedom outside the group, since it is engulfed by the practico-inert, and free praxis is ephemeral, so I alienate this fragile individual freedom in the group by asking everyone to be the guarantor, on the one hand, of my individual freedom (consolidated through effort) and, on the other, of our collective freedom as reciprocity of this stabilized freedom. The pledge, Sartre claims, protects me from others and from myself. Humanity as pledged group would then be indissociably and necessarily mutual suspicion and mutual protection. Suspicion-Terror, Protection-Terror. This reciprocity, which he had not envisioned in the ideological analysis of revolutionary right (*droit révolutionnaire*) is now, for Sartre, the basis of his analysis of the social and political bond. However, the logic of revolutionary right (*droit*) is indeed that of reciprocal freedoms that are self-limiting, or support and assume their free movement. Reciprocity, when domination is no longer in effect, even makes it possible to conceive that the freedom of some increases the freedom others, which Bakunin asserts when he affirms that the freedom of others increases his own freedom.

---

41 Ibid., 442
42 Ibid.

Conversely, when limits are crossed by a relationship of domination, it is up to each and to all to resist the oppression. I am struck by this proximity between the Sartrean socio-political philosophy, and the revolutionary juridical theory borne by the natural law of the Declarations of 1789 and 1793, which also create social and political bonds. Indeed, we can regard the Declarations as established figures of what Sartre calls the pledge. There is in the idea of resistance to oppression and in the idea of maintaining in the face of tyranny, the imagination of a praxis of constant vigilance and of a violence in reserve, which is not constitutive of an independent daily life, but which guards against the dissolution of society through domination. As in the moment of Tennis Court Oath, the group becomes a "requirement" (*exigence*) through the Oath—and therefore, for Sartre, through a free praxis—and not through an external pressure exerted on the fused group. This is why in Sartre, the Terror is a sacred terror, which does not pertain to the theologico-political but rather to an Oath which must always be invented in a situation, and to free praxis sustained by effort.

This effort is one of resistance to oppression, an inalienable natural right in the Declaration of 1789 (article 2) and the keystone of that of 1793, since resistance to oppression is the consequence of other rights of man (article 33), and freedom is only thinkable if it is genuinely shared by all. Ultimately, this is not so far from what Bakunin says when he defends the idea that freedom is not individual but is dependent on the freedom which exists in the social body, in society as such. As he writes:

> I am only truly free when all the human beings around me, men and women, are equally free. The freedom of others, far from being a limitation or negation of my freedom, is on the contrary its necessary condition and confirmation. I do not become truly free except through the freedom of others, so that the greater the number of free people I am surrounded by, and the more profound and broad is their freedom, the further it extends, the more profound and broad does my own freedom become.[43]

This assertion of Bakunin's in fact repeats, in my view, article 34 of the Declaration of 1793: "There is oppression against the social body when a single one of its members is oppressed: there is oppression against each member when the social body is oppressed." We are truly free only insofar as each is free. The pledge consists of having to maintain this freedom, even at the cost of life. Liberty or death.

---

43 Mikhail Bakunin, *L'Empire Knouto-Germanique et la révolution sociale 1870–1871* (Paris, Institut international d'histoire sociale, Champ libre, 1982), 173. Translator's rendering.

6

THE QUESTION OF DIALECTICAL TIME, OR THE INANITY OF THE NOTION OF THE REARGUARD

The question of time is central to the *Critique of Dialectical Reason* and to the Sartrean reflection on History. The dialectic imposes a time in movement, "ongoing." Totalization as a requirement of the Truth of knowledge (*Vérité du savoir*) is not fixed but, because it is dialectical, is constantly inscribed in a quest. It could be called an "ongoing effort of totalization." The Truth is always in a process of becoming. To a certain extent, dialectical Reason—which is Reason in touch with Being as defined by Sartre, namely as fundamentally historical—does not aim to make completed and consultable knowledges, with tidy and distinct objects, available. For Sartre, knowledge only has the power to enlighten in the movement that links being and knowledge (*connaissance*) in one movement of being. Through the involvement of the being caught up in this search for the Truth of Man, each event is a gateway to totalization. But this totalization is not totality. Living knowledge is never completed and certain; it is not an archivable sum but a movement, the consciousness *for* humans of belonging to a whole *as* a human. The dialectic of totalization and the whole cannot be understood without this human temporality, without human time being consciously apprehended as a historical condition. As such, for Sartre, dialectical reason is opposed to analytical and positivist reason, which proved its legitimacy in the eighteenth century but which, according to him, is "behind us."[1]

---

1 Jean-Paul Sartre, *Critique of Dialectical Reason* (London: Verso, 2004), 823.

Chapter 6

PROGRESS OF EMANCIPATION, DISCONTINUITY OF HISTORICAL EFFORTS

This "behind us" draws a timeline which is one of "progress," with an order of objects and relations which obeys it. Tomorrow is inventing. It is question of inventing "a new form of Reason, that is, a new relation between thought and its object."[2] However, this invention seems to invalidate analytical reason and its attempt at anthropology, its endeavor toward a knowledge of Man. Its temporality, where the past is past and the present is stretched toward a future which is by definition better, resembles "a rosy future."[3] This progress-temporality is critiqued in *Search for a Method* and in volume 2 of *Critique of Dialectical Reason*.

This "behind" could certainly have referred to a simple ordering of time: past, present, and future. But it in fact indicates the need for an advancement toward the better. It is indeed "progress." Yet this progress paradoxically blurs precisely this line of temporality by the very dialectic of the situations to be analyzed. He is himself involved in the effort that he describes, namely, that of the subject who strives for emancipation. If progress is ultimately preserved, it is not in the name of the arch of historical time—which can take various forms, even create aberrations, buckles, discontinuities—but of that being who does or does not emancipate themselves. Progress—the only one that Sartre thinks of—is emancipation. In this respect, the difficult reflexivity of the work, so dense on these questions of temporality, is that of this complex temporality of emancipation. If Sartre asserts that "chronological order" is, "from a dialectical perspective . . . always the most significant,"[4] he also affirms that his analyses are not historical in nature. Understanding how serial sociality can give way to fused groups and to humanity itself does not presuppose that seriality necessarily precedes the fused group.

> Who could claim that collectives come before groups? No one is in a position to advance any hypothesis on this subject; or rather—despite the data of prehistory and ethnography—no such hypothesis has any meaning. Besides, the constant metamorphosis of gatherings into groups and of groups into gatherings would make it quite impossible to know *a priori* whether a particular gathering was a primary historical reality or whether it was the remains of a group which had been reabsorbed by the field of passivity: in either case, only the study of earlier structures and conditions can answer the question—if anything can.[5]

---

2 Ibid.
3 *"des lendemains qui chantant."*
4 Sartre, *Critique of Dialectical Reason*, 821.
5 Ibid., 348.

Thus, as a gesture, emancipation is progress with respect to the freedom on which man is founded. This does not, however, entail historical progress, but rather sequences of emancipatory effort and sequences of relapse into passivity.

HISTORY APPEALS TO HISTORY: A CRITIQUE OF PROGRESS

The critique of historical progress emerging from the homogenous and empty time of Cartesian thought appears in some depth in note 2 of the chapter on the progressive-regressive method. There, Sartre criticizes Marxism, which, he says, "achieves the totalization of human activities within a homogeneous and infinitely divisible continuum which is nothing other than the 'time' of Cartesian rationalism."[6] He then refers to a *middle temporality*, the temporality engendered by the capitalist economy, which is capable of accounting for capital. "But the description of this universal container as a phase of social development is one thing and the dialectical determination of *real* temporality (that is, of the true relation of men to their past and their future) is another."[7] This true or real relation could today be called a "regime of historicity,"[8] that is, a way of arranging the different times of the lived experience of history. But these regimes of historicity are not given, they are constructed by humans in society. "One must understand that neither men nor their activities are *in time*, but that time, as a concrete quality of history, is made by men on the basis of their original temporalization."[9] Time is no longer an *a priori* given of consciousness, but a product of everyone's historical sociality.

Sartre then refers to the period when "Marxism caught a glimpse of true temporality when it criticized and destroyed the bourgeois notion of 'progress' which necessarily implies a homogeneous milieu and coordinates which would allow us to situate the point of departure and the point of arrival. But without ever having said so Marxism has renounced these studies and preferred to make use of 'progress' again for its own benefit."[10]

The only Marxist who has truly and directly critiqued progress is, in my view, Walter Benjamin in his *Theses on the Concept of History*. Benjamin

---

6 Jean-Paul Sartre, *Search for a Method* (New York: Vintage, 1968), 91.
7 Ibid., 92
8 On this notion of historicity, I refer back to the work of François Hartog, *Régimes d'historicité. Présentisme et expériences du temps* (Paris: Seuil, 2003).
9 Sartre, *Search for a Method*, 92.
10 Ibid.

is not afraid to think the "sacred," and "sovereignty" as such, just as Sartre sought to do in the historical moment of the postwar 1960s. The theses were published in *Temps Modernes* in 1947.[11] For Benjamin, the temporality of progress blinds Marxists (this applies as much to social-democrats as to communists). In calling progress into question, he invokes Blanqui. For Benjamin, Blanqui's *Eternity by the Stars* shows that blindness comes from phantasmagoria: "Blanqui's cosmic speculation includes the teaching that humanity will be gripped by mythical anguish as long as phantasmagoria occupy a place in it." "Humanity becomes a figure of the damned. Anything new it could hope for will be revealed as a reality which was always already present; and this novelty will be as little able to provide it with a liberating solution as a new fashion is able to renew society." Phantasmagoria, or the absence of lucidity, entails a pure repetition of the same cycle and hence does not allow for progressive emancipation. The only thing produced by a present caught in phantasmagoria is not emancipation, but an *illusio*.

For Benjamin, this *illusio* described by Blanqui of Second Empire France is also that of the 1930s, during which time the social-democrats, like the communists, are fascinated by technical progress. Benjamin is therefore desperately attempting to open the eyes of his contemporaries to the future that was being drawn. This drawing is so disconcerting that it was necessary to sound the "fire alarm" so as to stop the train of supposed progress, thus preventing it from crashing into the worst dehumanization. The critique of progress is, then, the critique of an imaginary where humanity is given once and for all, decidedly in motion toward extension and maturation and without risk of collapse. As we know, Marxist actors in the history of the 1930s remained blinded, grave symptoms of which were the refusal, in Germany, of life-saving alliances on the left against Nazism, and the German-Soviet nonaggression pact. As for the effects, they remain immeasurable. Walter Benjamin was not heeded, and the insights, although considered fundamental, are disavowed. Fundamental, in effect, because the "[d]ialectic as a movement of reality collapses if time is not dialectic; that is, if we refuse to recognize a certain action of the future as such."[12] But, Sartre says, it would here take too long to study the dialectical temporality of History. He wishes only to "indicate the difficulties" and "formulate the problem."

---

11 Walter Benjamin, "Thèses sur le concept d'histoire," *Les Temps modernes*, no. 24 (October 1947): 623–34.
12 Sartre, *Search for a Method*, 92.

Sartre returns to this problem directly, in my view, at the very end of volume 2 of the *Critique of Dialectical Reason,* on the page titled "History Appeals to History." It is here that the dialectic takes on all its historical meaning. This dialectic is the drawing into of relation of different histories (as we have just seen with the storming of the Bastille and the Liberation of Paris in 1944) and thus different times, which creates the very possibility of the totalization or incarnation of history, an enveloping totalization, always unachieved because it is unachievable for the individual who is conscious of History. "[E]very history, as soon as relationships in the present or past are established with other histories, is the incarnation of History."[13] Every particular history therefore incarnates universal History. "(Temporal) History appeals to temporality as consciousness to consciousness: it can be comprehended and revived (by its practical exploitation) only through a historical praxis defining itself by its temporal development."[14] The analogical comparison of the storming of the Bastille with the Liberation of Paris sheds light on this day in a way that, if not new, is at least particularly vivid. The singular-universal of every event puts humanity in play again, re-totalizes it, frees it each time; and these events are like Parisians in the same city, joined together without need of a leader or great divine organizer. The only order comes from beings precisely insofar as they are historical and not simply natural or serial.

Sartre then imagines what a non-historical being would be. "An absolute mind without *development* (intuition) could not *comprehend* History."[15] If freedom is not altered by historical conditioning, monuments or archives will not acquire a sense of Totalization, will not incarnate History, and will remain partial objects with fleeting presence, even without presence. "[A] free practical organism will be able (in monuments, etc.) to rediscover the former presence of other free organisms, but not History itself. This free organism must himself be historical: i.e. himself conditioned by the interiorization of his bond in exteriority with the totalization; himself an incarnation; himself History. Conversely, he discovers himself as historical in his own movement of restoration of made history."[16]

What is said on this page is not only that the mode of relations which perpetuates a history in History is itself historical (which is to say, it evolves) but also, from my point of view, that this relation can cease if the relation which is historical consciousness ceases. If this relationship is no longer

---

13 CDR. vol.2 pg. 453.
14 Ibid.
15 Ibid.
16 Ibid.

maintained, no longer transmitted as an experience of humanization, historical consciousness is lacking.

In this way, Sartre is extremely close to Walter Benjamin, who explains that what we call "History of Civilization," which "makes an inventory, point by point, of humanity's life [. . .] riches thus amassed in the aerarium of civilization henceforth appear as though identified for all time. This conception of history minimizes the fact that such riches owe not only their existence but also their transmission to a constant effort of society—an effort, moreover, by which these riches are strangely altered."[17]

For Sartre, this failure of historical consciousness is in fact a failure of social and political consciousness, a failure which Sartre knew as a young man, when he could believe in a freedom that was not conditioned by its social and material inscription in the world.

True knowledge of History therefore depends on two determinations. On the one hand, that of temporal movement as material movement and of the place given to the future in this material movement and, on the other, that of the consciousness of being Historical *qua* historical being—that is to say, conditioned by material and temporal historical experience. This question of dialectical time, then, effectively combines Marxism and Existentialism, praxis and the true knowledge of dialectical Reason.

In seeking to make "History the Truth of Man," it is a question of promoting dialectical time and of exiting a new antinomy: that which opposes being and Truth. For Sartre, "Materialist monism, in short, has successfully eliminated the dualism of thought and Being in favour of total Being, which is thereby grasped in its materiality. But the effect of this has only been to re-establish, as an antinomy—at least an apparent one—the dualism of Being and Truth."[18] Truth is not given to being but only to nature. It is therefore a matter of asserting that by reintegrating thought in material givens, one is also reintegrating the consciousness of time, and in this way dialectical materialism is a materialism of being and not of nature alone. For the problem is there, the confusion of Man and Nature. In effect, "[t]his difficulty has appeared insurmountable to modern Marxists. They have seen only one solution: [. . .] to eliminate man by dispersing him into the universe. This enables them to substitute Being for Truth. There is no longer knowledge in the strict sense of the term; Being no longer manifests itself in any way whatsoever: [. . .] The dialectic of Nature is Nature without men. There is therefore no more need for certainty, for

---

17 Walter Benjamin, *Arcades Project*, Trans. Howard Eiland & Kevin McLaughlin. Cambridge, MA: Belknap, 1999. 14.
18 Sartre, *Critique of Dialectical Reason*, 1:26.

The Question of Dialectical Time, or the Inanity of the Notion of the Rearguard 81

criteria; even the attempt to criticise and establish knowledge becomes useless. Knowledge of whatever form is a relation between man and the world around him, and if man no longer exists this relation disappears."[19] In his critique of the dialectic of Nature, Sartre insists on the question of temporality. According to him, it is in the "aftermath" of the discovery of the dialectic—defined as the relations between man and matter and between men and each other—that men of knowledge wanted to unify this knowledge in a dialectic of Nature, making men disappear. "The attempt to find the movement of human history within natural history was made only later, out of a wish for unification. Thus the claim that there is a dialectic of Nature refers to the totality of material facts—past, present, future—or, to put it another way, it involves a totalisation of temporality."[20] For Sartre, the dialectic of nature is nothing other than a sort of Kantian idea. In his view, not only can human history not be folded into natural history, it is not even of the same order of knowledge. The knowledge of dialectical Reason is historically situated. "Consequently, this materialism, if it exists, can be true only within the limits of our social universe."[21] Contrary to the knowledge (*connaissance*) of nature which can produce immutable laws valid for action, dialectical Reason produces a knowledge (*savoir*) carried by being insofar as it is historical, a situated knowledge which for all that, claims a different kind of Truth, one which is known through the effort of a consciousness at work. "But if it were merely the inert expression of this rise, or even of revolutionary praxis, if it did not direct its attention back upon this rise so as to explain it, to reveal it to itself, how could we speak of a progress of consciousness? How could the dialectic be regarded as the real movement of History unfolding itself? Like philosophical liberalism today, it would be no more than a mythical reflection."[22]

PARTIAL HISTORICAL OBJECTS, OR DIALECTIC OF HISTORY

This theorization may appear absolutely abstract and indifferent to empirical analysis. But the question of historical time is the basis of the historical analyses carried out by Sartre. These analyses allow him, on the one hand, to thwart the fetishization of progress as a movement of History known in

---

19 Ibid.
20 Ibid., 29.
21 Ibid., 33.
22 Ibid., 25–26.

advance and, on the other, to oppose analytical positivism when it claims to be the sole source of empirical knowledge. They also allow him to thwart the discourse on history which asserts that it is nothing more than contingency devoid of meaning, at least of rational meaning.

The Sartrean effort thus consists of wanting to undermine this idea of history as irrational and meaningless without accepting the reconstruction of meaning we find in Hegel. Constituted when all is finished, this meaning becomes useless, or rather ineffectual insofar as knowledge of the past no longer acts on the present or the future. What worries Sartre with regard to this conception of history is ultimately that it leads human beings to a fatalist attitude, and eventually to a position that denies the responsibility assigned to everyone in history, a responsibility which, through true knowledge (*connaissance*) reaches precisely Enlightenment.

So this complex temporality allows him to show the ideological and historical complexity of the political positions of revolutionary social groups who are trying to emancipate themselves, and who are thus striving to "progress" in the Sartrean sense, and who have nevertheless been described by Marxist historians as "rearguards." It is not just the notions of rearguard and vanguard that Sartre calls into question but also the temporal analysis that they imply. When Sartre foregrounds uncertainties around the interpretation of the demand for the taxation of prices and wages claimed in 1793 by the *sans-culottes*—the temporal analysis—he deploys a conception of the historian's work consistent with dialectical materialism as a materialism of the Truth of Man.

Here again he seeks to confront the so-called vulgar Marxists: are the *sans-culottes*, asks Sartre, "as some Marxists have dared to say the rear guard of the Revolution?"[23] Like Georges Lefebvre, Sartre presents the *sans-culottes* as a heterogeneous "popular front" made up of "petit-bourgeois, artisans, workers." This social group suffers from the subsistence crisis and acts on the Convention and the Municipality by promoting an "ethical conception of bourgeois property"[24] and not by proposing another conception of property. However, this conception appears to some as a residue of paternalistic feudalism which guarantees to each a minimum of subsistence by authoritarian measures, and to others an anticipation: obtaining democratic rules of protection which fall under credit rights and, more specifically, the right to existence, which must take precedence over economic liberalism. The invention, in a way, of regulation. The same demand thus

---

23 Sartre, *Search for a Method*, 120.
24 Ibid., 118.

belongs to the past as a residue and to the future as a requirement (*exigence*). The bourgeoisie sees only the authoritarian residue and this "horrifies" it, Sartre tells us, "not out of immediate class interest." "These members of the convention, for the most part poor—intellectuals, lawyers, petty officials— had an ideological and practical passion for economic freedom."[25]

We can clearly see the timeline as it unfolds in this example is far from being linear, because the *sans-culottes* make the Revolution insofar as they pull history toward the future, whatever one says about them. But in the truth of this future, bourgeois capitalist exploitation is masked from them by the ethical imagination. By refusing their demands, the bourgeoisie prepares the return of the Bourbons and hastens the end of the Revolution, all while being determined to bring about liberalism. . . . Knowing the outcome teleologically does not help to know which force would be progressive or reactionary, and it is thus the entanglement of complex temporalities which makes the temporal movement of this history—a past projected into a democratic republican future, a present which prevents the Revolution from triumphing in the immediate, but which is nevertheless pregnant with a future desired by the bourgeoisie. . . . As the truth of the situation cannot be revealed, in place of the economic question, the political question takes precedence among the Montagnards, who defend the suffering people.

Note that the Montagnards are also Convention members, and that Sartre, while specifying what is irrelevant in the analysis of the *sans-culottes* as reargaurd, misses in this passage the precise analysis of the conflict at the center of the Convention and even at the heart of the bourgeoisie. The method he advocates, we can see, is difficult to maintain from beginning to end without passing once again through an analysis of the different groups that confront one another. But here it has the great merit, in my view, of showing how different times come together: the present of visible conflict; the past of experiences of protection as a familiar place; the monumental past, to the extent that it encourages some to act (the *sans-culottes*) but is fundamentally repulsive to others (the members of the Convention); the future requirement of the regulation of liberalism in the liberal critique of liberalism which confronts the present exigencies of savage liberalism. This liberal critique of liberalism offers an alternative critique to that of communism, and Sartre generally eschews it. Here he only presents it as a policy of pity for the suffering people, whereas it is less pity than the demand for justice associated with compassion, which makes it possible to incisively formulate this critical politics in which economics is subordinated to politics.

---

25 Ibid., 119.

Of course, as totalization in motion, no history is completed or can be completed. We can always go further and clarify thought, analysis, consciousness, without this necessarily going through a profusion of archival knowledge, but rather a profusion of questioning, and changes in the question. To this end, Sartre offers a specific conception of history as a discipline: "problem history." as opposed to history as accumulated knowledge. Here again he is close to Walter Benjamin.

Indeed, when Benjamin vehemently protests against a history which adheres to the notion of "unbreakable progress," he is fighting against the German communists and their conception of historical materialism. He fights with the optimism of his interlocutors at a moment when the worst is being realized under their eyes, but when they nevertheless persist in the belief that technical progress, including Soviet progress, will lead to emancipation. He fights with those who continue to cling to this arrow of the future and refuse to understand that the only way out is to interrupt time. "It may be that revolutions are the act by which humanity, travelling on the train, pulls the emergency brake."[26] Benjamin is aware of the coming catastrophe, and of the fact that the repetition is sometimes a catastrophe, precisely because it leads to repeating the catastrophe. It is thus a question of reconstructing a history made up of complex webs, detours, regressions, bifurcations, and advances, against the imaginary of a ribbon that unfolds smoothly. Revolutionary violence is the violence of hindrance, produced by resistance to a shared obviousness. This is the emergency brake, an action of braking, certainly, but above all "a memory that saves you." a relationship to history that opens up in the pulsation of the desperate present. Indeed, "if the present alone is the time of politics, then in the present any event of the past can acquire or retrieve a higher degree of actuality than it had at the moment when it took place."[27] This relationship to the present does not freeze any knowledge because even the past that has been described exposes itself in its uncertainty, its worry, its gamble, like the present which it illuminates so as to escape defeat.

If, then, it is a question of addressing history head-on, and of the history of the vanquished in particular, it is in order to "organize this pessimism," to confront the "bad poem of the social-democratic spring" as well as the illusions of the communists. The past, far from being ordered by the present, becomes again "a jungle" where you have to clear a path for

---

[26] Walter Benjamin, "Notes préparatoires sur les thèses sur le concept d'histoire," trans. M. de Gandillac (Paris: Denoël, 1971), 190. Translator's rendering.

[27] Walter Benjamin, "Sur le concept d'histoire," in Écrits français (1940) (Paris: Gallimard, 1991), 342.

thought. The French Revolution is a part of this jungle of the past of the 1930s, and remains both central and fleeting in this questioning of progress. Against the Marxist conception of the French Revolution as an illusion for having been carried out in Roman clothes, Benjamin resumes a Marxian position which, far from devaluing the *illusio,* makes it a driving force. Certainly, it is necessary to distinguish between the Roman costume as a motor of action in 1793 and the *illusio* of the Jacobin costume in 1848, but he valorizes the ability of the French revolutionaries to rearrange time with a view to emancipation. Thesis XIV of the *Theses on the Concept of History* is where he replaces this supposed illusion with a flair for the present.

> History is the subject of a structure whose site is not homogeneous, empty time, but time filled by the presence of the now. Thus, to Robespierre ancient Rome was a past charged with the time of the now which he blasted out of the continuum of history. The French Revolution viewed itself as Rome reincarnate. It evoked ancient Rome the way fashion evokes costumes of the past. Fashion has a flair for the topical, no matter where it stirs in the thickets of long ago; it is a tiger's leap into the past. This jump, however, takes place in an arena where the ruling class gives the commands. The same leap in the open air of history is the dialectical one, which is how Marx understood the revolution.[28]

Historians work in the arena, but actual revolutionary history is none other than this dialectical leap. This is why the Revolution is neither a continuity of time nor a clean slate but a rearrangement (*réagencement*) of times. The historian of the French Revolution must therefore grasp how this is carried out.

In this way, we can consider the *Critique of Dialectical Reason* as firmly rooted in another Marxist tradition,[29] that which grants an important place to the sacred and the critique of progress, and which seeks to invent a historical knowledge grounded in a familiarity with the lives of those on whom revolutionary praxis depends. This is a tradition that has not given up on understanding the French Revolution, far from it.

Sartre's questioning of time thus falls within the regime of questioning left fallow since the disappearance of this figure of Marxist dissidence during the Second World War. When he works on ideology, he works on the dialectical effort that allows individuals, even a society, to face contradictions so as to overcome them in a loop of time where language must be disentangled (*désenglué*) and serve precisely to traverse past and present time to bring about

---

28 Walter Benjamin, *Illuminations,* trans. Harry Zohn (New York: Schocken, 1937), 261.
29 This other tradition is affirmed by Michael Lowy and Daniel Bensaïd in an article on Blanqui as a heretical communist (http://www.danielbensaid.org/Auguste-Blanqui-communiste).

another future, a change in the situation, a rupture. When he works on the May–June 1789 moment, he works on the uncertainty which, in terms of temporality, is called "waiting," "suspense," the "leap." But he also works on a practico-inert which could be called "remnants," or as he puts it so well: the "indissoluble past in the present." It is thus the event, once again as a fact of rupture, which he analyzes in order to show that its advent in time does not stem solely from the present but from what he describes as the necessary articulation for bringing it about: a past which is sometimes unrecognized and indissoluble in the present, an already imaginable future and a line of sight for action, a present made up of decisions, anticipations, and leaps. It is, then, an event which ties together tradition, its subversion, its permanence, and the new, the unheard of, the incredible. Far from an event that is thoroughly ineffable, Sartre shows how the evental rupture is partly directed, and partly a result of what he calls magic. Recognizing one's part in the magical and even the sacred means recognizing that the timing of the event does not come from the lone decision, even if it is shaped by it. It is the recognition that time is not an object of mastery but the mysterious condition of possible openings. "The future is at once transcendent and cut from the present, at once formidable and veiled as a secret in the heart of the present."[30] We are thus very far from the line of progress, since what Sartre describes in the effort of emancipation is an imbrication of active timelines, without the active subject truly knowing it or being able to know it. Finally, when he analyzes the tearing-away from the practico-inert that is the emancipatory act, it is once again temporal stakes that capture his attention: those of creation and then foundation. There was nothing, or more exactly, the practico-inert reigned, and then something arrives, namely a fused group (*groupe en fusion*) which is capable of freedom. "Apocalypse" is, then, the central temporal category. Ultimately, what he calls "foundation through fraternity-terror" and the "oath" is an act which seeks to counter time, to obstruct its undermining work. Undoubtedly all work on History is also work with time, but in these texts of Sartre's, it is not only a question of working with it but also of thinking it, categorizing it, and making the categories of time useful for the process of synthetic knowledge of a truth in the making, inventing ones that are missing from the knowledge of revolutionary phenomena. The Sartrean effort consists of constructing a history that no longer makes time the invisible hand of historicity. To this end, he obliges every historian to make lived time a principle of analysis of each situation, each event. He obliges them to consider this materiality as foundational to another way of doing history.

---

30 "Manuscrit Mai–juin 1789," *Études sartriennes*, no. 12 (2008): 93.

CODA

Before placing this reading of Sartre on the French Revolution in dialogue with his commentators and detractors, I would like to show how his propositions resonate with my own work.

As I began my training as a historian, the critique of the major social categories in Marxism—"bourgeoisie" and "proletariat"—was, in my view, if not fully achieved, at least very advanced. This critique took an analogous form to that of Sartre. Far from the simplistically unified "bourgeoisie," historians pluralized the approach to groups with shared interests, treating them as cleaved, complex, and resistant to preconstructed notions. Girondins and Montagnards were certainly bourgeois, but what is common to a lawyer and ship owner, a landowner and a journalist? Shaped by unique social situations, the groups that compose what we call the bourgeoisie should not be too quickly subsumed by abstraction if we want to understand what marks a break. Régine Robin, in her 1970 thesis *French Society in 1789* in which she studied the list of grievances of Semur-en-Auxois, showed that this concept should not be abandoned but rethought. She invents the notion of the "Ancien Régime bourgeoisie," for whom capital rests on the wealth of land and office—a firmly Ancien Régime framework—but whose aspirations for political power unites them with the classical capitalist bourgeoisie.

In the 1980s, the social and economic question was still very present in the presentation and defense of the Marxist current of revolutionary historiography, but few theses were undertaken on these subjects. Of course, Michelle Vovelle still spoke of a "floating proletariat" in his books, but the qualifier is already a distanciation. The critique of vulgar Marxism is now well known, and it is precisely within Marxist circles that it is deployed by the heterodox against the orthodox. I, for my part, was trained at the Sorbonne by those who were heterodox—Michel Vovelle, Françoise Brunel, and Jacques Guilhaumou—who have never adhered to the schematic and readymade approaches of the vulgar Marxists. They fought against the orthodox currents embodied by Claude Mazauric and Albert Soboul.[31] Nevertheless, they retained from the latter his valuable analysis of the *sans-culottes* and popular sovereignty, and affirmed the necessity of renewing the acuity and finesse of the historian's mode of questioning, so as to make the story of the Revolution a site of fascination rather than an inheritance to peruse.

---

31 Note, however, that Albert Soboul in 1968 had nevertheless shown some libertarian tendencies in the demonstrations in which he participated.

The Sartrean reflection on ideology is not, we have seen, a reflection on a neat theory which immediately offers itself as such. It is a complex system to describe. Ideology can be seen in the efforts people make to clarify the contradictions between an obsolete but still hegemonic ideology, and the ideology to come which offers the possibility of resolving certain contradictions. As a result, it is above all a reflection on mediations, and specifically on language and its use by actors who are thoroughly traversed with contradictions, are trying to name them so as to overcome them and bring about another world. This sometimes happens in a conscious and explicit way—this is what Sartre calls a political position—and sometimes in a more confused way. Actors are thus inhabited by a language that outstrips them.

These questions were at the heart of the renewal of the history of the French Revolution in the 1970s and 1980s in the field of discourse analysis in the wake of Régine Robin's pioneering work. In her thesis on Semur-en-Auxois titled *French Society in 1789*,[32] she foregrounds language as inherently consequential and not a mere representation of a reality which provides the historian with a reservoir of information. But it is not Sartre who initiates this desire for discourse analysis, but Althusser. Régine Robin recounts the publication of Althusser's essay "Contradiction and Overdetermination" in 1965 in *La Pensée*, which addressed contradiction in Hegel and Marx and which functioned as the motor of this line of inquiry. Robin's major book *History and Linguistics*, published in 1973, takes stock of these theoretical issues and the experimentations that historians had already undertaken. Michel Foucault, Levi-Strauss, and Jacques Lacan are also called upon by the young historian, who finds her discipline too distant from their innovative thought. In the meantime, she had forged a strong alliance at Nanterre with the Department of Linguistics. And we have here the collection of intellectuals with whom Sartre battles in an article published in 1966 in *Arc*, in which he responds to his detractors by claiming that their thought in fact rejects history, and as a result, Marxism. This includes Althusser, moreover, who despite being a Marxist, privileges structures over human action in his analysis of history. Sartre reproaches these authors for having reversed a classic error on the question of mediations: language was "nothing," now it is "everything." The structuralists seem to believe that all thought passes through language, whereas in the past it had been denied any real, active function. Not everything is a sign, Sartre asserts. He thus resists the grip of structural linguistics as it is being

---

32 Régine Robin, *La Société française en 1789, Semur-en-Auxois* (Paris: Plon, 1979).

propagated in a dominating way, including in the renewal of Freud in Lacanian psychoanalysis. Among the initiators of French discourse analysis, in fact, Lacan plays an important role, especially for Michel Pêcheux, one of its originators.

When I examine the history of the French Revolution, and particularly in discourse analysis, the word *ideology* spurs an indissociably epistemological, methodological, and historiographical reflection.

Epistemologically, it is a question of recognizing the central place of language in the historical process. History as a learned discipline, seeking to understand what drives the movement of History, must understand that language is a historical actor and not a tool that actors activate at their will. We must therefore track the history of languages in their articulation with social formations in a double movement: that of language creation within established social groups, and the function of often obsolete languages at the heart of social groups who are inhabited and operated *by* them.

From a methodological point of view, it is a question of asserting that no text is transparent to its reader. It is not about finding, in the archive, information to be verified, but languages to be deciphered, both in terms of their social inscription and their functioning within what can be considered the mental structure they make visible. It is therefore important to identify both linguistic regularities and linguistic events. The latter form the basis of an efficient invention within social worlds, which themselves fold back on their social and political practices, on their praxis.

These different categories of discourse analysis oblige historians methodologically to form an alliance with linguistics. Linguistic events are also often enunciative events, and it is thus a matter of reintroducing context into a pragmatics of situations and games of enunciation. The complexity of the interactions of actors, grasped here in Sartre's analysis of May–June 1789, which is a kind of socio-analysis of everyone's position as it is actualized in arguments and strategies, has become, in the hands of discourse analysis, a pragmatics of enunciation. This pragmatics of discourse observes the play of "I," "we," "you"—shifters and verbal temporalities. But for language to become an event, it is necessary to show how it constitutes a rupture in a course of movement. The linguistic event is certainly part of enunciative reversals, but within thematic and semantic paths. The analysis of Marxist discourse by Althusser, a linguistic and psychoanalytic (Lacanian) structuralist, seems to me to ultimately pursue concerns quite close to those of Sartre. It puts language at stake in ideology and the event, as a tipping point and site of political efforts, but also of the pragmatic uncertainty of history which is always ultimately dependent on interaction between humans that do not have a good understanding of what they are doing but are determined to do it—neither pure subjects of freedom nor mere agents of a history that exceeds them. Nevertheless, this work goes on in the shadows because this current remains marginal for both epistemological and political reasons. Althusserians are heterodox on all fronts.

However, the discourse analysis of the historians is at once new and already worked on, by Sartre among others. Roland Barthes, in his *Writing Degree Zero* published in 1953, had set out the perspective of a "history of political modes of writing" as "the best of social phenomenologies."[33] He had already pushed this project quite far, studying among other things the French Revolution, which had even given him material for his opening remarks: "Hebert, the revolutionary, never began a number of his news-sheet *Le Pere Duchene* without introducing a sprinkling of obscenities. These improprieties had no real meaning, but they had significance. In what way? In that they expressed a whole revolutionary situation. Now here is an example of a mode of writing whose function is no longer only communication or expression, but the imposition of something beyond language, which is both History and the stand we take in it."[34]

His concerns seem to me to be quite close to questions of dialectics as Sartre thematizes them in the same historical conjuncture, though he published them seven years later. The dialectic here is that of Tradition and History as a site of invention.

> It is under the pressure of History and Tradition that the possible modes of writing for a given writer are established; there is a History of Writing. But this History is dual: at the very moment when general History proposes—or imposes—new problematics of the literary language, writing still remains full of the recollection of previous usage, for language is never innocent: words have a second-order memory which mysteriously persists in the midst of new meanings. Writing is precisely this compromise between freedom and remembrance, it is this freedom which remembers and is free only in the gesture of choice, but is no longer so within duration.[35]

Barthes analyzes this "freedom which remembers" in relation to the French Revolution in the form of a fairly convincing atonement.

---

33 Roland Barthes, *Writing Degree Zero*, trans. Annette Lavers and Colin Smith (Boston: Beacon Press Books, 1970), 25.
34 Ibid., 1.
35 Ibid., 16–17.

Baudelaire spoke somewhere of the "grandiloquent truth of gestures on life's great occasions.' The Revolution was in the highest degree one of those great occasions when truth, through the bloodshed that it costs, becomes so weighty that its expression demands the very forms of theatrical amplification. Revolutionary writing was the one and only grand gesture commensurate with the daily presence of the guillotine. What today appears turgid was then no more than life-size. This writing, which bears all the signs of inflation, was an exact writing: never was language more incredible, yet never was it less spurious. This grandiloquence was not only form modelled on drama; it was also the awareness of it. Without this extravagant pose, typical of all the great revolutionaries, [. . .] the Revolution could not have been this mythical event which made History fruitful, along with all future ideas on revolution. Revolutionary writing was so to speak the entelechy of the revolutionary legend: it struck fear into men's hearts and imposed upon them a citizen's sacrament of Bloodshed.[36]

In this passage, both the notion of myth and that of entelechy resonate with the questions that Sartre poses to the Revolution, since writing would be the force, the active power present in matter, in this instance blood which has been shed. This blood, then, is the passive power which awaits the act, and this transmutation through writing produces precisely the mythical dimension of the Revolution which becomes the landmark of all future revolutions. But by this very fact, Barthes's analysis also distances itself from that of Sartre who, in his quest for truth seeks to found it upon something beyond myth, namely dialectical reason.

There is therefore in every present mode of writing a double postulation: there is the impetus of a break and the impetus of a coming to power, there is the very shape of every revolutionary situation, the fundamental ambiguity of which is that Revolution must of necessity borrow, from what it wants to destroy, the very image of what it wants to possess. Like modern art in its entirety, literary writing carries at the same time the alienation of History and the dream of History; as a Necessity, it testifies to the division of languages which is inseparable from the division of classes; as Freedom, it is the consciousness of this division and the very effort which seeks to surmount it."[37]

He thus clarified the relation between a social situation, the possibilities of language, and the freedom of the writer in this dialectized temporality of

---

36 Ibid., 21–22.
37 Ibid., 87–88.

the past and present which prohibits the belief that the line of time, when it comes to this effort, is only linear. But the effort assumed this figure of the writer as a singular actor. What became henceforth almost lamentable was this very same figure.

I can remember a certain dogmatism asserting the autonomy of social discourse without passing through the actors who at once (evidently) spoke it but could also subvert it. What had changed is that, by no longer speaking of the actor or the writer, we were no longer speaking of writers either, but of language as a given structure which has changed and evolved, but without it being explained how people managed to make them change. In the same movement, it was thus impossible to make these questions of discourse analysis hang together, where language became an object to be dissected thanks to linguistic tools, far away from any sensory phenomenology, and equally far from the question of writing history that would not be bland writing. Jacques Guilhaumou defended the absence of the historian in a pure assembly of archives that could do without meta language. It was no longer a question of dialectically understanding History—thanks, among other things, to written language—but of describing the languages of a historical moment. What had given this matter an exhilarating character was not the beginnings of Barthes or Sartre but the structuralist attack on the subject, the actor, and on the freedom of the subject as such in favor of the positive valuation of the position of scientific knowledge.

Nevertheless, the fact of having been immersed in discourse analysis since my first steps into research, the questions of an epistemological moment that continued that of the 1960s had, without my being consciously aware of it, made these problems familiar to me.

In 1982, Michel Vovelle had published a collection of articles titled *Ideology and Mentalities*, where he attempted to present his own point of view on these notions, so as to show that ideology and mentalities were not two ways—one Marxist and the other not—of speaking about the same thing, but rather two ways of understanding the famous question of complex mediations between the real life of men and their collective imaginary. If, according to him, texts were vehicles of ideology, and the aim was to grasp mentalities, then evidence of these mentalities had to be sought in other sources: gestures which attest to them, rituals, images, festivals, testaments. Ideology, in his view, wavers between clear thinking and the hazy ether of ignorance. This gap between ideology and mentalities, however, is subverted by the very idea of revolutionary mentalities. The event creates new mentalities in a forceful rupture. It seems to me, then, that the categories invoked resonate with the fused group because for these mentalities to be entirely different but mentalities all the same, the question of emotions comes into play, in particular those studied by Georges Lefebvre in the 1930s, namely, fear and hope. But we must also bring in the question of a temporality that includes the future in the present by this very hope. Revolutionary mentalities are thus opposed to long-term prisons which, for their part, are the place and the result of a non-programmable transmutation. Far from Lukacs's "carnivals of subjectivities," the revolution of mentalities is a process of subjectivation that does not arise from the free subject, but rather from a subject who is caught in a new revolutionary sociality that transforms them through praxis.

In 1985–1986 I was a bachelor's student, and Michel Vovelle's course dealt with the revolutionary mentality. In the resulting book, Vovelle investigates precisely if it is possible to change human beings in ten years. He wants to show that the event is indeed a specific moment, the producer of "irreversibles"[38] in the articulation of lived emotions and the political event, through logics that are not so far from Malraux's and Sartre's notion of *Apocalypse*.

All these ways of reflecting on the consistency and the effectivity of revolutionary rupture in society seem to me today perfectly congruous with the Sartrean project of the *Critique*. If the question of revolutionary emotions had been more or less absent from discourse analysis, I could find it in the analysis of mentalities. The conjunction of socio-critique of texts, which had never ignored social formations, and the analysis of highly formalized discourses in linguistics and the analysis of mentalities had, without my knowing it, given me a certain familiarity with what I eventually discovered in Sartre's thought.

What would remain missing for me was the question of the sacred and its relationship to the emotions and to the establishment of the pledged group. Missing, too, was the critique of progress that makes it possible to study history in its relation to actuality and the present, and not as mere accumulation.

Certainly, enunciative pragmatics can have as one of its aims the return to the emotions, but the category of emotions is never named as such. For me, however, emotions constantly surface in my work on the figure of the foreigner during the French Revolution: in the very writing of revolutionaries steeped in the eighteenth-century recovery of pathos, but also in the motives that animate the decisions taken with respect to so called "foreigners" (*étrangers*). As for the emotions which engage the historian, or are signs

---

38 *producteur d'irréversibles*.

of their commitment, they are vigorously expelled by the discipline, which even refuses Georges Duby's positions in his response to the demand for an ego-history. Simply for having spoken of subjectivity and intuition, of flair, he was aggressively criticized. If Jacques Guilhaumou knew that his work on the death of Marat was a way for him to metabolize the death of the Communist Party, he said nothing of it in his text.

In my view, on the contrary, we should not relegate the historian's subjectivity back of the book but foreground the quest they sets in motion. The relation to the present of political praxis and its questionings should be clearly legible and clarified. Writing the history of the figure of the foreigner in the revolutionary period is simultaneously a reflection on the present situation of "foreigners" in France—in the folds of France's complex history, at once intimate and collective. The Sartrean subject who is conditioned by history is the one I seek to put into practice. Doing history, for me, means recognizing that I am historically constituted, and that it is a matter of making this constitution speak, in addition to realizing the necessity of historical work, the work of the historian. It was Walter Benjamin and Nicole Loraux, then, who allowed me to allow myself these back-and-forths that were forbidden, despite their being accused of subjectivism and anachronism. Here, too, Sartre is very familiar, since the crime of subjectivism very much arises from the antinomy of Truth and Being. In the very same way, subjectivity is always accused of making positive knowledge, which is by definition objective, disappear. Involving subjective being consists in making the positive truth disappear. For my part, I am betting on a truth that, to the contrary, could only come about in this necessity of being. Not because being is entirely historical—it is also singular—but above all because it is the place where the need for a social group is expressed, and because I accept this condition of historical work as a quasi-anthropological given. I can only work on the history of the French Revolution because this history resonates with the social imaginaries of my group. Their disappointed or fulfilled hopes, their desires to know, their present aspirations. To this end, yes, the history that I want to produce is always located in space and time, and at the same time aspires to the universal singular, Sartre's "ongoing totalization" in its relation to other times and other places. Anachronism thus seems to me the condition of the historian's work, a necessity.

Nevertheless, anachronism does not necessarily imply adherence to dialectical History. The anachronistic method, as described by Nicole Loraux in 1993, seems to me to be mixed with elements of positivism and psychoanalysis.

To better understand what happened in the 1980s and 1990s, we must continue down the path of the 1960s. We will take up the criticisms of Sartre, first by Lévi-Strauss then by Foucault, followed by the Lacanian use of Freud, in alliance with linguistics, for a project of resuscitating psychoanalysis—just as Sartre had sought to revive Marxism—a project in which he crossed paths with the spirit of the Enlightenment and the French Revolution.

Let's follow the path.

II

REBUKING SARTRE AND HIS FINAL HUMANIST OBJECT: THE FRENCH REVOLUTION UNDER SCRUTINY

DIFFRACTIONS

The Sartrean elaboration of dialectical Reason placed a specific history at the center of its development, that of the French Revolution, both because it was a possible site for the analysis of an *initiating* (*initié*) and thus a surpassing of the inertia of the practico-inert by the fused group and then the pledged group, and because it was already one of the central historiographical objects of Marxists and communists. Criticizing vulgar Marxism required addressing a salient object of shared interest. The development of the Sartrean approach to the Revolution took place from 1945 to 1960, alongside a number of Marxist and communist historians whose work Sartre gradually came to use, cite, and criticize in his manuscripts, and to an extent in the *Critique*. By gathering primary historical knowledge, he was able to develop his own method and thus his own point of view. The more his dialectical conception of history progresses in theory, the more he appropriates the object "French Revolution" in a unique way, fashioning it into a genuinely Sartrean object. As we have seen, this process allowed him to test, in a historical revolutionary situation, his concepts of the practico-inert, fused group, and pledged group which are at the heart of his conception of incipient freedom.

Nevertheless, the reception of the *Critique of Dialectical Reason* did not precipitate a debate among the historians with whom Sartre critically engages. The debate centered around great intellectual figures who actually reject the Sartrean conception of history. The latter assumes that going beyond "structures"—or in Sartre's language, the practico-inert—happens through people's appropriation of their lived contradictions. These contradictions, which at some point in history become unbearable or dangerous, force them to invent other ways of being in the world, to exit serial inertia to become free and active in history. We can see that the practico-inert cannot, in the end, be identified with structures, even if Sartre will accept speaking in these terms.[1]

To understand the effects of the Sartrean reflection on the object "history of the French Revolution," it is therefore necessary to turn to these opponents of Sartre, who react to him by relying successively on each other. This succession draws a series that we have often called "structuralist," but its unity consists less in the adhesion to structuralism than in calling human freedom into question, since it constitutes the Truth of history and its dialectical specificity.

When Sartre, at the end of the *Arc*[2] issue devoted to him, is interviewed by Bernard Begaudeau, this series appears out of order. He is initially annoyed by the success of Michel Foucault's book *The Order of Things*,[3] then returns to Lévi-Strauss's structuralism, evokes the decentering of the subject in Lacan and the rejection of history in Althusser's Marxism, and ultimately pleads once again for Marxism as a "task to be accomplished."

There is very little discussion of literature except as a "contestation which contests itself," which cannot but abolish itself with its focus on formalism. For Sartre, the work of art implies the aim of meaning, and not just form. Once again, Sade makes it possible to explain the knots of meaning produced by a thinking subject caught within the limits of their own inertia. Sade is thus the example that makes it possible to conceive of the articulation of ideology and literature. As Lacan tells us in his 1959–1960 seminar, with Sade we have another story for the French Revolution. Not one of time and of science, but a story of supposed revolutionary heroes, of cruelty and ethics.

In any case, Sartre seeks to show that the temporality of going-beyond (*dépassement*) is what constitutes humanity, which ultimately allows him to rediscover the claims of the Enlightenment. It is precisely because they are capable of being free to think and thus to do in the face of their condition, that human beings are human. And it is because this thought can imagine other worlds that there is history and not just a series, the latter being the mere repetition of the practico-inert or immutable structures.

---

1 Indeed, if speaking of structures, we accord them complete autonomy vis-à-vis praxis, then we cannot assimilate the practico-inert to structure, since the latter is a practice that turns back against itself through the bias of worked matter. Praxis, along with matter, is primary in Sartre; this is why he develops a materialism of the world (world = the praxis-matter relationship) and not a materialism of matter.

2 "Jean Paul Sartre répond," *L'Arc*, no. 30 (1966).

3 Michel Foucault, *The Order of Things* (London: Routledge, 2005).

For Sartre, doubting that which is near to his heart constitutes, in his terms, a "logical scandal." He thus asserts that positivism can win all the territories of humanity it claims to investigate, and ground the human sciences, but that this would be the death of philosophy and the regression of the intelligibility of history. To castigate Foucault, he evokes the return of the "magic lantern" when we already have the cinema.

Our ambition here is not to address the entirety of this debate head-on, but to attempt, in the words of Sartre, a partial totalization of what is at stake in the object "French Revolution," with the knowledge that it is enveloped by an enveloping totalization that involves the status of history as a discipline in the 1960s.

We begin by revisiting the way that Lévi-Strauss responds to Sartre in the final chapter of *The Savage Mind*,[4] where the question of the French Revolution not only does not disappear but in fact constitutes the climax, in my view, of a matchless philosophical and epistemological debate *then opened*. The French Revolution serves as a line of sight both when it comes to thinking about peoples assumed to be without history but in possession of myths, and when it comes to thinking the mythical status of history for peoples who may believe that their history is a true knowledge in Truth (*un vrai savoir en Vérité*): the peoples of the West. For Lévi-Strauss, it is a question of demonstrating that, in the end, the social function of this knowledge is analogous to that of myth.

This is also the heart of our inquiry. How did the history of the French Revolution lose its monumental force since the 1980s and the bicentenary? Does wanting to retrieve this force entail reconnecting it with a mythical conception of history? And despite everything, since this is a criticism that was explicitly made to me by the Althusserian historian and linguist Jacques Guilhaumou, what does it mean to reconnect with a mythical conception of history?

Must we work on Althusser in a direct way? This strikes me as difficult. There are too few texts, perhaps none, that approach the subject of the French Revolution head-on, so I would have to come at it through consequences. Althusser played a big role for a generation of historians of the French Revolution who, at the time and subsequently, made him their fulcrum for proposing another approach to the Revolution and history from within Marxism and communism. Among them are Régine Robin, and later Jacques Guilhaumou. Since at the outset of my master's studies in the history of the French Revolution, Guilhaumou had given me

---

4 Claude Lévi-Strauss, *The Savage Mind* (London: Weidenfield and Nicolson, 1966).

Régine Robin's *Histoire et linguistique* (1973) as a first reading assignment, it was through my initiation into French discourse analysis, which gathered Althusserian Marxism, psychoanalysis, and Foucault, that I encountered this intellectual history. Here I will have to untangle the web that then led me to adopt methodological approaches without fully understanding exactly what was playing out in an apparent battle between the ancient and the modern.

In Robin's book, a chapter is devoted to Michel Foucault, and I will return to what Foucault was able to bring to historians of the French Revolution all while persistently rejecting this subject. I will try to show why and how he rejects it, but also how his analyses of the period of the Iranian Revolution and counterrevolution, during which time he was an intellectual reporter of sorts, are of profound relevance for thinking revolution in general and the French Revolution in particular, provided that we dispense with his prejudices.

Finally, I will try to understand how, without really responding to Sartre but nevertheless working within this configuration, Lacan's rereading of Freud and reinvention of psychoanalysis, without really responding to Sartre but nevertheless working within this configuration is theoretically connected to Sartre's attempt to reinvent Marxism as a philosophical, historical, and political task. I am once again struck by an undeniable contemporaneity, as Lacan's seminar "The Ethics of Psychoanalysis" dates from 1959 and "Kant with Sade" from 1963. Lacan, like Sartre, tackles the enigma of Sade and the contemporary stakes of his use of reason. Because ultimately that is what it is about. The *Critique of Dialectical Reason* follows well from Kant's *Critique of Pure Reason* and *Critique of Practical Reason*, the first being considered by the young Hegelians[5] as anti-metaphysical and wonderful, and the other as a regression to pathetic bourgeois moralism. These anti-ethical positions were taken up by Adorno and Horkheimer, but were they really by Lacan?

We know the cover of the Seuil edition of *The Ethics of Psychoanalysis*, where Man Ray's 1938 bust of Sade—quite unsympathetic, incidentally—is situated in front of a burning Bastille. Double cruelty, cruelty redoubled, cruelty against cruelty? What does this image say, which suddenly repositions the French Revolution as a moment to interrogate in relation to this ethical and historical question of cruelty in action? Mythical signage? It was 1986, another historical and political configuration entirely.

---

5 See on this point Slavoj Zizek, "Kant: With or Against Sade?" *Savoirs et cliniques*, 2004, 89–101.

What do the generations who came to psychoanalysis after Lacan say about the French Revolution? How are they heard? And with which historians do they agree? For in the meantime, a historiographical current of the French Revolution, inscribed in this anti-Sartrean lineage, has gained momentum and made its honey from Althusserian and Lacanian structural critique of history, displacing the concerns which animate historical work on the French Revolution. It is necessary to linger here in order to understand not only what was unfolding at the apparently commemorative event of the bicentenary, but also what was playing out in its unspoken intellectual backstage, perhaps without them even being aware of the stakes. Doing so allows us to appreciate the extent to which the 1980s were a culmination of the battle over reason and its abilities to bring about a more human world. We must still ask ourselves, once again, what "more human" means when it comes to history and its social function, particularly—but not exclusively—in Western societies, since Iran takes center stage of the interrogations of the meaning of "revolution," and what the concept itself owes or does not owe to the event of the French Revolution.

There are complex interconnections that must both be unfolded and preserved in order to understand in the intellectual conjuncture of the 1960s and 1970s, and what was conferred on us in the 1980s.

7

THREE HUMANITIES IN ONE: EUROPEAN, COLONIZED, SAVAGE

When Sartre prepares and writes the *Critique of Dialectical Reason*, and makes the French Revolution a foundational *intitium,* France is faced with its own incoherence. On the one hand, it reconnects with the French Revolution so as to turn its back on Vichy, and on the other, denies it when the event is called upon to convey the legitimacy and necessity of decolonization.

THE MISSING CONTEXT OF DECOLONIZATION: JEAN POUILLON, SARTRE, AND LÉVI-STRAUSS

The first to have understood the link between the American Revolution, the French Revolution, and the necessity of decolonization was Hô Chi Minh in the Vietnamese declaration of independence: "All men are created equal. They are endowed by their Creator with certain inalienable rights, among these are Life, Liberty, and the pursuit of Happiness." These immortal words are drawn from the American 1776 Declaration of Independence. Taken broadly, these words mean: all peoples on earth are born equal; all peoples have the right to live, to be free, and to be happy. The French Revolution's 1791 Declaration of the Rights of Man and Citizen also proclaimed: "Men are born and remain free and equal in rights." Here we have inalienable truths. However, for more than eighty years, French imperialists had been denying their principles:

> Liberty, equality, and fraternity have violated our Fatherland and oppressed our fellow citizens. They have acted contrary to the ideals of humanity and justice. [. . .] The truth is that we have wrested our independence from the Japanese and not from the French. The French have

fled, the Japanese have capitulated, and Emperor Bao Daï has abdicated. Our people have broken the chains which for nearly a century have fettered them and have won independence for Vietnam. [. . .] We, the provisional government of the new Vietnam, representing the entire Vietnamese people, hereby declare that from now on we break off all relations of a colonial character with France, cancel all treaties signed by France on Vietnam, and abolish all privileges held by France in our country."[6]

One year later, Admiral d'Argenlieu cut off ongoing negotiations with Hô Chi Minh and bombed Haiphong.

Jean Pouillon—the friend of Sartre's with whom he had created, in 1942 along with Merleau-Ponty and Desanti, the intellectual resistance movement *Socialisme et Liberté*—is at the time a political columnist for the *Les Temps Modernes* and secretary of parliamentary debates in the National Assembly. When he attends Léon Bloom's announcement of this political catastrophe, which he describes as highly affected, he decides, with his friend Sartre, to make it the focus of the December 1946 editorial of *Les Temps Modernes*. Mauriac replies in *Le Figaro* and attacks Sartre. But the French-Indochina war is well underway, without the majority of the deployed French soldiers knowing why they have been sent to fight the Japanese. The war becomes bogged down. In August 1953, an issue of *Les Temps Modernes* is dedicated this Indochina war. Jean Pouillon, still a secretary of the National Assembly, writes an article titled "From a Politics of Negation to the Nothingness of a Politics."[7] In it, he calls for negotiations with Hô Chi Minh and the withdrawal of the expeditionary force—without success, as we know. His position is that of a number of anthropologists aware of the relations of domination that prevail between colonizers and colonized. But Sartre did not wait for Jean Pouillon and had already supported the campaign in favor of Henri Martin. This young communist and former member of the Resistance had returned from Indochina stupefied at how France repressed the Vietminh and the freedom of the Vietnamese in general. Alerting his compatriots to what was transpiring there, he was arrested in March 1950 and condemned to five years in prison. He was released in 1953 after serving three years. The campaign for Henri Martin had allowed the Communist Party to step out of its isolation, thanks to *Les*

---

6 Declaration of Independence of the Democratic Republic of Vietnam, September 2, 1945, signed by Hô Chi Minh, president.
7 Jean Pouillon, "D'une politique de négation au néant d'une politique," *Les Temps modernes*, Viêt-Nam, double issue 93–94, Gallimard, 1953.

Temps modernes and *Esprit*, and also to the personal recognition of Michel Leiris, Hervé Bazin, Vercour, and Jacques Prévert.

Yet this same Jean Pouillon, at the instigation of his friend Sartre, writes an article in 1956 (also in *Les Temps Modernes*) on the work of Lévi-Strauss. He is dazzled by structural anthropology. The corner has been turned for those heading down the path of ethnology without abandoning philosophy but rather taking seriously the need to account for the common humanity and the radical alterity that lies at its core. However, Jean Pouillon does not adhere to the displacement of historicity that he detects in the work of Lévi-Strauss. Instead, he aligns with Sartre's positions on the historical dialectic.

He then becomes close to Claude Lévi-Strauss and attends his seminars. In 1960, when the *Critique of Dialectical Reason* appears, Jean Pouillon is solicited by Lévi-Strauss to come speak in his seminar. Three two-hour sessions are thus dedicated to Sartre's book.

POETICS OF A COMMON THOUGHT

Lévi-Strauss provides his view of Sartre toward the end of *The Savage Mind* (1962), in a chapter titled "History and Dialectic." He explains the necessity sharing this view in the short preface:

> If I have felt obliged to give expression to my disagreement with Sartre regarding the points which bear on the philosophical fundaments of anthropology, I have only determined to do so after several readings of the work in question which occupied my pupils at the École des Hautes Études myself during many sessions of the year 1960–1. Over and above our inevitable divergences I hope that Sartre will recognize above all that a discussion to which so much care has been given constitutes on behalf of all of us a homage of admiration and respect. [8]

This preface allows us to appreciate the intensity of a conflict of ideas which aims, not so much at destroying the other's positions—divergent more than opposed—but at evaluating them, and thus being able to assess one's own position among intellectuals heavily invested in precisely the same questions. There is also a necessary reciprocity of respect, so that this conflict of ideas can take place despite epistemological differences that might appear

---

8 Lévi-Strauss, *The Savage Mind*, xii.

irreconcilable but which ultimately, it seems to me, can be seen as compatible within a common poetics of knowledge.

Indeed, since analytical, or scientific reason makes it possible to recognize the dignity of the so-called savage mind and thus of all synthetic thought, Lévi-Strauss proposes a path which leads to reaffirming the power of human reason in all its forms, without hierarchical competition. It consists in recognizing each other's power and dignity. This poetics then leads him to doubt the existence of a radical gap between dialectical reason and "savage" thought, which also draws bold conclusions, sometimes false but not always. He thus values dialectical reason as human reason, which, in the end, is shared by so-called savages (including those whom he rebukes Sartre for having qualified as "stunted humanity") and the so-called civilized. The latter, too, even if they do not want to admit it, require this allegedly savage thought—mythical or perhaps dialectical, even synthetic—in order to live. Before entering into an analysis of the chapter in question, "History and Dialectic," I would like to revisit this poetics which demonstrates the equal dignity of types of thought.

The issue underpins the first chapter on the sciences of the concrete. Lévi-Strauss was careful to begin this chapter with a statement from Balzac which connects the Savages of anthropology of the far-away with the peasants of anthropologists of the nearby: "For studying out a question in all its bearings, there are no folk in this world like savages, peasants, and provincials; and this is how, when they proceed from thought to action, you find every contingency provided for from beginning to end."[9] Of course, it is a question of knowing if the "beginning to end" is the synthesis effectuated by the thinking subject, the subjective synthesis that makes it possible to totalize what is lived. Dialectical reason, applied to an empirical analysis always to be renewed, produces knowledge. But for Lévi-Strauss, this knowledge distinguishes itself from scientific knowledge, which is repeatable and cumulative.

Lévi-Strauss then strives to show that magical thought is not as far as we assume from analytical thought, the very analytical reason that, for him, grounds and presides over science. Lévi-Strauss thus questions the grounding of "all thought" in analytical classification or the requirement of order: "The thought we call primitive is founded on this demand for order. This is equally true of all thought but it is through the properties common to all thought that we can most easily begin to understand forms

---

9 Honoré de Balzac, "The Collection of Antiquities," *The Complete 'Human Comedy,'* Golden Deer Classics. Cited by Claude Lévi-Strauss, Œuvres complètes. *La Pensée sauvage*, 557 (The passage is not included in the English edition of *The Savage Mind*).

of thought which seem very strange to us."[10] Further on, he asserts that so-called magical thought anticipates science by having faith, without knowing it, in deterministic causality. "One can go further and think of the rigorous precision of magical thought and ritual practices as an expression of the unconscious apprehension of the *truth of determinism*, the mode in which scientific phenomena exist. In this view, the operations of determinism are divined and made use of in an all-embracing fashion before being known and properly applied, and magical rites and beliefs appear as so many expressions of an act of faith in a science yet to be born."[11] The advent of science therefore depends on this unconscious (in the sense of non-reflexive) competence, the competence to act on faith. And for Lévi-Strauss, it is precisely this unconscious apprehension that connects with science as the conscious advent of the knowledge of determinations. Hence his claim that "it is therefore better, instead of contrasting magic and science, to compare them as two parallel modes of acquiring knowledge. Their theoretical and practical results differ in value [. . . ,] Both science and magic however require the same sort of mental operations and they differ not so much in kind as in the different types of phenomena to which they are applied."[12]

In this unfolding of time which links the "savage" and the civilized, Lévi-Strauss goes as far as asserting that certain scientific methods exist in "savage thought" well before existing in science. Progress is no longer on the side of civilization. The latter is not only dependent on savage thought as its foundation, but its progress is but the retrieval, via another path, of that which has already been thought by the so-called savage. "For it seems to be the case that man began by applying himself to the most difficult task, that of systematizing what is immediately presented to the senses, on which science for a long time turned its back and which it is only beginning to bring back into its purview. In the history of scientific thought this 'anticipation-effect' has, incidentally, occurred repeatedly."[13]

It is thus not a question of denying the value of mythical history when Lévi-Strauss engages with Sartre on this point, but rather of evaluating it as such by recognizing in it all its value and its possible failings, which are not the same as those of science; and also of recognizing that certain domains of knowledge and action—and political action in history is perhaps one of these—can only fall within this register of common thought. The chapter

---

10 Lévi-Strauss, *The Savage Mind*, 10.
11 Ibid., 11.
12 Ibid., 13.
13 Ibid., 11–12.

of polemical dialogue, "History and Dialectic," is surrounded by two moments that clarify this common thought.

The immediately preceding chapter is called "Time Regained," following Marcel Proust's expression. Recall that the latter aimed, through art, at the transmutation of sensory reality in the work of art, whether pictorial or literary. Reason, always engaged, assumed an intuitive and sensory relation to the world. Art was thus the fruit of a sensory reason which is able to make a work out of sensations; sensations lived for the first time, and sensations retrieved in their temporal density in the work. For Lévi-Strauss, this capacity for "time regained" belongs to those societies said to have no History but which do in fact have it, another history, obeying complex rules which are like rules of art in relation to time. By effectively involving sensible thought in his demonstration, Lévi-Strauss affirms that history is not a Western attribute, but simply functions differently in other societies. Ultimately, it is even the case that the history of these societies is not so remote from the history of Western societies, so long as history is understood as science—or more exactly, as method—and not as narrative (*récit*).

A loop is thus formed from the first chapter, "Time Regained," to the assertion made in "History and Dialectic," which could be summarized thus: "Your history, my dear Jean-Paul, is not more in the Truth than the history of my stunted savages. Like yours, it is 'mythical.'"

Immediately thereafter, we find a moment of writing and thought that I find exceptionally elegant. Once again, it is titled *la Pensée sauvage*, but this time, it refers to the fine "flower." Lévi-Strauss deploys an ethnographic exercise on the meanings ascribed, in the thought which explores Flora, to the flower called the "Wild Pansy" (*Pensée Sauvage*). He also recounts stories of wicked stepmothers, unhappy incestuous couples, and orphans. Analytical thought tells a series of stories about savage thought (*pensée sauvage*) and arranges them for our greatest pleasure in a Prévert-esque succession made of immortals and thoughts . . . but in which scientific thought doubtless remains itself an orphan of savage thought.

Of course, magical thought, savage thought, and synthetic or dialectical thought are not exact synonyms, unless it is a question of valuing their power to understand the world as a power that makes it possible to make use of the world. There is thus decidedly something recurrent in Lévi-Strauss's work on savage thought. At every turn, it leads to the affirmation that far from having to put these modes of thought into competition with one another, these savage, magical, synthetic, dialectical, mythical, and scientific modes of thought should be affirmed—we must affirm them as common modes of thought, just as we must defend the commonness of humanity. Of course, as a member of the scientific community, who takes that position in the world seriously, he values science and its practical usage in spite of everything. However, to be proud of what you do does not entail devaluing what others do, but simply the recognition of one's singular historical location—a contingency.

It remains to be understood what Sartre meant when he spoke of societies without history, by "Man" as a "stunted and misshapen being."[14] We must make sense of what this involves in terms of the imagination of common thought and common humanity, the unity of man and the diversity of cultures.

"MAN IS THIS STUNTED AND MISSHAPEN BEING"

Sartre's "stunted man" appears in his reflection on the scarcity of material goods, and what is engendered by such shortage in terms of indissoluble contradictions for humanity until abundance replaces it. According to him, scarcity is a condition of possibility of History, which is generated by the assumption, on the part of societies, of contradictions to be overcome or surpassed as a result of this scarcity. But he is aware that scarcity does not *ipso facto* determine human historicity, and that the absence of scarcity does not make it disappear, even if this hypothesis is not verifiable in this instance. Ultimately, in the vocabulary that Sartre adopts, History is a "mode of temporalization," or a "form of temporalization." History is thus a way of doing things over time, a way that stems from scarcity but not necessarily because of this scarcity. Man as the "stunted and misshapen being" is man engendered by ideology, says Sartre. Societies without History are societies that do not make scarcity a historical motor, but rather accommodate it in such a way as to live in pure repetition. He adds in a parenthesis: "It is true that many groups which here settled into repetition have a legendary history; but this is irrelevant, for legend is a negation of History, its function being to reintroduce the archetype into sacred moments of repetition."[15]

What Sartre does not appear to understand is the possibility of being content with scarcity, that this contentment might be a renunciation or simply a choice, even though he does consider both possibilities. He cannot recognize himself in an ideology from out of which the choice would be made to be "a stunted misshapen being, hardened to suffering, and he lives

---

14 Jean-Paul Sartre, *Critique of Dialectical Reason* (London: Verso, 2004), 126
15 Ibid., 126–27.

in order to work from dawn till dusk with *these* (primitive) technical means, on a thankless threatening earth. [. . .] If a state of equilibrium is established within a given mode of production, and preserved from one generation to the next, it is preserved as *exis*—that is to say, both as a physiological and social determination of human organisms and as a practical project of keeping institutions and physical corporate development at the same level. This corresponds ideologically to a decision about human 'nature.'"[16]

This decision validates Sartrean humanism, since it is indeed a free choice which is at issue, but nevertheless a choice that perplexes him. In short, the idea that this choice, at once ideological and practical, could produce political and social benefits, that on the questions of surplus labor or the State, beneficial and exemplary alternatives could be found, does not seem to strike him, even while such ideas traverse the thought of the postwar period of 1945–1960. This traversal is exemplified by the highly clarifying article of Claude Lefort, "Historicity and Society without History," which advances, under the guise of "stagnant history," the claim that that there is another way to knowingly inscribe oneself in history. This very same split is later found with Pierre Clastres's *Society against the State* (1974), the primitive society of abundance in Marshall Salhins, or the concept of "molecular development" in Deleuze and Guattari. Here, there seems to be no apprehension of a freedom that, far from being frozen in the mode of the oath in order to remain free, might choose to maintain the chronic instability of the fused group, essentially creating stability through a relation to the legendary and not through a relation to the State, which always captures freedom.[17] What worries Sartre is not this capture of freedom by the institutions that are ultimately another name for the oath, it is that in the future, Man will no longer be able to make history with time. He fears that History as he has defined it is a way of being in the world that disappears from lack of will to live and overcome the contradictions of scarcity.

For Sartre does not consider History a "natural" human given, or in his vocabulary, an "essential necessity." He believes it is the Marxists and the idealists that think this. And he adds: this conception "reinstates necessity and unity everywhere."[18] But some societies can completely ignore other societies; unity is not proven. The temporalization which aims at repetition is not a cessation of lived history but rather another way of working

---

16 Ibid., 126.
17 See in this regard the way that Miguel Abensour deploys the notion of "insurgent democracy," which dethrones the State to return the role of political community to civil society which taken from it, in *Democracy Against the State: Marx and the Machiavellian Moment*, trans. Max Blechman and Martin Breaugh (Cambridge, UK: Polity, 2011).
18 Sartre, *Critique of Dialectical Reason*, 126.

with time, a way of doing that is in fact recognized as such by Sartre but which he despairs of, as is evident in the derogatory vocabulary he employs.

However, it seems difficult to me—without bad faith—to maintain that in the 1950s and 1960s Sartre hierarchized peoples as civilized Westerners and non-Western savages, or to imagine that he only values, for example, the Vietnamese insofar as they betray Western acculturation in their arguments for sovereign independence. He clearly distinguishes between Westerners with History (but it is not immutable and can cease), the colonized who are caught between colonizing Western civilization and their own civilization that is more or less proximate to Western History in their relation to time, and those who are called "primitive" or "savage," who were not colonized but nevertheless know misfortune. This misfortune is the impossibility of maintaining a distance from the State and voluntary servitude: theirs, too, is a mode of being in the world which is not immutable. Savage politics is like History: it must be actively desired to be maintained. As for this desire, we must recognize that Sartrean experience offers it no light, unlike the experiences of anthropologists who do not make it a point of reference for thinking another human freedom linked to another history. Thus, Clastres writes: "The history of peoples without history is . . . the history of their struggle against the State." When the State appears, with its separation of politics and economics and its relations of domination, then History struggles against an effective State for the benefit either of another form of State (another form of the Oath) or of the reinscription of savage politics before misfortune—what Miguel Abensour calls "anarchic, insurgent democracy" that dethrones the State and returns the role of political community to civil society, from which it was dispossessed. Sartre's thinking on the colonized and decolonization never fits into this hypothesis. The reconquest of freedom on the part of the colonized is, for him, inscribed in History.

COLONIZED, WANTING FREEDOM

The 1961 preface to Frantz Fanon's *Wretched of the Earth* is extremely clear. Firmly maintaining his dialectical conception of History, Sartre defends no transcendental position, no false universality, no hierarchy.

> As long as the status of "native" existed, [. . .] we saw in the human species an abstract premise of universality that served as a pretext for concealing more concrete practices: there was a race of subhumans overseas

> who, thanks to us, might, in a thousand years perhaps, attain our status. [. . .] Today the "native" unmasks his truth; [. . .] since the others are turning into men against us, apparently we are the enemy of the human race; the elite is revealing its true nature—a gang. Our beloved values are losing their feathers; if you take a closer look there is not one that isn't tainted with blood.[19]

Further on, he returns to the manner in which Europeans invented a "subhuman" in Algeria, invoking Fanon's text: "Not so long ago, Fanon recalls, a congress of psychiatrists deplored Algerian criminality: these people are killing themselves, they said, it's not normal; the cortex of the Algerian must be underdeveloped. In Central Africa others established that 'the African uses his frontal lobes very little.' These scientists would do well to pursue their research in Europe, and especially among the French."[20] If the French are tearing each other apart in their positions on decolonization, is it because their frontal lobes are shrunken? Recognizing the equality of intelligence, as Lévi-Strauss does, is a battle that converges with his radical positions on the Algerian War.

In his famous preface, Sartre effectively defends the same conceptions as those he defended in the *Critique of Dialectical Reason*. The dialectic is that of the native and the European colonizer, or accomplice of the colonizer. It is a revolutionary dialectic in which those who were "terrorized become terrible." Sartre thus uses the expression of the French revolutionaries at the time of Marat's death. The violence suffered returns to those who inflicted it so as to reconquer freedom-humanity.

In this theoretical context, Sartre asserts the following at the end of his piece:

> This is the last stage of the dialectic: you condemn this war but you don't yet dare declare your support for the Algerian fighters; have no fear, you can count on the colonists and mercenaries to help you make up your mind. Perhaps, then, with your back to the wall, you will finally unleash this new violence aroused in you by old, rehashed crimes. But, as they say, that is another story. The history of man. The time is coming, I am convinced, when we shall join the ranks of those who are making it."[21]

---

19 Jean-Paul Sartre, preface to *Wretched of the Earth*, by Frantz Fanon (New York: Grove Press, 2004), iix.
20 Ibid., lx.
21 Ibid. lxii.

Only people who renew their freedom in action make history, for Sartre, to the extent that history is a way of becoming human by becoming free. Evidently, his definition of the human as a category which is at once historical, political, and philosophical is extremely restrictive. If everyone has the same capacity for freedom, everyone makes a different, historically and culturally constrained use of it. But in a revolutionary situation, revolutionaries alone embody the singularity of the human. "Man" is thus not a natural given, a human kind, but a free and political self-construction in each situation. Dehumanization occurs through inertia, that is, one's capture by the practico-inert.

Because of this, however, the "natives" are only the acculturated, who use their freedom to rediscover this violence suffered-returned, freeing themselves through the formation of a fused group. We thus find a definition of the free human as the one who enacts this de-serialization through the activation of the ubiquitous potential for freedom, constructing thereby a collective freedom.

None of this, however, broaches the question of a humanity that is not caught in the historical melee of decolonization. Thus, it does not bear on all of humankind. It does not bear on the "savage" who was never colonized.

Of course, Sartre stresses that societies said to lack history and be "founded on repetition" "have begun to interiorise our History, because they have been subjected to colonialism as a historical event. What historialises them, however, is not a reaction to their *own* scarcity."[22] All of these terms would make today's researcher or reader of "post-colonial studies" bristle, but the notion of passivity must be resituated in relation to his theory seriality and its opposition with the fused group, and not to a value judgment about the capacity to resist. The fact remains, however, that on this precise point he does not account for "savage" societies which could self-"historialise" in Sartre's sense by forming a State without being colonized. His whole concern is to affirm that "counter-praxis"—unintended ends of intentional actions, human actions which unwittingly deteriorate and thus lose the certainty of the gestures of temporal development; a counter-praxis which is not passivity—also makes History. It is also interesting to note that at this precise point, Sartre gives a definition of historical intelligibility for acting subjects as "certainty within the complexity of temporal development," and unintelligibility as the loss of this certainty.

---

22 Sartre, *Critique of Dialectical Reason*, 126.

Faced with this argument, Lévi-Strauss unfolds the heart of his thought. By identifying dialectical reason with History, and History with humanity, Sartre excludes peoples supposed to lack history and

> the prodigious wealth and diversity of habits, beliefs and customs is allowed to escape; and it is forgotten that each of the tens or hundreds of thousands of societies which have existed side by side in the world or succeeded one another since man's first appearance, has claimed that it contains the essence of all the meaning and dignity of which human society is capable and, reduced though it may have been to a small nomad band or a hamlet lost in the depths of the forest, its claim has in its own eyes rested on a moral certainty comparable to that which we can invoke in our own case.[23]

To this historical totalization and sort of moral hierarchy of situated peoples—a hierarchy which relies on the degree of emancipation achieved—Lévi-Strauss opposes a conception of the singular-universal, where every distinct society embodies this universal of human life as both particular and universal regardless of their organizational form. He thus proclaims a common morality that leads to the equalization of intelligences and dignity, which owes nothing to what is called development or acculturation but much to the postulate of common humanity irrespective of differences between modes of life.

Without a doubt, this moral question is in part tied the experience of the World War II, the non-recognition of this common humanity, and to Lévi-Strauss's inability to prevent the deportation of his parents because he himself was in Brazil. This postulate of common humanity is not scientific but indeed moral, though it does also entail a certain conception of the human sciences.

There remains, for us, the questions posed by the notion of underdevelopment which then saturates the public space, and which implies a certain idea of time as progress through development. In the 1960s, this notion covered both colonized peoples in the figure of the "native," and that of "savages," effectively considered as belonging to the Stone Age.

Lévi-Strauss also battles with this notion when he underscores the equal dignity of all social forms, and the tremendous quality, indeed the great power, of the modes of thought which prevail in the places described as savage and underdeveloped, the same places that Sartre claims humanity is "stunted and misshapen." Does humanity and dignity pass through the

---

23 Lévi-Strauss, *The Savage Mind*, 249.

Western form of history, with its belief in progression and its moral hierarchy of peoples based on their degree of freedom or emancipation? This is the question that Lévi-Strauss directly poses to Sartre. Besides, if we accept a critique of progress, should we not, like Clastres, consider the "savages" and their "savage politics" that opposes the State as more emancipated than all the state forms put together? The debate then assumes the form not just of a political-philosophical debate but a disciplinary and epistemological one.

For Lévi-Strauss, the "truth of man," if it is a way of speaking of his "being," cannot be exclusive to a single regime of historicity or a single geographical location, but "resides in the system of their differences and common properties."[24] He thus reproaches Sartre's "egocentrism" and "naïveté," which he associates with Sartre's incapacity to decenter himself, an incapacity tied to "the allegedly self-evident truths of introspection."[25]

This is why the insinuation that the "being in humanity" of the "savage" "does not belong to him in his own right" and is the "function of his being taken hold of by historical humanity," either in the context of colonialism or as a scientific claim, is both a moral and a scientific error. Let us underscore once again that the societies labeled "primitive," or against the State—described by Clastres and Salhins in an often critical[26] dialogue—are societies of decision, and thus are societies where being in humanity has no need of the colonial presence, or of decolonization. The human science that is able to address humanity without discrimination is thus an anthropology rooted in ethnography, not Sartrean History.

This debate is also taking place within anthropology at this time. Beginning in 1959,[27] George Balandier asserts that certain ethnologists, including himself, "have accepted the upheaval of the 'primitive' universe and its methodological consequences. They are more sensitive to fissures, to heterogeneity, to movements of de-structuration and re-structuration of traditional societies which are now in the process of transformation. They are more sceptical of the privilege that every particular discipline claims—anthropology or sociology—in posing as the arbiter of 'the universality of the propositions established by social sciences,' in the revealing formula of

---

24 Ibid.
25 Ibid.
26 In particular, Pierre Clastres discusses at length Marshall Sahlins's book *Âge de pierre, âge d'abondance* (Paris: Gallimard, 1978).
27 "Tendances de l'ethnologie française I," *Cahiers internationaux de sociologie*, Paris, PUF, 27 (December 1959): 11–22.

G.P. Murdock.²⁸" When Balandier underlines the need for ethnologists to study, not traditional societies per se, but their ongoing mutations in the contemporary world in precisely this context of decolonization, he takes up the term (in 1956) "Third World" alongside Alfred Sauvy, who introduced it in 1952. In both cases, the notion is borrowed from the French Revolutionary imaginary and its revolutionary Third Estate. This is essentially how both authors explain the term. In his article published in *L'Observateur* on August 14, 1952, Sauvy makes explicit reference Siyès's pamphlet. "We gladly talk of the two worlds, of their possible war, of their coexistence, etc., too often forgetting that there exists a third, the most important one. [. . .] It is those that we call [. . .] underdeveloped countries [. . .]. This Third World which we ignore, exploit, despise [. . .] also wants to be something."²⁹ The notion was taken up and amplified by Georges Balandier, when in 1956 he edited the volume titled *Third World*. The French revolution bridges History of the Sartrean type for peoples who are *a priori* outside of its field of action. The countries of the Third World are thus qualified as potentially revolutionary countries on account of their demand to be considered within common History.

Boulandier therefore wishes to highlight the stakes of establishing connections between different societies and the problem of underdevelopment. What concerns him, then, are the discrepancies due to the inequality of their relations, which are never established on the basis of reciprocity. When Balandier returns to the notion of the Third World in a 2003 interview with *L'Express*³⁰ he is particularly clear:

> This expression has enjoyed worldwide success. But it often gave rise to misunderstandings. For us, it was not about defining a third collection of nations alongside the two blocs (capitalist and Soviet) during the Cold War. No, it was a reference to the Third Estate of the Ancien Régime, that part of society that refused to 'be nothing,' according to the abbé Sieyès. This notion therefore designates the claim of third nations who want to be inscribed in History. After a long eclipse, the initiative is being taken by several countries in the course of modernization: Brazil, India, South Africa. At the recent Cancun conference, they affirmed a strong identity in the face of Western powers. Is this not the beginning of a renaissance of the Third World?³¹

---

28 G. P. Murdock, "Sociology and Anthropology," in *For a Science of Social Man*, ed. J. Gillin Macmillan, New York, 1954, 270; Alfred Sauvy, *L'Observateur*, August 14, 1952.
29 Sauvy, *L'Observateur*.
30 *L'Express*, October 9. 2003.
31 Ibid.

The question of the Third Estate, like that of the Third World, consists of asking what measures would make it possible for one's own voice and own historicity to be heard, despite crushing relations of domination.

It seems to me beyond doubt that in this respect, the questions of the equalization of dignities and voices, of freedom as non-domination, are ones that unite Sartre, Lévi-Strauss, and Balandier. But for Sartre, who lacks a conception of "savage" politics, this dignity remains tied to the Western form of history via the historical situation of decolonization. This is also the case for Balandier. Only Lévi-Strauss maintains the equal dignity of all cultures and regimes of historicity, freely elaborated by people who know what are they are doing, without submission to a State or to scarcity. Whereas Lévi-Strauss casts references to the French Revolution as ethnocentrism or a failure to decenter, Sartre and Balandier make it a monument which remains exemplary. Of course, it is a question of decentering, but in a different way.

8

FINISHING A BOOK, CONCLUDING A DISCUSSION

In *The Savage Mind*, the discussion with Sartre takes place in the final chapter, as a conclusion to the book. But how can a book be concluded with a polemic?

A DIALOGUE BETWEEN TWO MARXISTS: SARTRE AND LÉVI-STRAUSS

Lévi-Strauss is clear, for those who may not have already understood, that this discussion has been taking place throughout the whole book: "In the course of this work I have allowed myself, not without ulterior motive, to borrow a certain amount of Sartre's vocabulary. I wanted to lead the reader to face a problem, the discussion of which will serve to introduce my conclusion. The problem is to what extent thought that can and will be both anecdotal and geometrical may yet be called dialectical."[1]

Lévi-Strauss persistently conducted this discussion on a dual plane: moral and political on the one hand, epistemological on the other. Here we will attempt to better discern the epistemological stakes, as he invites his reader to do by interrogating the notion of "dialectical reason." If the aim of such a reason is totalization, he says, then savage thought achieves it better than Sartre, who "lets seriality escape" and "excludes schematization," which are the foundation and crown of "savage" classificatory thought. But in discussing the notion of dialectical reason, he is perhaps, in this precise place, reluctantly defending the Sartrean view of History. For in fact Sartre, pushing toward a moving totalization, cannot include

---

1 Claude Lévi-Strauss, *The Savage Mind* (London: Weidenfield and Nicolson, 1966), 245.

a schematism that would arrest this movement of "totalization without a totalizer." As for Seriality, it relates precisely to that in history which has not yet been dialectized, that which renders people inert, entirely subjected to the practico-inert, and not to the movement of their conquest by freedom or emancipation. Hence this dialogue is, so to speak, deaf. Nevertheless, in discussing dialectical reason, Lévi-Strauss immediately shows that he wishes to discuss it as a Marxist, with a detractor of vulgar Marxism. Thus, he affirms: "Although in both our cases Marx is the point of departure of our thought, it seems to me that the Marxist orientation leads to a different view."[2] From the second page of this conclusion, it is clear that Lévi-Strauss misses the scope of the Sartrean proposition as a Marxist proposition, since he rejects the possibility that Marxism could lead to Sartre's point of view. He refuses a mode of thinking that cannot conceive itself as cumulatively producing knowledge, but which demands the ceaseless movement of qualitative adjustments to a situated truth. Yet for Sartre, there is no renunciation in considering these adjustments as the fruit of human History, quite the contrary. Provided that we make the effort to direct them in the temporal to-and-fro of the present to the past, the past to the present, in connection with political praxis, they even bring about a historical consciousness which may very well have a universal purview. Totalization always remains open to the uncertainty of history in action in the present. Praxis works with schemas of interpretation, but they too are never completely fixed. Historical consciousness as synthetic consciousness is indeed a universal-singular that totalizes in a situation. This is a dialogue between the deaf, since as we have seen, the question of human dignity resides, in Lévi-Strauss's work, in a conception of the universal-singular of each human group who, differences aside, totalize this human dignity.

Well upstream from this conclusion, Lévi-Strauss had nevertheless noted his point of agreement on the notion of praxis, which for him too is not reducible to practice. It consists of "modes of intelligibility in the form of conceptual mediation between matter and praxis." "If, as I have said, the conceptual scheme governs and defines practices, it is because these [. . .] are not to be confused with praxis which—and here at least I agree with Sartre—constitutes the fundamental totality for the sciences of man."[3] In a Marxist vein, he adds: "Without questioning the undoubted primacy of infrastructures, I believe that there is always a mediator between praxis and practices, namely the conceptual scheme by the operation of which matter

---

2 Ibid., 246.
3 Ibid., 130.

and form, neither with any independent existence, are realized as structures, that is as entities which are both empirical and intelligible."[4] For Lévi-Strauss, these conceptual schemas are "unequivocal constitutive units," while Sartre asserts that these modes of intelligibility can only be conceived by passing through a conceptual scheme which must depend on "details." Only empirical details make it possible to achieve a sufficient degree of relevance to be worth "truth" and therefore dialectical science. So, yes, detail and the conceptual go together in Sartre, or in Lévi-Strauss's terms, "the anecdotic and the geometric." It is on this condition, for Sartre, that effectiveness in terms of knowledge arises, and makes it possible to consider conceptual schemas as more than just "fetishes."

Lévi-Strauss then defines his conception of the dialectic of superstructures, from the empirical (his way of working not with details but with facts) to conceptual simplicity (the science of fact), and from conceptual simplicity to synthesis of meaning (systems of signs). The synthetic operator, or scientific knowledge, thus transforms the fact into the *sign*. Where Sartre seeks to account for a moving process, Lévi-Strauss strives to account for that which makes it possible to decipher signs which have become (or almost become) immutable facts, as in language. The point of agreement on *praxis*, from which rituals and myths arise for Lévi-Strauss, does not lead them to give "dialectic" the same meaning because the schema of intelligibility in Sartre is elaborated in a movement that does not lead to the same conception of the use of signs.

History for Sartre cannot be intelligible as a system of signs, but only as an unstable grammar that constantly reforms itself. Yet when Lévi-Strauss asserts that his anthropological work consists of identifying these systems of signs, he also proposes a distribution of tasks, even if he relativizes it by including ethnology as an auxiliary discipline of history. "It is to this theory of superstructures, scarcely touched on by Marx, that I hope to make a contribution. The development of the study of infrastructures proper is a task which must be left to history—with the aid of demography, technology, historical geography and ethnography."[5]

He goes on to say that ethnology is a psychology. There is thus a very explicit conflict that is not only epistemological but territorial. Insofar as Sartrean History grants a place to the phenomena of fear, the crowd, the pledge, to the emotions in general and the singular appropriation of language by individual actors (as he demonstrates in the case of Sade, for

---

4 Ibid.
5 Ibid.

example), it too could affirm that history is a kind of psychology. Lévi-Strauss cannot identify with a discipline of history that would have the sole vocation of dealing with infrastructure, especially since he has just called into question the theory of stages as a fetishized conception of social relations.

Throughout the work, therefore, the discussion is internal to Marxism and what we are entitled to understand by the word "dialectic," and in turn what we are entitled to expect from history as a discipline.

When he returns to the phrase "dialectical reason," Lévi-Strauss asserts that, for him, it ultimately consists of "courageous reason," "tensed by its efforts to transcend itself."[6] And this effort is "constitutive"; "it is the bridge, forever extended and improved, which analytical reason throws out over an abyss; it is unable to see the further shore but it knows that it is there, even should it be constantly receding."[7] Seeking to build bridges between the protagonists of this discussion, this constitutive moment resembles that which occurs for a fused group, and the temporality of this constitutive effort strongly resembles that which makes it possible to think progress and the horizon of anticipation it produces. A progressing temporality brought back to its constitutive moments, everything suggests that this dialectical reason in Lévi-Strauss is much closer to classical Marxism than that of Sartre. But there is no contempt for Sartrean dialectical reason, just a desire to clarify and demonstrate the artificiality of an overly forced difference in Sartre between analytical and dialectical reason.

What Lévi-Strauss considers as a "forced difference" is in fact the interval between what we could call a scientific naturalism and a philosophical humanism. Indeed, Lévi-Strauss goes as far as wanting to reintegrate culture in nature, and in fact asserts the identity of all the sciences whether they are labeled human or natural or even exact, thanks to an approach he qualifies as agnostic. Nevertheless, if this is the objective, the science of the 1960s had not arrived there, so to speak. This naturalism is an ambition supported by the effort of analytical reason, which rears up in dialectical reason in order to surpass itself. But it will take, according to Lévi-Strauss, many more courageous leaps to reach the goal. Let us note, however, that this conclusion finishes with the possibility of analytical reason's recognition of what he calls the scientific spirit: the material dimension of communication, which exists in itself, independent of the transmission and reception of information, and which has to do with meaning. Lévi-Strauss

---

6 Ibid., 246.
7 Ibid.

shows that this material dimension had intuitively been known quite early by the "savage mind," which interprets material signs and makes them speak, whereas the scientific mind—thanks to the science of communications—makes them the fulcrum for new technology. For Lévi-Strauss, the intuition of "savage thought" can thus be restored its rights. It gave all its weight to this material existence of information as a physical phenomenon to be interpreted in a sensory mode. But it is indeed under the auspices of the scientific mind and therefore of analytical reason that this reunion and this recognition can take place. "Savage thought," like dialectical reason, is intuition of natural facts, and therefore for Lévi-Strauss—consequently, a materialist Marxist—it falls to scientific-analytical reason to demonstrate them. The leap is made by the first mode of reason, but the cumulative effort by the second.

Lying beneath this question of the validity of dialectical reason and of the very possibility of speaking about it is the status accorded to "savage thought" in the Sartrean theory being discussed. The whole book aims to demonstrate that this mode of thought is not that of "stunted man," but that of multiple fascinating societies with reflexivity and inventiveness in the pursuit of their ends. The refusal to classify humans, whoever they are, as "stunted" is, moreover, characteristic of the ethnologist.

Finally, Lévi-Strauss calls "history" a capacity to shape time in order to obtain either the repetition of social forms or their transformation. He explains precisely this in the immediately preceding chapter, "Time Regained." In it he shows that "this regained time," in what he calls mythical history, consists in taming diachrony and synchrony through a complex set of skills. Thus, "mythical history thus presents the paradox of being both disjoined from and conjoined with the present. It is disjoined from it because the original ancestors were of a nature different from contemporary men: they were creators and these are imitators. It is conjoined with it because nothing has been going on since the appearance of the ancestors."[8] He shows that the rites of control operate on the side of synchrony, whereas historical or commemorative and bereavement rites operate on the side of diachrony. The former move from the past toward the present by entrusting the living with the task of personifying distant ancestors, the latter from the present toward the past through the creation of heroic figures. This is how that past is changed into present, and the present into the past. Ultimately, in mythical history, the reality that matters is not truth in the sense of authenticity, but the evocation of contingency that provokes emotions.

---

8 Ibid., 236.

Yet in the couple hot history/cold history that Lévi-Strauss constructs, history is directed in both cases at the lived present. Hence why the anthropologist puts them both in the category of myths.

Cold history is mythical because it is an affirmation of a society's will to persevere in its being and in its form, despite its contradictions and by religiously managing them, we might say. Hot history, or Western dialectical history, whose function is essentially, for Lévi-Strauss, assimilated to that of a myth, uses contradictions to transform societies with a view to a more desirable present, that is to say, more emancipated, a world where human freedom is active.

But Lévi-Strauss does not believe in this freedom. According to him, Sartre makes history "the last refuge of a transcendental humanism: as if men could regain the illusion of liberty on the plane of the 'we' merely by giving up the 'I's that are too obviously wanting in consistency."[9] Lévi-Strauss rejects the hypothesis of the pledged group as a group of free men. What he refuses is the foundational hypothesis of the Sartrean project, the human condition as a condition of freedom, which he here reduces to an *illusio*.

It is this supposedly free man—who believes himself to be superior compared to, in Sartre's vocabulary, men of serialized repetition, or again those stunted men, men of mythical history—that Lévi-Strauss thinks must be radically rejected. In his view, the human sciences do not need to find the "Truth of man," but to "dissolve" it. The spirit of his work is the dissolution of man. It is to be done with human nature in the name of a consciousness of the multiplicity of ways of being in the world. It is therefore about breaking free from a timeless and ethnocentric conception of humanity. This, he claims, is the work of science, and with this aim the human sciences can utilize analogous methods to the sciences of nature. To this extent, he takes a position firmly against Sartre, who had vilified scholars who study societies the way we study the chemical properties of matter.

But there is no hierarchy among the types of reductions of the complex to the simple. To reduce is to allow for the rearrangement of complexity so as to render it more intelligible. "The idea of some general humanity to which ethnographic reduction leads, will bear no relation to any one may have formed in advance."[10] However, if the effort at understanding is really an achievement of meaning, Lévi-Strauss insists as a Marxist and a Freudian on the fact that the meaning achieved is *"never the right one,"* and that "superstructures are *faulty acts* which have 'made it' socially."[11] Thus

---

9 Ibid., 263.
10 Ibid., 247.
11 Ibid., 253–54.

the effort of understanding can without damage be science fiction and not science, because for Lévi-Strauss, "the real question is not whether our endeavour to understand involves a gain or a loss of meaning, but whether the meaning we preserve is of more value than that we have been judicious enough to relinquish."[12]

But what did Sartre mean, in searching for this "Truth of man," if not the search for the conditions of possibility of an emancipation at work in human praxis?

We therefore have a deaf dialogue between two ways of conceiving disalienation. Yet it is undeniable that Sartre missed the historical function of myth produced by "savage thought," insofar as, for him, it only pursues and leads to repetition and not the transformation of the world of those who act, and he only ascribes History to the resolution of contradictions as a vehicle of emancipatory transformation. His History cannot be conceived without granting a place to human freedom in history. His Truth is this existential condition of being condemned to be free. When he seeks the Truth of man in History, he seeks his freedom there in its modifying actions and not in immutable signs.

Sartre in fact denies that there is freedom in knowingly wanting to repeat a social state, in wanting to bring it to life, sometimes even keeping it sheltered from the clutches of relations of domination. He negates the possibility that repetition is not just serial inertia and hence effectively dead, but issues from the finesse of an action that allows for the perseverance of social being with great sophistication.

It is in the logic of a historical condition that makes it possible to live the present that Lévi-Strauss locates the proximity of Sartrean history and that of the "primitives," which the latter excludes for not having historical consciousness. It is also here that he finds the real problem posed by the *Critique of Dialectical Reason*, which comes down "to the question: under what conditions is the myth of the French Revolution possible?"[13] Lévi-Strauss responds to Sartre with the claim that he has hardly strayed from the Marxists he criticizes.

This rendering of the object "French Revolution" as an object of narrative or the fabrication of history is placed by Lévi-Strauss in his turn at the heart of the polemic that animates the final chapter of *The Savage Mind*. At the precise moment where he asserts that the French Revolution, as Sartre takes hold of it in the *Critique of Dialectical Reason*, is a myth, he provides

---

12 Ibid., 253.
13 Ibid., 254.

a definition of myth, not as conceived by the so-called savages, but as it is conceived in the West, and thus contributes to the study of what he calls the "mythology of our time."[14]

THE FRENCH REVOLUTION AS A MYTH, ACCORDING TO LÉVI-STRAUSS

What, very precisely, does Lévi-Strauss say:

> The contemporary Frenchman (*l'homme contemporain*) must believe in this myth. [. . .] But it does not follow that his meaning, just because it is the richest (and so most suited to inspire practical action), should be the truest. Here the dialectic turns against itself. This truth is a matter of context, and if we place ourselves outside it—as the man of science is bound to do—what appeared as an experienced truth first becomes confused and finally disappears altogether. The so-called men of the Left still cling to a period of contemporary history which bestowed the blessing of a congruence between practical imperatives and schemes of interpretation. Perhaps this golden age of historical consciousness has already passed; and that this eventuality can at any rate be envisaged proves that what we have here is only a contingent context like the fortuitous "focusing" of an optical instrument when its object-glass and eye-piece move in relation to each other. We are still "in focus" so far as the French Revolution is concerned, but so we should have been in relation to the Fronde had we lived earlier.[15]

According to Lévi-Strauss, therefore, the French Revolution as an object of storytelling occupies the place of effective myth.[16] Its efficacy, he maintains, lies in offering consistency of practical meaning—the knowledge of what we have to do as an agent—and a truth that is in and of a situation, which is not scientific truth. It is this congruence that he calls "historical consciousness": that through which history makes it possible to know what we have to do in the present. It allows for the articulation of "interpretive schemas" and "practical imperatives," a congruence from which a certain intellectual and political comfort follows. Those who, since 1945, have

---

14 This is not unrelated to the publication, in 1957, of Roland Barthes's *Mythologies*.
15 Claude Lévi-Strauss, *La Pensée Sauvage*, 254.
16 In this regard, recall that George Lefebvre's response to Alfred Cobban had invoked the mobilizing Sorelian myth of the general strike as projection toward the future, and asserted that the French Revolution remained a similar mobilizing myth.

faith in the French Revolution may also simultaneously have the feeling of being right, effective but also just, the feeling of doing the right thing.

Note that, as a result, historical consciousness is not buttressed by the historian's knowledge but by mythical knowledge, the famous "myth of the French Revolution."

Nevertheless, in this very condensed passage, myth is not another science, but is a non-science. Both myth and "savage thought" are at odds with the history of the historians, who have the responsibility, as men of science, of distancing themselves from the situation. Myth allows for action in the situation, scientific history for the contemplation of a true past.

A conception of the historian's scientific truth emerges that is by definition different from historical truth that is lived, or used by present historical agents, since the scientificity of the historian's work lies precisely in the creation of this difference through distanciation—the separation from contingency.

If we continue in the text, the temporal definition of this contingency oscillates between the simple effect of temporal distance, of ineluctable separation from the past, and a more complex contingency understood metaphorically as optical adjustment.[17] On the one hand, Lévi-Strauss only speaks of homogeneous and empty time, that of capitalism, in fact. On the other, he speaks of a more subtle conception of time: the adjustment between two movements, that of the studied object and that of the present situation. In the words of Walter Benjamin, "if the present alone is the time of politics, then in the present any event of the past can acquire or retrieve a higher degree of actuality than it had at the moment when it took place."[18] Clearly, two conceptions collide here. The second conception is related by Lévi-Strauss to what Sartre calls "historical consciousness," that is to say, to the momentary possibility of collectively interiorizing history, of intensely living this interiority induced by the time, but which will prove to be a myth for the "men of a future century."[19] However Lévi-Strauss does not consider this mythical relation to the past as a defect, far from it. He is very specific about this: "I am not however suggesting that man can or should sever himself from this internality. It is not in his power to do so and wisdom consists for him in seeing himself live it, while at the same time knowing (but in a different register) that what he lives so completely and intensely is a myth."[20]

---

17 Ibid.
18 Walter Benjamin, "Sur le concept d'histoire" (1940), in *Écrits français* (Paris, Gallimard, 1991), 342. Translator's rendering.
19 Lévi-Strauss, *The Savage Mind*, 255.
20 Ibid.

128   Chapter 8

For Lévi-Strauss, it should be assumed that people only act thanks to myths, but that intelligibility is scientific.

This passage on the French Revolution, where one senses that Lévi-Strauss is settling some scores not only with Sartre but with the Left, thus poses a direct problem, that of historical truth or truth in history, and of what one can expect from this famous Sartrean Truth if the history it deploys is mythical. It is also a question of understanding what connections this conception of Truth has with the question of temporality in history.

In fact, Lévi-Strauss reproaches Sartre for creating confusion between human history as a totality (that is, History), the historian's history as "true knowledge," and history as past experience—singular totality or precise details in Sartre's vocabulary—to be jointly analyzed by analytic and dialectical reason.

However, Levi-Strauss asserts, if we refuse to identify humanity and History because in Sartre's logic this excludes a part of humanity from humanity, all that is left is the history of historians as a "method without an object."

HISTORY, A METHOD WITHOUT AN OBJECT

Lévi-Strauss then proposes to show that in this instance, time is no less continuous than space, and that history is a discontinuous knowledge (*connaissance*) which cannot be totalized. "In so far as history aspires to meaning, it is doomed to select regions, periods groups of men and individuals in these groups and to make them stand out, as discontinuous figures, against a continuity barely good enough to be used as a backdrop."[21] Lévi-Strauss thus analyzes time as a classification procedure, in a similar way to how Buffon can classify species. To each type of time, a corresponding knowledge. Lévi-Strauss demonstrates that the code of history, owing to the discontinuity of time, cannot be the date but rather the class of dates, "where each date has meaning in as much as it stands in complex relations of correlation and opposition with other dates."[22] Each class of dates, he says, is defined by a frequency, which he also calls a "domain." "Historical knowledge thus proceeds in the same way as a wireless with frequency modulation: like a nerve, it codes a continuous quantity—and as such an asymbolic one—by frequencies of impulses proportional to its

---

21 Ibid., 257.
22 Ibid., 259.

variations."²³ Information theory is a place where one can think the materiality of signs and thus a common thread. History is no longer History with a capital *H*, but a site of encodable information on the past. It is in this respect, and this respect alone, that Lévi-Strauss grants history a certain truth-value and scientificity.

Logically, he then deploys an analysis of degrees of information and intelligibility contained in different "classes of time" and "types of history."

"What makes history possible is that a sub-set of events is found, for a given period, to have approximately the same significance for a contingent of individuals who have not necessarily experienced the events and may even consider them at an interval of several centuries."²⁴

It will be noticed that here we are in the second conception of time, neither homogeneous nor empty. It is the conception of history that involves bringing two situations into relation: the situation of those who lived a period of history, and the situation of those who are going to read about this period of history. "History is therefore never history, but history-for. It is partial in the sense of being biased even when it claims not to be, for it inevitably remains partial—that is, incomplete—and this is itself a form of partiality."²⁵ For Lévi-Strauss, "a truly total history would cancel itself out—its product would be nought."²⁶

But is such a history, which is equal to zero, not precisely cold history? What happens to the charge of mythical history? Does cold history actually have a greater claim to being scientific than hot history?

It is at this precise point that arguments arise concerning the possibility of a dialectical history of the French Revolution.

> When one proposes to write a history of the French Revolution one knows (or ought to know) that it cannot, simultaneously and under the same heading, be that of the Jacobin and that of the aristocrat. *Ex hypothesi*, their respective totalizations (each of which is anti-symmetric to the other) are equally true. One must therefore choose between two alternatives. One must select as the principal either one or a third (for there are an infinite number of them) and give up the attempt to find in history a totalization of the set of partial totalizations; or alternatively one must recognize them all as equally real: but only to discover that the French Revolution as commonly conceived never took place.²⁷

---

23 Ibid.
24 Ibid., 257.
25 Ibid., 257–58.
26 Ibid., 257.
27 Ibid., 258.

What Lévi-Strauss says of the French Revolution could be said of any historical period, but here it seems to be specific because what is evoked are the protagonists of a political conflict, the Jacobins and the aristocrats as two fighters in the ring, as Sartre described them in the *Critique*. Taken with Sartre's metaphor, Lévi-Strauss appears to speak more of "points of view" than partial totalizations. Effectively, Lévi-Strauss is in the logic of history "for," "one-sided because partial," whereas Sartre speaks of the Truth of the fight as a whole and only thinks of partial totalization with a view of this totalization of the fight.

While missing the stakes of the partial totalizations described by Sartre thanks to the metaphor of struggle, Lévi-Strauss points to an issue with the operative disciplinary approach. But whereas contemporary historical science of this debate does not recognize that it adopts a point of view—it wants to be objective—this is precisely what Lévi-Strauss asserts. In short, no history can claim to be scientific knowledge, and it always falls under fiction. There are no solid, scientific links between the totality of human history, historical narratives, and partial histories, whether lived or recounted. Nevertheless, if the possibility of a historical narrative is contingent, then in this case, one can also imagine that one can, or will be able to, write the history of the aristocrats and the Jacobins together without, for all that, annulling history, but restoring to it its combative dynamic. Such an exercise is more complex, more perilous, but it is imaginable.

The question is whether the synthetic and totalizing point of view developed to analyze a fight in a ring can be relevant to a historical rupture.

To demonstrate this possibility, Sartre thinks the situation in its complexity, and in particular the action-reaction of different elements within it as partial totalizations, aristocrats versus Jacobins. But the signifying points of view can only coincide from a retrospective position, already knowing how the story ends. It is the knowledge of what follows that would allow Sartre to make history intelligible, and this would mean committing the epistemological crime of teleology or of anachronism.

This is why Lévi-Strauss appreciates Sartre's work as a historian when he remains analytical in his explanations of partial totalizations, explanations that work a single point of view, a particular praxis. It is also why he ascribes a lesser worth to Sartre's analyses that claim to be deploying dialectical reason, which fall back into the ruts of Marxism that he criticizes, smothering the purported object of analysis with rationalizations, concepts, and knowledges.

The foundational discipline would then be ethnology in that it utilizes the famous progressive-regressive method that searches for structures underneath the facts, but knows nothing of structures the moment it analyzes facts. Space, unlike time, would not lead to a teleology.

One is tempted to say, like Lévi-Strauss, that this history is strongest and most interesting when it deploys analytical reason. But despite everything, what makes it possible to think or to apprehend this history as dialectical? First, I believe, is the very fact of a taste for detail whose goal is not erudition but political understanding, an awareness of the functioning of the political for consciousness today. A dialectical history of the Revolution is possible, not as a dialectic of points of view, not as a synthesis of partial totalizations, but as a dialectic of situations. Nevertheless, this "focused" dialectic is ultimately rejected as unscientific by Lévi-Strauss. He does not think that the coming and going between past and present produces non-arbitrary intelligibility, he does not believe in this production of Enlightenment and thus rejects the cognitive character of dialectical reason. He thus folds science into analytical reason, which is alone capable of dissolving, classifying, and recomposing elements to produce, despite everything, a surplus of meaning. If Lévi-Strauss restores the dignity that is owed to "savage thought," it is insofar as it is analytical and not because it might be dialectical or poetic. Indeed, he does so because it classifies and quantifies. If what we call "logical" and "pre-logical" thought are united, it is ultimately in scientific naturalism. "For it seems to the case that man began applying himself to the most difficult task, that of systematizing what is immediately presented to the senses, on which science for a long time turned its back and which it is only beginning to bring back into its purview."[28]

---

28 Ibid., 11.

9

MICHEL FOUCAULT AND THE FRENCH REVOLUTION

A Misunderstanding?

Before 1983, Foucault had practically never written on the French Revolution.[1] One even gets the sense that he carefully avoided this object of historical examination. In his great work *The Order of Things*, published in 1966, his periodization does not include the revolutionary knowledge (*le savoir révolutionnaire*) between the classical age and post-Kantian modernity. Would the Enlightenment, like the French Revolution, fall outside the *épistémê*? Can they really be included in the "classical age" without damage? In his *History of Madness in the Classical Age*, he addresses with precision the short period that separates the end of the general Hospital and the beginnings of a medicalized madness. This is the moment when the power to distinguish between reason and unreason belongs to the citizen and, even more precisely, to the family in the form of family courts established in 1790. It is the moment of a transition, where the virtue that prevails in the asylum differs in no way from that which prevails in society. Foucault thus speaks of the necessity of "assuring an ethical continuity between the world of madness and the world of reason."[2] This requires an adjustment between social norms with respect to madness and the behavior of the mad, with the understanding that the mad belong to a common humanity which must

---

1 According to Roger Chartier, "From *The History of Madness* to *Discipline and Punish*, the French Revolution is present in all of Foucault's major works. In none of them, however, is it considered as the time of a total or global rupture, reorganizing the field of discourse, knowledges, and practices. What is essential lies elsewhere: in the shifts that crossed the Revolution and in the continuities inscribed in the *durées* that surpass it." "Foucault et les Historiens, les historiens et Foucault," in *Au risque de Foucault* (Paris: Éditions du Centre Pompidou, 1997), 230.
2 Michel Foucault, *Madness and Civilization* (New York: Vintage, 1988), 259.

be recognized despite the fear that some may provoke.³ After *The Order of Things*, however, this careful analysis of what happened in the Revolutionary period did not reoccur.

The French Revolution is thus a foreclosed object in Foucault's work, including when he discovers a living revolution in Iran in 1978. The French Revolution seems to fall back on what he calls "bourgeois or revolutionary democracies" and "definitions of Islamic government." He declares that, far from being imprecise, "they seemed to me to have a familiar but, I must say, not too reassuring clarity. These are basic formulas for democracy, whether bourgeois or revolutionary, [. . .] Since the eighteenth century now, we have not ceased to repeat them, and you know where they have led."⁴ What is implicitly vilified is the bourgeois domination of the parliamentary regime. The Marxist notion of bourgeois revolution appears to emerge. In *Discipline and Punish*, he had taken on this interpretation in terms of bourgeois revolution. "Historically, the process by which the bourgeoisie became in the course of the eighteenth century the politically dominant class was masked by the establishment of an explicit, coded and formally egalitarian juridical framework. [. . .] But the development and generalization of disciplinary mechanisms constituted the other, dark side of these processes."⁵ Of course, he did not distinguish between different revolutionary moments, moments in which the prison did not have the same function.⁶ But beyond the immediate philosophico-political concern, the word "Revolution" itself connotes, for Foucault, a largely inadvisable participation in French identity. He thus declares that the question he confronted upon return from Iran—"Is this revolution?"—was one that he refused to answer. It was a refusal to engage with "a whole opinion in France that does not take any interest in what is not from our country except at this price."⁷ Would the French not take interest in Iran unless it presented them with a national parallel? A revolution compared to the French Revolution as its ultimate referent? We cannot be quite so precise, but the word "revolution" as a universal is the only one which, according

---

3 Cf. Mathieu Potte-Bonneville's *Michel Foucault l'inquiétude de l'histoire* (Paris, PUF, 2004), 47 sq.

4 Michel Foucault, *Dits et Écrits, 1976–1979* (Paris: Gallimard, 1994), 692. Translator's rendering.

5 Michel Foucault, *Discipline and Punish*, trans. Alan Sheridan (New York: Vintage, 1995), 222.

6 The disciplinary prison, which introduces other pains than just the privation of freedom, far from corresponding to the period of Terror, for example, is post-Thermidorian, as is shown by Christine Tarakanov in her thesis titled "Le Carcéral: désir d'humanité et changement révolutionnaire. La prison des Archives parlementaires, et les archives du département du Nord, 1789–1799," under my direction in January 2016.

7 Foucault, *Dits et Écrits, 1976–1979*, 716. Translator's rendering.

to Foucault, would allow the French to leave "home" (*chez nous*), it being understood that the "outside," through the magic of comparison, then becomes once again a familiar "home." Yet Foucault's aim in diagnosing the present is to de-familiarize it, to singularize it. Like all comparisons that fabricate contiguity, the comparison with the French Revolution appears to him as an illegitimate one.

The fact remains that even in 1978, Foucault avoided the word "revolution," preferring to speak of "insurrection." In doing so, and this is something quite rare, he appeared content with the commonsense understanding of both revolution and the history of the French Revolution. He had already explained this unavailability of the word "revolution" well before the Iranian revolution and counterrevolution. "Since 1789, Europe has changed in accordance with the idea of revolution. European history has been dominated by this idea. It is precisely this idea that is in the process of disappearing at the moment."[8] He then asserted that revolution was a Western concept, caught in the crisis of Western thought and the crisis the Western universal, and finally in a crisis induced by Marxism. The only concession he made to a possible rapprochement between what was happening in Iran and the French Revolution came in response to the publication of François Furet's *Interpreting the French Revolution* in that same year of 1978. While it is certainly the case that François Furet explicitly refuses to reduce the revolutionary event to economic and social structures in the manner of Marxist history, he remains far from an insurrectionary or popular perspective. Furet is interested in elites, whereas Foucault is interested in common people who carry out a "bare-fisted revolt." Foucault seeks to discern how the will of the Iranian people is "one, stubborn, efficient," how "the upheaval of a whole society stifled civil war,"[9] whereas Furet makes popular uprising the decisive factor of political violence and civil war. As a historian of the revolutionary period who worked between 1990 and today, I can only be surprised at what I feel to be a misunderstanding, a de facto alliance whose meaning lies in an explicit and common sympathy for a third party, the weekly *Le Nouvel Obeservateur* and its desire to be a site of synthesis for a new left that is no longer tied to "Marxism" and "Jacobinism."

But if this is enough to understand why Foucault cites François Furet and not Albert Soboul, it does not suffice as an explanation of his aversion to the French Revolution as an object of knowledge.

The question might seem anecdotal.

---

8 Ibid., 623.
9 Ibid., 701.

How can we fail to recognize that Foucault was himself insurrectionary in his relationship to knowledge (*savoir*)[10] and politics, and simply say "too bad" that he did not work on the period of the French Revolution? In fact, since my earliest work as a historian of the French Revolution, at several points and in a number of ways, Foucault has been very illuminating for me. But at a time when the French Revolution has more than ever fallen back on the standard Tocquevillian narrative, the latter functioning as the authoritative figure in François Furet's *Interpreting the French Revolution*, it seems important for us to unravel the enigma. It is as a result of the power of the Tocquevillian narrative that an important part of "post-colonial studies" rejects any value in this historical and political moment, refusing to consider all of the work done by historians of the French Revolution to critique this standard narrative.

In light of this misunderstanding, we must return to the publication of *The Order of Things*.

THE ORDER OF THINGS: A LINK IN THE CHAIN OF DEBATES OPENED BY SARTRE AND LÉVI-STRAUSS

In 1967 Balandier asserts that

> structuralism is in fashion: debates, erroneous interpretations, exploitations of the term, the application of the notion of 'structures' to the most diverse fields, and the wide diffusion of works that are difficult understand proves it. Drawn out of the domain of specialists, structuralism is almost always abused, so much so that all amalgamations become possible: combinations are generally made of Lévi-Strauss, Lacan, Althusser, and Foucault, which confuse and misuse their projects.[11]

If this is not an amalgamation based on a shared epistemological project, what is it based on? Certainly, it is not simply the focus on structures which, as Balandier reminds us, is already in Marx, but rather the decentering of the subject, and the famous "death of man," if by "man" we understand the centered and self-conscious subject.

However, in this affirmation of decentering and the "death of man." Foucault plays an essential role, with a succession of publications and debates that led, little by little, to foreclosing the knowledge (*connaissance*) of

---

10 See Diogo Sardinha, *L'Émancipation de Kant à Deleuze* (Paris: Hermann, 2013).
11 Georges Balandier, *Civilisés, dit-on* (Paris: PUF, 2003), 71, article published in 1967 in *Le Nouvel Observateur*. Translator's rendering.

the revolutionary period. Because this revolutionary period was chosen by Sartre as emblematic of History in Truth and thus human freedom, rejecting Sartre as a relic of the nineteenth century led *ipso facto* to emptying the "terrain" that goes with this epistemological hypothesis.

Foucault is very familiar with the debate between Sartre and Lévi-Strauss, and like everyone from his generation, he knows the French Revolution well. Is it not the expression "supreme being," so strongly attached to the revolutionary event, that leaves his lips when he is interviewed by Pierre Dumayet for the ORTF on June 15, 1966. He connects the space of freedom and moral inventiveness opened up by the death of God to his own announcement of the death of man. Even if, as Judith Revel asserts,[12] he cites historians more than he does Sartre, Lévi-Strauss, or Lacan—that famous constellation—the latter are, in spite of this, explicitly present and literally inhabit Foucault's thought. For a Foucault in front of the media, it is a question pursuing the debate opened by Sartre and Lévi-Strauss while preserving the singularity of his own work.

With *The Order of Things*, he claims to have done an "ethnology of western culture," what anthropologists henceforth called the "ethnology of the proximate." In this regard, he argues that Western culture is as foreign to us any other culture, and that believing that we are conscious of our culture and our history is a delusion. It is as foreign as the tribes declared by Sartre to be "without history" in the *Critique*. In doing so, he proposes a third theoretical position for those who wish to assert his relevance for anthropological/ethnographic/ethnological questions, alongside Sartre's *Critique of Dialectical Reason* (in which Sartre also claimed to be doing anthropological work) and the work of Lévi-Strauss. Here, the term "anthropology" is perhaps made unavailable. If "man" is no longer central, anthropology is itself perhaps cautioned against, in favor of what are called the "human sciences."

Without being explicitly addressed, the question of the French Revolution remains present at least in the background. Foucault mentions it in the June 15 interview as a hinge between a time without the preoccupation with the human as such and the beginning of the nineteenth century—in which the categories *human* and *humanism* ultimately make possible, a century later, the advent of the human sciences on the debris of humanist philosophy, Marxism, and Existentialism. With the death of man, Foucault can no longer connect his work with political engagement. Say goodbye to the myth of the French Revolution as a schema that harmonizes knowledge,

---

12 Judith Revel, "En relisant *Les Mots et les choses*," in dossier fabula n° 31, op. cit.

belief, and action. To explain this dissociation, Foucault asserts, with the words of Lévi-Strauss and Barthes, that this work has destroyed "a myth," that of Man, without a new mythology being "reconstituted." The work to be undertaken, according to him, must unseat not only philosophical myths but also historical and political ones.

With respect to history, there is no continuum or succession from one situation to another, but a void, a discontinuity. With respect to action and knowledge, Foucault claims that "henceforth, thought (*la pensée*) is no longer there to prescribe to people what they must do." He suggests a "colder morality to his interlocutor. Hence there are at least three terms from this interview which I believe follow from the debate opened by Sartre and Lévi-Strauss: (1) knowledge (*savoir*) in the human sciences as a methodical scientific knowledge and not as philosophical work; (2) myth, which should be debunked in favor of the knowledge of knowledge (*du savoir sur le savoir*); (3) the coldness of moral invention as opposed to the warmth of humanist commitment or the subject of revolutionary history.

PRACTICO-INERT/THEORETICO-ACTIVE: OF A HISTORY THAT WOULD NO LONGER BE ONE

Two months earlier in an interview with *Lettres françaises*, Foucualt had already explained his work by differentiating himself from Sartre, without citing him but instead invoking his concept of the practico-inert: "rather than seeking to explain this knowledge (*savoir*) from the point of view of the practico-inert, I seek to formulate an analysis of what we could call the 'theoretico-active.'"[13] The knowledge of which he speaks makes it possible for a specific society at a specific time to generate theories, practices, opinions, and institutions. It is a foundational knowledge, which is simultaneously unknown and necessary for a society to be more than a mere collection of individuals but rather constituted from end to end by what Foucault calls the "conditions of possibility" of knowledge. Ruptures are identified when these conditions of possibility are renewed, that is, when the organizing principle, or in Foucault's terms, "constitutive and historical knowledge"—the "subsoil of our consciousness of meaning"—changes and transforms every discourse.

---

13 Michel Foucault, *Dits et Écrits, 1954–1969* (Paris, Gallimard, 1994), 498–99. Translator's rendering.

He claims that the advantage of this type of research is that it "avoids all problems of the priority of theory in relation to practice and vice versa." He says he is researching "isomorphisms." What is thus rejected is the idea that the diachronic principle is necessary for all understanding, and certainly the idea of an "existence which precedes essence." If the organizing principle weighs on an epoch, there is no need to refer to the specific acts of a free subject to explain his choices, his decisions. Foucault thus explains that the sciences of "man" in fact lead "to the disappearance of man rather than his apotheosis."[14] Let us note the proximity of this expression "the disappearance of man" to Lévi-Strauss's "to dissolve man," from the latter's engagement in the debate on the *Critique of Dialectical Reason* in *The Savage Mind*.

But if "Man is dead," it is not just because human nature has been rejected. Sartre also rejected human nature when he asserted the creative freedom of individuals, who are masters of their destinies and as a result do not depend on a creator to fashion their futures but depend instead on their capacity to forge their own quest for life and meaning. Now, it is precisely this freedom that is challenged. It becomes tenuous, rare, and fragile. This is the "death of Man." The expression itself buries the free man. Certainly, from Sartre's point of view, it is not only individual acts that condition historical situations, but also the practico-inert, the force of "worked matter," physical or ideal, and it is this worked matter that operates in a concealed way and so prevents us from being fully conscious of what we are doing. Hence the idea of inertia, of something which weighs heavily on us and prevents us from forging ahead with clear awareness, which makes it so that everyone is *of* their time such that "their time" is more than just a fashion or "the spirit of the times" but a foundation which is both common and tied to our specific individual experience. But whereas in Sartre it was a question of going beyond the practico-inert to become free, in Foucault, the theoretico-active does not obstruct but rather "permits." It is the soil of history, a nourishing soil, no more conscious than the practico-inert, but Foucault does not care about consciousness. Humans no longer choose, but are nourished by the structure of their epoch, which is no longer presented as an alienating constraint but as a given that makes thinking possible. In Foucault, the concept of consciousness, like that of Man, seems to belong to the nineteenth century. And it is precisely to its survival that he seeks to deliver a deathblow.

---

14 Ibid., 502.

In all these respects, Foucault's work, which undoubtedly has other wellsprings, emerges above all in opposition to the *Critique of Dialectical Reason*. But in order to oppose it, he must obscure it, rejecting it point by point in such a way that, it seems to me, there emerges a Foucault who is at once distant and proximate to Sartre. Thus, in May 1966 in *La Quinzaine littéraire*, he asserts: "One thinks within an anonymous and constraining mode of thought which belongs an epoch and a language. This mode of thought and this language have their laws of transformation." We might say that Sartre's notion of "philosophy-world," philosophy, which acts on us "like the moon pulls the tide," is just as far from a subjective conception of thought and hence could also be conceived as "that thought before any thought, that system before any systems." The dividing line, however, is drawn at the place given to the famous "free man."

Foucault's *épistèmê* is "the ground on which our 'free' thought emerges and scintillates for an instant."[15] He takes this expression up again in the June 15 interview, where he refers to the individual as a "scintillation on the surface of formal systems." In his 1970 inaugural address at the Collège de France, this scintillation had become a "slight gap," a "happy wreck," the "point of possible disappearance" of discourse, itself qualified as a "nameless voice" which precedes him or her who speaks by "lodging" them in the "interstices," as if in a "calm transparency, profound and indefinitely open."

But back to the TV interview. Like Lévi-Strauss, Foucault begins by paying homage to Sartre as a great philosopher, but only so as to dismiss him as a man of the nineteenth century, it being understood that the nineteenth century is the century of Man with a capital *M*, so dear to Sartre. Certainly, with this "scintillation," freedom has not completely disappeared, an important gap for Lévi-Strauss, too. But if this filial formation remains present and even acknowledged, the young thirty-eight-year-old kills a father figure. In another interview, with C. Bonnefoy in the June 1966 *Art et loisirs*, he clearly refers to the sixty-one-year-old when he mentions "the man of the nineteenth century's magnificent and pathetic effort to think the twentieth century." Foucault states that "Sartre did everything he could to integrate contemporary culture, that is to say advances in psychoanalysis, political economy, history, sociology, and dialectics," and concludes that "in this sense Sartre is the last Hegelian, and I would even say the last Marxist."[16] The word "pathetic" turns the generational gap into an implicit rivalry. Sartre, Foucault tells us, is not contemporary, he is

---

15 Foucault, *Dits et Écrits, 1954–1969*, 515.
16 Ibid., 541.

surpassed and outside the time, and hence without use. In other words, he is already as dead as "Man."

Sartrean Truth is therefore supplanted by Foucauldian necessity. The passage from one historical sequence to another no longer depends on any subject, whether individual or collective, but on the uncontrollable and constitutive historical ground of each sequence. The revolutionary event as rupture, certainly determined in part by this ground and the practico-inert but also by active political wills, becomes henceforth difficult to conceive. Herein lies the initial collateral damage suffered by the object "French Revolution," a Sartrean object and one which is adequate to his theories, but an object that appears incompatible with Foucauldian theories.

The conflict between these two men and two generations, these two currents of thought, becomes an open one in the fall of 1966, when Sartre releases his famous interview at *L'Arc*, in which he asserts that Foucault's work attests to the particular structuralist refusal of history.

"What do we find in *The Order of Things*? Not an archeology of the human sciences. The archaeologist is someone who searches for traces of a disappeared civilization so as to reconstruct it. It studies a style that was conceived and put to work by men. The style was then able to imposes itself as a natural situation, taking on the appearance a given. It is nonetheless the result of a praxis whose development the archaeologist traces. What Foucault presents us with, as Kanters saw well, is a geology: the series of successive layers that form our 'soil.'"[17]

"I do not dispute the existence of structures, nor the need to analyze their mechanisms. But structure is, for me, but one moment of the practico-inert. It is the result of a praxis that outstrips its agents. All human creation has its element of passivity, but this does not mean that it is subjected through and through." Sartre concludes thus: "Man is perpetually out of step with the structures that condition him, because he is something more than what he does, than being what he is. I therefore do not understand why we would stop at structures: for me, it is a logical scandal."

A response from Foucault appeared in *La Quinzainne littéraire* in March 1968, in which he claims that Sartre is much too occupied with his own work to have read *The Order of Things*, and as a result, "what he says cannot be pertinent."[18] He then asserts that he did not give his consent to its publication, and that for eighteen months he reflected on the objections he faced "by Sartre, among others." Foucault still prefers believing that

---

17 "Jean-Paul Sartre répond," *L'Arc 30: Sartre Aujourd'hui*, October 1966.
18 Foucault, *Dits et Écrits, 1954–1969*, 666.

he has not been read rather than misunderstood in his displacement of the practico-inert for the theoretico-active which grounds the autonomy of the "system" in relation to the free wills of subjects.

Doubtless, Foucault is interested in the question of the history of knowledges and of thought. But this history is not what Sartre considers History. Even if human History as a totality and as the Truth of Man is not or is no longer that of all historians, Sartre called on the latter to save history as a homogeneous discipline, as a system of history, we might say. Thus he writes: "A historian today may not be a communist; but he knows that one cannot write serious history without foregrounding the material aspects of the life of men, relations of production, praxis—even if like me he thinks beyond these relations, of the 'superstructures' that constitute relatively autonomous domains."[19]

A FOUCAULT VERY CLOSE TO LÉVI-STRAUSS

Foucault's generation values work on these autonomous domains and affirms that it is precisely a question of producing this autonomization, guaranteeing a scholarly knowledge which would make it possible to no longer confuse the past and the present and to escape the imaginary of an eternal human nature. Foucault also takes advantage of the French publication of Ernst Cassirer's book on the Enlightenment to show how the latter had, as a kind of precursor, autonomized the statements of the Enlightenment from their situations and their enunciators. "Cassirer proceeds according to a sort of 'foundational abstraction': on the one hand, he effaces individual motivations, accidents of biography, and all the contingent figures that populate an epoch; on the other, he suspends economic or social determinations. And what then unfolds before him is a whole inseparable fabric of discourse and thought, of concepts and words, statements and claims which he attempts to analyze in their own configuration." "He isolates an autonomous 'theoretical' space from all other histories (of individuals as much as of societies): and under his eyes, a heretofore silent history is discovered."[20] Cassirer's method therefore opposes that of Sartre, who tries to hold everything together through a figure of "man" who is thoroughly traversed by the practico-inert. And in fact, the debate over the practices of historians is at the same time a debate over the subject "man"

---

19 "Jean-Paul Sartre répond," *L'Arc 30: Sartre Aujourd'hui*, October 1966.
20 Foucault, *Dits et Écrits, 1954–1969*, 548.

as Lévi-Strauss presents him in his final works. The valorization of the work of abstraction and scholarly unveiling thanks to abstraction, and of the comparative classification of givens separated from their contingency, was already causing Sartre's "man" to disappear. With man out of the picture, different kinds of cuts in time will be privileged. If on both sides, there is a rigor of the archive, only the question of the relevant timescale creates the division of the field. Now, let us recall that this question of classes of time was an important issue in Lévi-Strauss's argument for history as a method without an object, but a method which must precisely interrogate the relevance of the rupture in time.

Foucault does not cite Lévi-Strauss, and explains in June 1967 that in terms of history, the new adventure is that of Fernand Braudel, François Furet, Denis Richet, Emmanuel Leroy Ladurie, the researchers in the Cambridge school of history, and the Soviet school.

However, in this matter of periodization, it is explicitly a question of rejecting the revolutionary scansion. Fernand Braudel, particularly in his article published in 1958 in *Les Annales ESC* titled "The Long Durée," regards the facts of revolution as "epiphenomena," as a "pathetic inconvenience." What matters are "masses of slow history." As for Emmanuel Leroy Ladurie, his way of approaching anthropology is to assert that the time of history is in fact "still."

"These historians pose the very difficult problem of periodization. We realized that the obvious periodization punctuated by political revolutions was, methodologically, no longer the best possible form of scission." "Every periodization cuts out a certain level of events in history, and conversely, each layer of events calls for its own periodization. [. . .] We thus reach the complex methodology of discontinuity."[21] Here again we see Lévi-Strauss ventriloquizing, because it is this very discontinuity of signs of historical method that he had taken great care to describe so as to construct comparable classes of objects. Foucault, however, does not dwell on this question of object classification, but emphasizes that "the old opposition between the human sciences and history (the former studying the synchronous and the non-evolutionary and the latter analyzing the dimension of incessant major change) is disappearing: change can be an object of analysis in terms of structures, the discourse of history is populated with analyses that it lends to ethnology and sociology, to the human sciences, and thus perhaps for the first time, we have the possibility of analyzing as an object a collection of

---

21 Ibid., 586.

materials which have been left aside over time through signs, traces, institutions, practices, works, etc."[22]

The Foucauldian method is truly novel in its project of autonomizing the discursive object as a means of access to a theoretical subsoil that governs the surface. However, if he reverses the Marxist point of view in which the infrastructures dominate superstructures, he is not content with the traditional history of ideas that places the great thinkers at center stage. It must be recognized that the borrowings from history by sociology and other human sciences nonetheless date from the 1930s, with, among others, the creation of the journal *Annales* by Marc Bloch and Lucien Febvre. This is not what is new. Labrousse works on the economics of price, Febvre on mental tools, which is another way of speaking of a theory of the foundations from which human actions and beliefs unfold; Marxists are attached to great scansions and thus define a succession of historical periods linked to socioeconomic structures: slavery, feudalism, capitalism. . . . We do not see great novelty here. There remains a new use of these questions of temporality and periodization. Rejecting the vital time of events by relating it to that of revolutionary scansions had not been done, for precisely these different temporalities, the long time of structures, the time of conjunctures, and the event came from Marxism. Foucault oversimplifies and makes de facto alliances with the historians who reject the value of the event in general, and the revolutionary event in particular.

He thus finds not the words, but the prosody of the Lévi-Strauss of *The Savage Mind* when he replied to Sartre and rejected the use of the French Revolution as a myth that is useful to citizens. But Foucault broadens the subject to a mode of doing history. "For many intellectuals, distant respect [. . .] for history was the easiest way to align their political consciousness with their research or writing activity. In the eyes of some, history as a discipline constituted the last refuge of dialectical order: in it, rational contradiction could be saved."[23] Foucault concludes that "it would mean attacking the great cause of the revolution to refuse such a form of historical speaking."[24] It is clear that the historians who are cited are those that either fundamentally rejected the French Revolution as a pertinent object of analysis (Braudel, Leroy Ladurie) or subverted the history of the Revolution from top to bottom by abandoning the very idea of studying the days of the Revolution. The latter foregrounded the political and discursive dimension of a historical moment which could have occurred

---

22 Ibid.
23 Ibid., 584.
24 Ibid., 586.

without actors since everything had played out in advance of the irruption of the people on these famous days (Furet and Richet).

In doing so, alongside Lévi-Strauss, Braudel, and Furet, Foucault in fact stages a combative debate over the aims of history.

For Michel Foucault, his philosophical work consists in "diagnosing the present,"[25] borrowing the word "diagnostic" from Nietzsche. It is a question of "stating what the present is, stating how the present is different and absolutely different, that is to say from our past."[26] He singularizes the present, the "today," whereas the *Critique of Dialectical Reason* makes each partial event the possibility of a totalization in lived experience, of giving oneself "one's own light" for action, in praxis. With Sartre, therefore, the past is not separated from the present. They are contiguous. If this contiguity breaks down, then History may fade away. Effectively, in the words of Sartre, "history calls for history," and it is the subject who, through his investigation, his gaze, his readings made possible and effective by his political praxis, gives meaning to history. "That also means that every history, as soon as relationships in the present or past are established with other histories, is the incarnation of History."[27] Every singular history, then, incarnates universal History. But Foucault, in affirming the death of man as the subject of history, clearly asserts that such a conception of history is, in his view, obsolete. When Sartre criticizes him for not taking history into account, he is reproaching him for no longer supporting this contiguity of the past and present, and the historical consciousness that goes with it.

Sartre had made the French Revolution the laboratory for that which prevents people from being free but also that which allows them, despite everything, to become free—a laboratory of emancipation in a conception of History, clearly discontinuous and even fragile, but always re-totalized in the consciousness of History.

In his response to Sartre, Foucault speaks of a reason that does not obey progress. Yet we know Sartre did not defend this idea of progress in the *Critique of Dialectical Reason*, even emphasizing that this category belongs to homogeneous capitalist time. The unfounded accusations based on rivalry continue, but the camps are now entrenched. History for the philosopher, according to Foucault, interweaves three myths: "continuity, the effective exercise of human freedom, and the articulation of individual

---

25 Ibid., 665.
26 Ibid.
27 Jean-Paul Sartre, *Critique of Dialectical Reason*, vol. 1, ed. Arlette Elkaïm-Sartre, trans. Quintin Hoare (London: Verso, 1991), 453.

freedom and social determinations."[28] He declares that this is the history he wants to kill, but in this assassination he also kills, in my view, any desire to revisit the question of revolutionary time, of the revolutionary moment, of revolutionary freedom. These are too obviously Sartrean questions, questions which have become, like Sartre in his view, "old-fashioned." Foucault thus commits parricide and kills the father along with the father's object.

So, is Foucault a historian of "cold history"? It would be moving too fast to describe him this way, but he effectively allies himself with historians who assert that the function of history is no longer to provide us with insights for today, but knowledges (*des savoirs*) for understanding a past that is separate from the present.

The revolutionary surged forth in Iran in 1978, yet Foucault still does not return to revolutionary history.

---

28 Foucault, *Dits et Écrits, 1954–1969*, 667.

10

THE FRENCH REVOLUTION

Between the Archaeology of Knowledge, Discursive Formations, and Social Formations

The Foucault of *The Order of Things*, *The Archaeology of Knowledge* and of *The Order of Discourse,* as well as the inaugural lecture at the Collège de France in December of 1970, is paradoxically entirely able to support a work on the French Revolution, with Foucault and despite Foucault. I speak from experience. If in my university education there was no attention given to Sartre, Foucault arrived in my master's studies as an essential figure of discourse analysis as it was elaborated by historians, and specifically with regard to the French Revolution, by Régine Robin and Jacques Guilhaumou in the wake of linguistics, Foucault, and Althusser.

ENCOUNTERING FOUCAULT IN 1986

When I began my work on the figure of the foreigner during the French Revolution, the aim was to grab hold of, not enunciating subjects, but discursive formations, the "it speaks" of a society, which later, at the Inter-University Research Center in Montreal[1] established by Régine Robin and Marc Angenot, we instead called "social discourse." It was a question of locating the ways a society put statements without an enunciator into circulation. "Without an enunciator" means without us really being able to ascribe to these enunciators a subject position creating, through their statements, processes of subjectivation, even if we could situate them socially and politically—a socially, non-subjectively-produced "sayable," therefore.

---

1 Inter-University Research Center in Discourse Analysis and Social Critique of Texts, in Montreal, Canada.

This would not prevent us from observing individual ways of appropriating social discourse, even of subverting it or breaking it through enunciative ruptures. But the postulate was that discourse was not the attribute of a subject free to say what they want, but that they respond to the famous conditions of possibility operative both in language and "the social," in the wider sense of the term.

This approach to discourses was at once structuralist and Marxist, and made it possible to no longer relate statements to politically and socially situated subjects but to identify which statements traverse which spaces. Thus, everything would not be brought back to immediate political struggles or to immediate positions, even if, in a second step, moments of rupture and discontinuity could also be analyzed in terms of these struggles directly inscribed in discourses. It was then a question of avoiding emphasis on a context external to discourses, while locating within discourse the ways that contexts are inscribed in enunciative traces. It is only in this way, and at precise moments of a work, that the subject of the enunciation—which is not, strictly speaking, the subject—made a return.

Nevertheless, in this enterprise of discourse analysis, *à la Françaises* we might add, three of Foucault's works were especially important: *The Order of Things*, *The Archaeology of Knowledge*, and *The Order of Discourse*. Moreover, in the articulation of discourse and history, Foucault congruously interrogated three issues that gave consistency to the ambitions of discourse analysis in the study of history: How to produce scientific historical knowledge? Which body of documents enables this production? What temporality should be made operational in this work?

The way of making scientific knowledge, for Foucault, lay in the connection between the history of the sciences and a mode of analytical reason defended by Lévi-Strauss in *The Savage Mind,* and by Foucault himself in his invocation of the work of Cassirer.[2] It lay likewise in discourse analysis and—as we shall see—its kinship with the scientific ambitions of the Marxist science extolled by Althusser. The latter thus shared the requisites of Lévi-Strauss and Foucault, which makes it possible to understand why he could be perceived, despite differences, as belonging to the same epistemological constellation and susceptible to alliances.

Then comes the way that the scholar, the scientist constitutes her corpus—a closed corpus or an open one—and above all how she thinks about the way she constitutes it in connection with the epoch she is studying. In the *Archaeology of Knowledge,* history had become "the work

---

2 See Michel Foucault, *Dits et Écrits, 1954–1969* (Paris: Gallimard, 1994), 548.

expended on material documentation (books, texts, accounts, registers, acts, buildings, institutions, laws, techniques, objects, customs, etc.) that exists, in every time and place, in every society, either in a spontaneous or in a consciously organized form."³ "History tends toward archaeology," Foucault thus tells us, because it describes documents in their functioning, their organization, rather than making them the site for deciphering "the traces left by men."

The history of knowledge conducted in this way made it possible to value different ways of conceptualizing discontinuity (threshold, rupture, scission, mutation, transformation), and even the irruption of events. From this point of view, archaeology was opposed to a serial history which, evidently, organized series in order to construct the continuum of history in its long *durée* and not its discontinuity. In *The Order of Discourse*, Foucault discusses this point and appears to credit historians of the long *durée* with a talent for bringing new seeds of events to light.

> It is often entered to the credit of contemporary history that it removed the privileges once accorded to the singular event and revealed the structures of longer duration. That is so. [. . .] I do not think there is an inverse ratio between noticing the event and analysing the long durations. On the contrary, it seems to be by pushing to its extreme the fine grain of the event, by stretching the resolution-power of historical analysis as far as official price-lists (*les mercuriales*), title deeds, parish registers, harbour archives examined year by year and week by week, that these historians saw—beyond the battles, decrees, dynasties or assemblies—the outline of massive phenomena with a range of a hundred or many hundreds of years. History as practised today does not turn away from events; on the contrary, it is constantly enlarging their field, discovering new layers of them, shallower or deeper.⁴

We can still hear the voice of Lévi-Strauss and his classes of time in what Foucault tells us here, and to this extent, *The Archaeology of Knowledge* remains indebted to the controversy of 1962. "But the important thing is that history does not consider an event without defining the series of which it is part, without specifying the mode of analysis from which that series derives, without seeking to find out the regularity of phenomena and the limits of probability of their emergence, without inquiring into the

---

3 Michel Foucault, *The Archaeology of Knowledge* (London: Routledge, 2002).
4 Michel Foucault, "The Order of Discourse," in *Untying the Text: A Post-Structuralist Reader* (Boston: Routledge and Kegan Paul, 1981), 68.

variations, bends and angles of the graph, without wanting to determine the conditions on which they depend."⁵

Foucault thus produces a critical epistemology of history as Tradition which bears some resemblance to the critique of progress in the 1930s. Like Walter Benjamin, and indeed myself along with Sartre, Foucault refuses to make Revolutions the necessary moment of coming to consciousness in the continuum of progress, a form of the incessant effort of consciousness at work. Each, albeit in different ways, in fact critiques the concept of progress and of teleology. However, with Foucault even the concept of Revolution is absent, whereas Benjamin and Sartre question its uncertainty.

Foucault affirms that history does not produce historical consciousness, if by that we understand the kind of consciousness originating in and revealed by Revolutions as an arduous achievement of freedom. History, in that case, would not be "scansion," but "becoming." It would be, "not an interplay of relations, but an internal dynamic; not a system, but the hard work of freedom; not form, but the unceasing effort of a consciousness turned upon itself, trying to grasp itself in its deepest conditions: a history that would be both an act of long, uninterrupted patience and the vivacity of a movement, which, in the end, breaks all bounds."⁶ Foucault once again refuses any role for the subjective swings of historical actors. Conversely for Sartre, the progression of time is uncertain and reversible because the subject exists, even though it is in fact rare and fragile while being determinative in each situation.

Nevertheless, in this question of documents and time, there is a genuine discursive issue: is discourse the prisoner of the long *durée*? Or like notarial data, the possible site of tacking retreats without them correlating only to actors? Can we identify, in an event such as the French Revolution, discursive events that inhabit and surpass it?

I admit that when I reread this passage from Foucault's *Archaeology of Knowledge*, which is quite vehement in its continued battle with Sartre, I could not help but smile at the thought of the titles of two my books: *Emotions, the French Revolution, and the Present: Practical Exercises in Historical Consciousness*, and *The Long Patience of the People: 1792, the Birth of the Republic*. I, who had started with the *Archaeology of Knowledge*, had failed to observe his requisites. There is a difficulty, perhaps even impossibility, of holding the positions elaborated in *Archaeology* when doing a history of the French Revolution today. How can the short time of a revolution and

---

5 Ibid.
6 Ibid., 14.

this archaeological ambition, which seems to dismiss visible actions, be held together?

But in fact, being less ironic about myself, the theoretical question was already the following: How can such an archaeology, which in its rejection of consciousness refuses the idea of any progress in history, as is effectively done by Benjamin and Sartre, produce a critical knowledge and not simply a description of documents? This critical knowledge could be called, not "historical consciousness," but the discontinuous collection of moments of historical knowledge ,which, despite everything, are revealing, even if they do not produce awareness in the researcher and their reader—knowledge as a kind of revolution, however, a revolution that is decisively against coming to consciousness and time as totalization, against History with a capital H as Sartre conceived it in the *Critique of Dialectical Reason*. But here again Foucault had misunderstood this totalization, which is always moving and not fixed in a Tradition. It is a totalization which is not a principle of unity, but a principle of the passage between times.

In short, how to redeem "historical consciousness" while accepting the dispersion of time, which despite Foucault's misunderstanding, could be called "detotalizing it."

This was the question that presented itself to me when I took up the question of the foreigner in direct relation to the present.

Agreeing to produce an archaeology, leaving behind the subjects of history, certainly, but in order to grasp a situation and return to the present ballasted by a knowledge of what allows us to pose new questions to it. Yet Foucault, while I was working on these issues from 1986 to 1994, had already to a certain extent responded to these questions.

Foucault had in fact given his lecture on Kant's *What Is Enlightenment* at the Collège de France in 1983, and the *Magazine littéraire* had published it in 1984.[7] In this lecture, it seems to me, he tackled all of this head-on in the following terms: "We can opt for a critical philosophy which would present itself as an analytical philosophy of truth in general, or we can opt for a critical thought which would take the form of an ontology of ourselves, and ontology of the present."[8] Foucault effectively makes Enlightenment the moment which questions, in a reflexive way, the link between rationality and its present, explicitly drawing into relation "life, experience, and science." Some of the terms that he repudiated in the 1960s thus return: the word "experience," in particular, though we could

---

7 Michel Foucault, *Dits et Écrits*, t. IV, 683.
8 Ibid. Translator's rendering.

say the same of the "present," the "sensible," and "knowledge" (*savoir*), or other combinations that enable us to grasp the present in its difference, to grasp the discontinuity of the present compared to yesterday and the next day, a present which announces nothing and does not produce the necessity of a continuous thread: the present as a site for tracking discontinuities proper to the moment, in its relation to the past and in the direct line of the *Archaeology of Knowledge*.

The ontology of the present is certainly not dialectical reason, but it nevertheless seems to affirm that, in the knowledge of the present, it is a matter of finding in the present the very place of questioning. The philosopher would have to "say the meaning" "to specify the mode of action that can be exercised within this present" (*What Is Enlightenment?*). We are very close to Sartre's "praxis." though all totalization, even partial, has been abandoned.

This is the epistemological framework of the undertaking. Nevertheless, I was unknowingly dependent on the debate of the 1970s and the way that it had been constitutive of discourse analysis.

REPLAYING THE POSSIBLE ALLIANCE BETWEEN FOUCAULT AND ALTHUSSER

In order to work on the concept of the "foreigner" in the revolutionary period, in the collection of the *Archives parlementaires,* I thus located semantic fields, thematic trajectories, fixed phrases, and enunciative reversals. I tried to grasp where and how tipping points became legible in the order of discourse. This is how I was able to locate the political meaning of the word "*étranger*"[9] closer to the notion of the "traitor" and "counter-revolutionary" than to our notion of the "foreigner" as someone from another people or country. In this way, I was able to understand how King Louis Capet was the quintessential figure of the foreigner during the Revolutionary moment. It is also how I was able to spot how the discourse on the English had gradually appointed the foreigner to the rank of criminals guilty of treason against humanity for having betrayed right (*droit*) and the language of right. This involved recognizing—in a procedure of discourse analysis that was no longer structural but configurational—discursive events that irrupt in the sayable and the audible. Here again, the analysis of the details and the force relations between different sites of discursive enunciation does not,

---

9 Foreigner, stranger. —Translator.

in my view, seem so distant from what Sartre had proposed in his analysis of May–June 1789.

What was playing out, for me, having studied revolutionary mentalities and discussed the concept of ideology with Michelle Vovelle, was the testing of discourse's entry into the field of Revolutionary history while a battle was unfolding between the economic and social history of the supposedly "real" Marxists, and the history of discursive practices, mentalities, representations among those who were not orthodox. Without my initially understanding it, what was playing out was to an extent the critique of orthodox Marxism by dissident Marxists connected with Althusser. In a certain way, it was another attempt at a possible alliance between Foucault and Althusser, such as was attempted in the 1970s, over fifteen years beforehand. Here again it was a question of being able to critique vulgar Marxism, but without ultimately renouncing the concepts of historical materialism, which were obscured in most of the human sciences according to Régine Robin[10].

If Foucault occupies an important place in her great work *Histoire et Linguistique* (1973) despite his anti-humanist positions with the understanding that "Marxism" can take a humanist form, it is to the extent that he makes it possible not to sink into a structural linguistics of discourse. The latter only functions in an intra-discursive way, without being articulated with an exterior to discourse. Régine Robin emphasizes the extent to which the question of the referent, which remains a question for historians, is not Foucault's question, and that he is only interested in the conditions of discourse, historically determined conditions of the sayable. According to her, however, this quest forces Foucault "to pose the problem of the emergence of non-discursive practices in discourse itself, the latter being conceived as a practice."[11] She then quotes passages from *The Archaeology of Knowledge*. Let us look at the first: "What made it [psychiatry] possible at the time it appeared, what brought about this great change in the economy of concepts, analyses, and demonstrations, was a whole set of relations between hospitalization, internment, the conditions and procedures of social exclusion, the rules of jurisprudence, the norms of industrial labour and bourgeois morality."[12] But if Foucault is praised for refusing the autonomization of discursive practices, Régine Robin just as soon laments the absence of a theory that connects these discursive and non-discursive practices. Their simple juxtaposition skirts the necessity for a theory, be it Marxist or not, of social formations and the processes at

---

10 Régine Robin, *Histoire et Linguistique*—translator's rendering.
11 Ibid., 85.
12 Foucault, *Archaeology of Knowledge*, 197.

their core that generate the play of history. For Régine Robin, this play of history is one of "instances and dominances," but even if this is the vocabulary of a situated Marxism, it must be recognized that with Foucault the withdrawal from a discursivity folded back on itself does not lead to the interrogation of the arrangements (*agencements*) operative between different types of practices in a in society that make its history. If the subject is not the operator of this linkage, then what is? What complex interrelationships produce change?

For Régine Robin, this connection is no more apparent in *The Order of Discourse* when Foucault suggests working on "serial regularities and inter-serial dislocations."[13] Whether it is to understand how the discourse on sexuality or poverty works, she tells us, it is about valuing specificities and discontinuities. Yet once again, if she praises this way of fighting against the anthropology of the subject and against hermeneutics, refusing to "imagine that the world turns towards us a legible face which we would have only to decipher,"[14] refusing historical continuity, too—closer in this respect to Canguilhem's history of the sciences than to the history of ideas—she ultimately laments the fact that discursive practices, as Foucault studies and analyzes them, are not, in the end, seriously inserted into other social practices. In the order of discourse, the history of discourse is made up of different discursive practices, but once more not the history of societies. Perhaps it is, despite everything, the history of knowledge as an autonomous domain.

However, after returning to the fundamentals of historical materialism, she arrives at the Marxist and then Althusserian conception of ideology, which allows her to reflect on the interconnection of discursive and social formations. "We propose to dwell on the concept of ideology, because it is through a theory of ideologies in their complex relationship with the economic base that a materialist theory of discourse can eventually see the light of day."[15] From here on, she breaks with Foucault precisely because of his distrust of this notion. "The notion of ideology is in my view difficult to utilise for three reasons. The first [. . .] is that it is in virtual opposition to something which would be the truth. Secondly, [. . .] it refers [. . .] to something like a subject. And thirdly, it is in a secondary position in relation to what must function as the base."[16] For Foucault, intervening with the concept of ideology meant setting the cat among the pigeons.

---

13 Robin, *Histoire et Linguistique*, 87.
14 Foucault, "The Order of Discourse," 67.
15 Robin, *Histoire et Linguistique*, 100. Translator's rendering.
16 Michel Foucault, "Vérité et pouvoir," *L'Arc* (1970): 20–21. Translator's rendering.

However, if Althusser's definition of ideology as practical ideology is cited as foundational, it borders others such as that of Gramsci. In this notion of practice, the subject is always absent as such, but the actant remains at the heart of the process. Following Althusser, practical ideology is "on the one hand complex formations of montages, concepts, representations and images, and configurations of comportment through attitude-gesture on the other, altogether functioning as practical norms that govern the attitude and the assumption of concrete positions by men in relation to the real objects of their social and individual existence and their history."[17] The reference here is to an unpublished work titled *A Course for Scientists*, cited by C. Glucksmann in *Nouvelle Critique* in April 1969. At this moment, *Nouvelle Critique* was the journal of the intellectuals of the Communist Party, in which these intellectuals never stopped debating over their practical tools because, according to the journal's subtitle, it was concerned above all with articulating intellectual practices and militant praxis. They called it a "Journal of Militant Marxism." If Foucault developed his thought in opposition to both Marxism and humanism, Althusserian Marxists were not set against Foucault. To the contrary, they read and discussed him, and from out of these discussions there arose seemingly improbable alliances, creating more links among some of them with Foucault than with the Sartre of the *Critique*. And yet such a definition of ideology seems closer to Sartre's practico-inert than Foucault's discourse. Gramsci and Poulantzas then enter the picture. For the former, ideologies are "historically necessary" and "form the terrain where men move and become conscious of their position,"[18] bringing consciousness back into the picture. For the latter, "ideology has the precise function of hiding the real contradictions and of reconstituting on an imaginary level a relatively coherent discourse which serves as the horizon of agents' experience."[19] We return finally to Althusser and his ideological state apparatuses, which give ideology a material rather than simply ideal existence.

Discursive practice thus stands on the ground of ideologies, themselves constitutive of social formations. But at the other end of the discursive chain, as close as possible to linguistics, "the traces of ideology in discourse are locatable at the level of explicit judgments, rationalizations, interiorized norms, values, modulations, assertions, complex phenomena through which the subject intervenes in his own discourse, etc.; mechanism of

---

17 Ibid. 102.
18 Antonio Gramsci, *Œuvres choisies*, Éditions sociales, 74, cited by Régine Robin, *Histoire et Linguistique*, 103.
19 Nicos Poulantzas, *Political Power and Social Classes*. 207, Verso, London, 1978.

selections, combinations of lexical units, pejorative and meliorative traits." Ultimately, Régine Robin speaks of an "asserted" that refers to "the individuality of the subject as a support," the famous "one is spoken by" which must replace "I speak" but ends up invoking something that "functions like subjectivity"[20] without actually speaking of a free subject. Of course, all of this is tied to a genuine quest, but the subject, albeit as decentered, makes a discreet return as something more than the subject of the enunciation. While the notions of instance efface the details and could be passed over with a fine-tooth comb by Sartre's critique of fetishized concepts, fine linguistic work brings these details back.

In the proposed analysis on social formations on the one hand, and ideologies and discursive formations on the other, in the eighteenth century, it is a question, through discourse analysis, of taking a position against the theory of an alliance of elites (the nobility and the bourgeoisie) proposed by François Furet in his article published in the prestigious history journal *Annales ESC* in March April 1971, titled "Revolutionary Catechism." Régine Robin replies that the places frequented by both the bourgeoisie and the aristocrats are "places where real contradictions are erased," which in reality resolve nothing because "equality always butts up against Ancien Régime privilege," except for "closed and recreational places like lodges, *salons*, and academies." However, Régine Robin tells us that "pseudo-egalitarian ideological subsystems do not prevent (on the contrary we would say that they contribute to) the development of aristocratic ideologies and ideological sub-systems, without possible compromise." Discourse analysis will allow her to demonstrate it. There is therefore a real historiographical gain which, when tethered to social formations, is at once very far from and quite close to Foucault, because what interests Régine Robin are the ways in which different discursive formations, with a common lexicon but very different modes of usage, function in relation to one another.

In the 1980s these questions were not resolved but displaced. Discourse analysis became more configurational, semantic, and already at risk of being reduced to a toolbox deprived of the theoretical stakes of its foundation. Nevertheless, it continues to carry out these debates and maintains its Marxist and scientific origins within it. This is the crossroads at which I chose to try to understand the "foreigner" in Revolutionary discourse, working on the question of the languages of the Revolution. My objective, then, is to grasp history in its folding and unfolding, its remanences,

---

20 Robin, *Histoire et Linguistique*, 104.

its inventions, its stops, and to this end I do not adhere to Foucault's conception of historical temporality. Without knowing it, I am on the side of historical consciousness. And in good conscience, I would add, since in the meantime Foucault had himself reworked an ontology which, while certainly not actually breaking with discursive formations—processes of subjectivation are connected to them—emphasizes "the patient form of our impatience for freedom" to which intellectual work contributes. He thus affirms, in essence, that the subject is an actor who freely carries out acts to access truth. With a "regime of truth" which makes it possible to isolate the free and reflected part of the subject in their own actions, without renouncing the anonymity of discourses, it seems to me that the gap between Foucault and Sartre had continued to shrink, without this ever being directly acknowledged. It seems to me that in my work, a syncretism took place, as through a precisely anonymous work linked to these epistemological discursive formations in which I had bathed and which led me to produce a work analyzing Revolutionary discourse, and then Revolutionary emotions in connection with our present. Certainly, it was a question of diagnosing the present, but also of identifying its remanences, the bubbles of another temporality that Nicole Loraux had, for his part, worked on in his invention of the notion of "controlled anachronism"[21] (*anachronism contrôlé*).

In this first part of my work, I sought to understand the enduring presence of the Foucault of *The Archaeology of Knowledge* within the text of his seminar "Society Must Be Defended," which at the time was being discussed by the Foucauldians at the ENS. The latter would be published the same year as my dissertation, 1997.

I think it pertinent to demonstrate how Foucault has since influenced certain constellations in my thought.

THE QUESTION OF "RACE WAR" DURING THE REVOLUTIONARY PERIOD

The "foreigner" was a political subject before being a social category, and it is thus a plurality of social forms that gave content to what indeed appeared to be a concept: officials who abuse their power, treacherous generals, formerly noble *émigrés*, the factious, the lazy, and then also foreigners in our

---

21 Nicole Loraux, "Éloge de l'anachronisme en histoire," *Le Genre humain*, art. Seuil, 1993, Paris.

current sense: the English, the Prussians, masked men such as Nacharsis Cloots. . . . However, a fixed phrase could contradict such an approach. It was found particularly in the statements of the decree of 26 Germinal Year II, in the phrase "nobles and foreigners."

If the nobles were figures of foreigners, this phrase was redundant, and if they were not, it had to be understood why, among the variety of figures of the stranger, the care was taken to isolate "nobles and foreigners."

Now, it was reading Foucault that ultimately shed light on this question for me. In effect, he asserted that the English revolts against the Norman conquerors, at the end of which the Magna Carta had been obtained, had given rise to specific measures for the expulsion of foreigners (less the Normans than Poitevins and Angevins, to be precise). Later, in the seventeenth century, the juridico-political discussion of the rights of the sovereign and the rights of people took place in England on the basis of this vocabulary given by the event of conquest, the relationship of domination of one race over another and the revolt, or the permanent threat of revolt of the vanquished against the victors.

A first interpretation could then be made. "Nobles and foreigners" were two types of conquerors, conquerors of yesterday, who had asserted that they were noble because they conquered, and potential conquerors of the moment who could conquer sovereignty by occupying the positions of the sovereign people. In effect, these nobles and strangers were both banned from strongholds and popular societies (*sociétés populaires*). Forbidden from places where the territory was defended, and from places where the law and its legitimacy were discussed, two places where conquest could subvert the sovereignty of the French people.

In fact, Foucault told us, the discourses of this struggle between races, or race war, were not the prerogative of aristocrats like Boulainvilliers in eighteenth-century France. The struggle between races inhabited the discourses of the absolutists just as much as the parliamentarians, inhabited the radical positions of the diggers or the levelers. Revolutionaries could thus reconnect with this struggle, which was in fact a binary struggle between victors and vanquished. The fixed phrase—"nobles and foreigners"—asserted that nobles and foreigners alike were to be regarded as the vanquished ready to revolt, and that this revolt should be anticipated.

However, was this still a struggle of races? The question was not without importance, because if the struggle between races in the archaeological and genealogical work of Foucault did indeed refer to a political struggle, it was still conceived between social groups defined as "folk" (*gens*), lineages, common blood, a common origin.

To go further, it was necessary to return to the Revolutionary archive and identify the processes of de-racialization at work in the discourse beginning in 1789.

In *What Is the Third Estate*—so since 1789—Abbé Sieyès had asserted that it was necessary to de-racialize social relations: "The Third Estate need not fear examining the past. It will betake itself to the year preceding the 'conquest'; and as it is nowadays too strong to be conquered it will certainly resist effectively. Why should it not repatriate to the Franconian forests all the families who wildly claim to descend from the race of the conquerors and to inherit their rights of conquest? If it were purged in this way, I think the nation might well recover from the thought that thence forward it would be reduced to the descendants of mere Gauls and Romans."[22]

This expulsion materialized at the moment of the meeting of the Estates General, where the statement of the same Sieyès, in the same text, was put to the test of the facts: "If we removed the privileged order, the nation would not be something less but something more."[23] Initially the nobles as such were excluded from the sovereign nation. They were excluded because they were defeated, and doubtless as nobles they were always ready to revolt, a political hypothesis confirmed by the emigration and treason of certain generals. By abandoning one's nobility, one could nevertheless become a citizen.

But this de-racialization, or this way of dismissing the war of races in favor of a simple war with its victors and vanquished, appeared not just in this text. It can be identified in arguments which themselves assert the necessity of renouncing the use of what Foucault calls "a sort of instrument, both discursive and political, that allowed both sides to formulate their own theses."[24] The question is no longer the racial origin but the political origin of the contractual foundation. In not participating in this foundation, the nobles redoubled their status as foreigners. But more fundamentally, when Saint-Just asks "What is a king next to a Frenchman?"[25] he not only opposes an aristocrat to the people, but power which issues from blood and power which issues from the political reconquest of sovereignty—a racialized greatness versus a political and historical greatness. To de-racialize greatness is to reinscribe it in the time of history as a shaping of the world, whereas blood fixed a tradition, outside of time.

---

22 Abbé Sieyès, *What Is the Third Estate?*, 120.
23 Ibid.
24 Michel Foucault, *Society Must Be Defended, Lectures at the Collège de France, 1975-1976*, ED. Mauro Bertani and Alessandro Fontana, Trans. David Macey, New York: Picador, 1997. 102.
25 Saint-Just, "Rapport sur la police Générale," presented to the Convention nationale on 26 Germinal, Year II (April 15, 1794), in *Œuvres complètes* (Paris: Gallimard, 2004), 752.

Thus, Saint-Just can still ask: "I would like to know who were, when Pompey lived, the ancestors from whom descend our current day kings? What claim did they have for their descendants to the government of Great Britain, Holland, Spain and the Empire? The passage of time has not caused us to forget reason for we know that these tyrants are nothing more than the grandchildren of labourers, sailors and soldiers who were men of far greater worth than they."[26]

The struggle of races is thus invalidated and treated as a political fiction in Sieyès as in Saint-Just. Relations of force are not fictional, there are indeed victors and vanquished, there is in fact struggle. It is the races which are fictional, which came to shatter the idea of a humanity that is not only one, but made up of individuals who are free and equal in rights and who cannot obtain their social and political status through birth, that is, through blood, through the body. It is thus a question of desacralizing the names of power—hereditary kings must be done with—and desacralizing the names of peoples. If territories have historical names, those that inhabit these territories also have historical names, and this history is not shaped by origin but by the relationship constituted by the same link to the laws of the country. "Where there are no laws, there is no homeland (*patrie*),"[27] declares Saint-Just. It is thus neither fathers nor mothers who make a homeland, but laws that we devise collectively when we have become a sovereign people. This sovereign people can develop procedures for including foreigners, which would not be experienced as procedures of conquest. The people includes those who are not of the same blood but recognize the rules of their political contract, its laws. When the title of "French citizen" is given to foreigners in 1792, this question of blood returns in the mode of metaphor as Lamourette speaks of "philosophical consanguity"[28] with the great men of the Enlightenment. There are peoples, however, they are not races but political institutions. There are positions of power, but they are not granted by heredity. Thus, there are indeed struggles to obtain power or territories or to recover them when they have been usurped, but these are not racial struggles—yes, there are wars, those of freedom against tyranny, political battles, yes.

Therefore, the study of the revolutionary period, more or less neglected by Foucault, can be illuminated by the long history of the discourse of racial struggle. The French Revolution operates in the manner

---

26 Saint-Just, Louis-Antoine, "Report on the General Police/Rapport sur la police generale (1794)," *Theoria: A Journal of Social and Political Theory* (2014): 76.

27 Saint-Just, *Esprit de la Révolution et de la Constitution, 1791*, in *Œuvres complètes*, 456.

28 Lamourette, *Archives parlementaires*, t. 48, 689. Translator's rendering.

of an "interruption" as Walter Benjamin understood it, a more subjective cessation in the manner of Sylvain Lazarus.[29] But if the period of the French Revolution renounces the racialization of politics, race forges another path. When it reappeared in the nineteenth century, it became an object of scientific knowledge. It is a question of understanding, with Foucault, how this knowledge comes to challenge the Revolutionary de-racialization of the nation, or more precisely the name "French," and creates a new discursive formation which one can hypothesize is operating in a singular way today.

In fact, another history begins. Another encoding. Another era.

As for ours, perhaps it is time, on the theoretical plane, to identify uses of history that require neither renouncing the Sartrean conception of history, which posits, despite everything, irrupting, insurgent actors, nor the Foucauldian conception of history, which allows us to better distinguish that which, in the present, is precisely pure present, for better but also for worse.

---

29 Sylvain Lazarus, *Anthropologie du nom* (Paris: Seuil, 1996). According to him, the revolutionary cessation takes place in interiority; it is a subjectivity which is interrupted, which is exhausted.

11

ON THE "IRANIAN REVOLUTION"

Retrieving the Missed Object, with Foucault and Despite Foucault

Perhaps we can now look back at the example of the Iranian Revolution to understand up to what point Michel Foucault was attentive to the passage between the French Revolution and this "Iranian Revolution," despite his obstinate refusal to examine the former.

Faced with the Iranian insurrection of 1978, Foucault, in his reports for the *Corriere della Sera*,[1] provided, in my view, a reflection on the possible uses of the word "revolution" to designate what was unfolding before his eyes. From the French Revolution to the Arab Revolutions, the reflection he weaves remains effective for understanding these moments of popular enthusiasm where it seems that a form of political spirituality, irreducible to the institutions they result in, seems to resurface. He nevertheless directs us toward a difficulty: the concept of "revolution" essentially includes insurrectional moments that create the emancipatory dynamic, and moments that congeal into political regimes that can effectuate a counterrevolution. The Islamic Republic for its part will crush popular aspirations for emancipation to the point of their disappearance. By analyzing the insurrectionary phase of the Iranian Revolution, that of a Shiism proper allied with Marxists and political liberals—the phase which is not yet institutionalized around the notion of an Islamic Republic—Foucault was perhaps unwittingly, without intending to be, a great thinker of revolutionary phenomena, with the precision of intellectual reporting.

---

1 It was at the behest of the Italian daily *Corriere della sera* that Michel Foucault visited Iran twice. The first time from September 16 to 24, 1978. The second from November 9 to 15, 1978. During these two stays, Foucault commented in a journalistic context on the fall of the Shah but above all on what seemed to him to be central: the event of a popular revolt.

We will thus have to return to what may remain an enigma: how, on the one hand, can one defend insurrectionary popular aspirations and political spiritualism and, on the other, reaffirm the refusal of the history of the French Revolution in the manner of François Furet? We must take up the case without resolving it too quickly. The evidence of political alliances for a new "second left," which continues to render any actualization of Marxist thought unavailable, seems insufficient to me. Rather, we must examine the functioning of a discursive formation, which owes a lot, in my view, to the debate of the 1960s and 1970s on ways doing history and the history of the French Revolution.

FOUCAULT INTERROGATES ENTHUSIASM: RETURNING TO THE CONTIGUITIES OF THE IRANIAN AND FRENCH REVOLUTIONS

In his analysis of insurrectionary Iran, Michel Foucault invokes the notion of "political spirtuality."[2] He refers to "a movement traversed by the breath of a religion that speaks less of the beyond than the transfiguration of this world."[3] In the France of 1978, the link between spirituality and politics, which had differentially inhabited all the revolutions of the seventeenth and eighteenth centuries in Great Britain, the United States, and France, appears to constitute an object of memory loss to which Foucault does not seem to have been an exception. Foucault knows this. When he makes his statement and accentuates the link between spirituality and politics, he says: "I can already hear French people who are laughing, but I know they are wrong."[4] "Political spiritualism" appears either to be an oxymoron or to fall back on the theologico-political, which Foucault rightly refuses. Yet Foucault proceeds as if the French Revolution did not also bear witness to a great crisis of Christianity. Between Jansenism, the Conciliar spirit, and the clash of two clergies—one which refused the Revolution and another which wanted it—the crisis was very real. In fact, Catholic spirituality played a foundational role in initiating the Revolution. On the theoretical plane, think of Abbé Sieyès or of Gregoire and their pamphlets. But also on the level of practice, think of the priests who were the first to decide to

---

2 On the notion of political spirituality in Foucault, see Julien Cavagnis, "Michel Foucault et le soulèvement iranien de 1978, retour sur la notion de spiritualité politique," in *Foucault une politique de la vérité. Cahiers philosophiques*, no. 130 (2012).
3 Michel Foucault, *Dits et Écrits, 1976–1979* (Paris: Gallimard, 1994), 716.
4 Ibid., 694.

join the Third Estate so that the Estates General could become the National Constituent Assembly during those days of May–June 1789 analyzed by Sartre.

Back to our initial investigation. Foucault, in observing the Iranian Revolution, shifts from the "system" to "the insurrectionary event itself." He senses that there is a strong temptation, at least among those around him, to draw the Iranian and French Revolutions into contiguity. But, he says, it would not be the French Revolution of Marxist historiography. He does not know this historiography well; in 1976, Michel Vovelle had published *Religion and Revolution: De-Christianization in Year II*.[5] Foucault turns his back on what he does not understand and adopts a blindly credited historiography which he likewise misunderstands but which has the wind in its sails. He is simply and obstinately conformist to anti-Marxism. But how can we follow him? Let us be clear that it appears *prima facie* as impossible.

To grasp this contiguity would require, in my view, a practice of observation that is more sympathetic to the object "Revolution" as a popular and insurrectional moment than François Furet was capable of. We are therefore going to try to demonstrate this contiguity, but also the gap between the French Revolution and the Iranian Revolution on several points. But we will do so by starting with another current that is critical of vulgar Marxist historiography, the one that we have attempted to clear alongside erstwhile Althusserians,[6] political theories of utopia,[7] Nicole Loraux's[8] "controlled anachronism," and political anthropology[9]—among other sources of inspiration—to enable a conception of history that puts the emotions at the heart of the political process.

With the Iranian Revolution and then the Iranian counterrevolution in 1978, Foucault encounters insurrection and enthusiasm while he continues to reject the notion of revolution.

> The Iranian movement did not experience the "law" of revolutions that would, some say, make the tyranny that already secretly inhabited them reappear underneath the blind enthusiasm of the masses. What constituted the most internal and the most intensely lived part of the uprising touched, in an unmediated fashion, on an already overcrowded political chessboard, but such contact is not identity. The spirituality

---

5 Michel Vovelle, *Religion et Révolution: la déchristianisation de l'an II* (Paris: Hachette, 1976).
6 I am as indebted to the Althusserians of discourse analysis as I am to the thought of Jacques Rancière, who broke with Althusser, in my way of thinking about history.
7 In particular the work of Miguel Abensour and his anti-statist conception of the Revolution.
8 Nicole Loraux, "Éloge de l'anachronisme en histoire," *Le Genre humain*, art. Seuil, 1993, Paris.
9 Particularly as developed by Marc Abélès and Henri Pierre Jeudy.

of those who were going to their deaths has no similarity whatsoever with the bloody government of a fundamentalist clergy. The Iranian clerics want to authenticate their regime through the significations that the uprising had. It is no different to discredit the fact of the uprising on the grounds that there is today a government of mullahs. [. . .] Hence, precisely, the necessity of underscoring what is not reducible in such a movement.[10]

I would add non-manipulable to "non-reducible," hence in enthusiasm.

In my view, this notion of enthusiasm makes it possible to pass between different revolutions and their preoccupations.

In Great Britain during the English revolutions, enthusiasm was synonymous with fanaticism, and this obliged philosophers to think about it. This was the case for Locke and his student Shaftsbury. The latter, in reflecting on the role of enthusiasm in the English revolutions, makes religion the dangerous principle of identification. However, unlike his detractors at the time, and John Locke in particular, he does not radically oppose enthusiasm. From his point of view, this emotion is a part of human nature and constitutes "good visionary spirit." Enthusiasm is "when the mind is taken up in vision and fixes its view either on any real object or mere spectre of divinity, when it sees, or thinks it sees, anything prodigious and more than human, its horror, delight, confusion, fear, admiration or whatever passion belongs to it or is uppermost on this occasion, will have something vast, 'immane' and (as painters say) beyond life."[11]

Enthusiasm, then, is "the feeling of recognizing a divine principle, but far from consisting of subjective feeling or an intimate conviction of divine inspiration, it is the feeling we experience when we are able to recognize an order and a harmony in the universe that testify to the existence of a divine principle in the world."[12]

If enthusiasm produces fury, the excess comes from the violence of the feeling of sociability and not from hostility between people. Shaftesbury's task is to understand how religion arouses enthusiasm, to consider its ambivalence, and to assert that, like all human ambivalence, it is subject to adjustment. It is about not depriving oneself of the good enthusiasm simply because it can become fanaticism.

---

10 Michel Foucault, "Is It Useless to Revolt?," in Janet Afary and Kevin B. Anderson, *Foucault and the Iranian Revolution: Gender and the Seductions of Islamism*, Chicago: UChicago Press, 2005. 265–66.

11 Lord Shaftsbury, *Characteristics of Men, Manners, Opinions, Times*, ed. Lawrence Klein (Cambridge, UK: Cambridge, 2000), 27.

12 Ibid.

One could argue that Foucault, by emphasizing the shared sensorium (*sensible partagé*) and mentality of the Shiites, sought to describe a good enthusiasm to explain the effectiveness of enthusiastic contagion in an insurrectionary situation. He asserted the following: "These men of religion are like so many photographic plates on which the anger and the aspirations of the community are marked. If they wanted to go against the current, they would lose this power, which essentially resides in the interplay of speaking and listening. Let us not embellish things. The Shi'ite clergy is not a revolutionary force."[13]

Thus, for Foucault, the clergy does not merge with the popular enthusiasm, but allows it to find a place, a form which, he says, can disintegrate if it does not respond to the aspirations that are being activated by anger. In fact, what the clergy provide is its capacity to function as a container. In the vocabulary of Sartre, the Shiite clergy thus "contains" Iranian society since in effect "a society is first of all the place which contains it."[14] This search for a "container" also existed during the French Revolution, in a sacredness which is no longer just linked to the Hall of the Estates, is not linked to the clergy, to a revealed religion, but to a civic sacralization of new political roles. Let us take an example.

When the so-called patriot ministers enter the ministry, a celebration is organized in Paris in the form of a banquet that culminates in the baptism of a small girl who embodies the republic to come—a Marianne *avant la letter*. The mayor of Paris, "Pétion, was received like the good father at the banquet. A victor of the Bastille, indulging in his enthusiasm, he swore in the name of his comrades, *loyalty* to the beloved mayor."[15]

This loyalty is addressed to the one who had defended the idea of putting the fugitive king on trial in 1791, to he who had lost in the elections to the person responsible for the shots fired at the Champ-de-Mars, namely Lafayette. His presence is at once a celebration of the day and an evocation of that other bereaved picnic of July 17, 1791, the incarnation of republican expectation.

When Pétion creates enthusiasm at the banquet of March 1792, he refuses to incarnate the expectation, and gives a lesson in political theory. "Citizens," cried Pétion, "it is not to a man that you should swear loyalty, it is to a nation, to a constitution."[16] The enthusiasm that is conjured, linked to both the worship of the dead at the Champ-de-Mars and the worship of

---

13 Michel Foucault, "Tehran: Faith against the Shah," *Foucault and the Iranian Revolution*, 202.
14 "Manuscrit *Mai-juin 1789*," *Études sartriennes*, no. 12 (2008), 85.
15 Le Moniteur universel, March 25, 1792.
16 Ibid.

life, should not be embodied by, fixed in, or identified with one body, one leader. During the French Revolution, this temptation to identify was strong, but it is experienced for a long time—from 1789 to 1794—as dangerous, which manifests in a complex desire for, but rejection of, such embodiment.

Similar events in 1791 and 1978 can again be compared. In both cases, the people's soldiers were made to fire at people—at the Champ-de-Mars on July 17, 1791 and during demonstrations against the Shah in 1978.

> The government, in an attempt to maintain order, is being forced to call on soldiers who lack both training and the willingness to follow orders. And these troops have the opportunity to discover that they are not dealing with international communism, but rather with the street, with the bazaar merchants, with workers, with the unemployed, men like their brothers, as they themselves would be if they were not soldiers: "We can make them shoot once, but not twice; in Tabriz eight months ago, 18 it was necessary to change the entire garrison; and even though we brought regiments to Tehran from remote corners of the provinces, it will still be necessary to change them rapidly." It was confirmed to me that on Black Friday at least one officer had been killed by his soldiers when he gave the order to shoot at the crowd, and also that some of the soldiers had committed suicide the next day.[17]

In July 1791, members of the National Guard also attacked their leaders, and some likewise committed suicide after having shot at their brothers.

Further on, Foucault adds: "In the political excitement, the dead were not forgotten, but given the veneration to which they were entitled."[18] I believe the same could be said of several political celebrations in March and April 1792. These celebrations were held both to avenge the dead of the Champ-de-Mars and to rediscover the passion for life. This includes the banquet we just referenced, but also the celebration of freedom on April 15, 1792.[19]

But whereas Pétion claims that one should not identify this religion and this aspiration with one body, the Iranians make revolution a struggle for the incarnation of sovereignty: expel the Shah, venerate Khomeini. It fails to heed the lesson in the control of identifications that can give the courage to fight and believe but can also turn the revolution into a counter-revolution.

---

17 Foucault, "Tehran: Faith against the Shah," 193.
18 Ibid. 201.
19 On these two celebrations, see my book *La Longue Patience du peuple, 1792, naissance de la République* (Paris: Payot, 2008).

for those who tried to understand what was going on in the heads of these men and women when they risked their lives, one thing was striking. They inscribed, on the borders of heaven and earth, in a dream-history that was as religious as it was political, all their hunger, their humiliation, their hatred of the regime and their will to bring it down. [. . .] As a result, the imaginary content of the revolt did not dissipate in the broad daylight of the revolution. It was immediately transposed onto a political scene that seemed totally willing to receive it but was in fact of an entirely different nature.[20]

There had been no lesson on erroneous identifications, on the necessary refusal of embodiments of the ideal.

Yet in the Quran, as in the French Revolution, the community can resist oppression. "It is justice that made law and not law that manufactured justice." It is necessary "to defend the community of believers against the evil power."[21] French revolutionaries, for their part, invoked a right of resistance to oppression in the Declaration of the Rights of Man and the Citizen, which borrows heavily from the first synods, where believers won against corrupted prelates.

In this way, religion "transforms thousands of forms of discontent, hatred, misery, and despairs into a *force*. It transforms them into a force because it is a form of expression, a mode of social relations, a supple and widely accepted elemental organization, a way of being together, a way of speaking and listening, something that allows one to be listened to by others, and to yearn for something with them at the same time as they yearn for it."[22] Foucault concludes: "This force refused to be embodied in an incarnation of power."

Nevertheless, it is this very embodiment in an incarnation of power that quickly ensues, namely that of Khomeini, who defines the government as Islamic, which is hardly reassuring for Foucault. "'These are basic formulas for democracy, whether bourgeois or revolutionary,' I said. 'Since the eighteenth century now, we have not ceased to repeat them, and you know where they have led.' But I immediately received the following reply: 'The Quran had enunciated them way before your philosophers, and if the Christian and industrialized West lost their meaning, Islam will know how to preserve their value and their efficacy.'"[23]

---

20 Foucault, "Is It Useless to Revolt?," 265.
21 Ibid., 201–2.
22 Ibid., 202–3.
23 Ibid. 206.

In my view, the whole question comes down to whether it is these formulas, or rather their perversion, which produce subjugation through enthusiasm for a venerated body, rather than enthusiasm for arguments over justice and right.

The figure of a Kohmeini and its uses in 1978 creates a gap between the experiences of the French and Iranian Revolutions. Khomeini is an incarnation in the full sense of the word, and no longer just a perceivable fragile plaque.

To this end, we can see that another way of doing the history of the French Revolution could have shed light on both the actors and commentators of the Iranian Revolution. This other way owes nothing to François Furet, despite his being the only historian whom Foucault credits in his intellectual report. We must attempt to elucidate why.

FRANÇOIS FURET AND MICHEL FOUCAULT: THE SAME ORDER OF DISCOURSE?

Deciphering François Furet's historiographical position in the political implications of his *Interpreting the French Revolution* can be done in different ways. One of the major accomplishments of the work produced by discourse analysis—whether Foucauldian or linguistic and textual—is to have shown how texts are generated, producing not only divergences but also common systems of references, inter-texts. In her 1974 book *The Revolution of Poetic Language*,[24] Julia Kristeva defined intertextuality as "the passage from one system of signs to another" in order to describe the process of the production of meaning in the circulations which exist between one text and another through citations, borrowings, or evocations.

Given that I wanted to show that Foucault's statements very precisely evoked those of Lévi-Strauss, particularly on classes of time and the analytical science capable of sweeping away the humanist dialectic and its myths, here I would like simply to work on François Furet's inter-text with regard to the debate I have delineated, beginning with Sartre's analysis of the revolutionary moment in the *Critique of Dialectical Reason* up to Foucault via Lévi-Strauss. It is a question of measuring François Furet's originality, a rare historian of the French Revolution because of his theoretical and historiographical engagement with the Althusserian historians discussed above. At the time of the bicentenary, the possibility of dialogue

---

24 Julia Kristeva, *La Révolution du langage poétique* (Paris: Seuil, 1974). Translator's rendering

and reciprocal recognition between Jacques Guilhaumou—longtime communist and Althusserian historian of the revolutionary period—and the current referred to as "critical history," tied to François Furet, became clearer. As Althusser had upended the theoretical taboos which reigned in the Communist Party of France, thus breathing new life into the identity of communist intellectuals, so François Furet had opened alternative historiographical perspectives by questioning this communist Tradition—rebaptized as "Jacobin"—of the French Revolution. Yet this historiographical alternative could be multiplied by going beyond a simple logic of social determinations and by leaving this famous "Tradition," while sharing theoretical and methodological postulates with political adversaries. It is these postulates that I would like to emphasize by locating this inter-text and showing how, in fact, they participated, against historians considered "militant," in an operation of depoliticization, which is in my view only apparent in the historiography of the French Revolution, which would lead to a disgust for the French Revolution, a disgust actually expressed by Foucault in 1978.

Like Lévi-Strauss, François Furet maintains that the myth of the French Revolution tends to replace history as the process of its recognition. Like Foucault, he decries the "contamination of the past by the present," another way of saying that any contiguity of past and present is harmful to historical knowledge as such. What he directly calls into question is in fact a teleological conception of the Revolution as a story of origins, whether it be that freedom or that of the bourgeoisie in the new version of this Tradition, which is perhaps the other name given to what both call the revolutionary *myth*. Thus "by becoming the positive or negative prefiguration of an authentically communist revolution [. . .] the Revolution has simply renewed its *mythology* at the expense of its impoverishment."[25] The question of the revolutionary myth is further linked to the impossibility of looking at it as such and analyzing it as a scholar the way Foucault analyzes a given discursive formation. As with Foucault in the June 1966 interview, it is as an ethnology that this analysis is qualified as impossible. "There is no possible ethnology in such a familiar landscape. The event remains so fundamental, so tyrannical in contemporary political consciousness that any intellectual distance from it is immediately equated to hostility—as if the relationship of identification were inevitable, whether it be of filiation of rejection."[26]

---

25 François Furet, *Penser la Révolution française* (Paris: Gallimard, 1978), 22. Translator's rendering.
26 Ibid., 26. Translator's rendering.

Chapter 11

In this desire for an ethnology of myth which butts up against the political consciousness that it has generated, Furet is thus the fourth among our thinkers after Sartre, Lévi-Strauss, and Foucault, to imaginarily play the ethnologist so as to cleanse the Tradition, the vulgate, the routines. In this undertaking of impossible ethnology, François Furet belongs indeed to this movement of thought. One recognizes both the discourse of Lévi-Strauss and that of Foucault, who took up Lévi-Strauss and his formulations.

Furet had always been aware of these debates, and from 1967 had, in an article titled "French Intellectuals and Structuralism,"[27] diagnosed the craze for structuralism as the sign of the end of ideologies, meaning the end of Marxism and of Sartre in French intellectual life. He thus asserted that "structural ethnology drew part of its influence from what it offered as an anti-history."[28] He makes of Lévi-Strauss "the inverted image of a the Sartrean man for whom the embeddedness in history and the emergence of revolutionary praxis impose the famous 'commitment.'"[29] He thus effectively links Lévi-Strauss and Foucault. "It is permissible to draw Lévi-Strauss and the work of Barthes and Foucault closer together. The areas of research are very different, but the methodological inspiration is shared: the attempt to take an ethnological look at contemporary cultures and societies."[30]

The French Revolution, as an object of history, has become a myth in this discursive formation. It could have, or should have been the object of an ethnographic analysis which would make it possible to identify the identity of a tribe, in this case that of the French. To do an ethnography of the French Revolution is to understand the French identity. For that matter, François Furet claims that "all histories of the French Revolution, which clash with and tear each other apart for two hundred years [. . .] in reality share a common terrain: they are histories of identity. There is thus no possibility, for a Frenchman in the second half of the 20th century, of an outsider's perspective on the French Revolution."[31] We can understand, then, why the object "French Revolution" is perceived by both Foucault and Furet as an eminently national object, it being understood that in France the "national" is said under cover of the "universal" in currents as different as the Catholics and the secular republicans. The universal is

---

27 François Furet, "Les intellectuels français et le structuralisme," *Preuves* 192, (February 1967): 3–12.
28 Ibid., 5. Translator's rendering.
29 Ibid., 7–8. Translator's rendering.
30 Ibid., 9. Translator's rendering.
31 Furet, *Penser la Révolution française*, 26.

colored differently, but it is always French, just like all the contending histories of the French Revolution.

For Furet and Foucault alike, the French Revolution—not as a historical fact but as a narrativized fact—is not just a myth, but a national-identitarian myth. Both the political myth as George Lefebvre understood it through Sorel, and the political myth which makes it possible to subjectivate one's place in the polity as Lévi-Strauss had analyzed it, disappear in the name of this national-identitarian myth. The operation of disqualification is complete. Sartre and his desire for a scientific dialectic are henceforth completely unavailable.

In Foucault's case, as we have seen, the step is quickly taken to say that the Revolution as a historical fact is adequate to its myth: national, bourgeois, and parliamentary. He, who opposes communist Marxists, repeats their commonplace. Here, Foucault undoubtedly has much to learn from Foucault, but this is another affair.

This treatment of the history of the French Revolution as a myth in François Furet's work is supported by his strong criticism of commemorative history, which cannot really distinguish itself from myth insofar as it honors ancestors as heroes. It is here that Sartre is present without being named. "It has long been fashionable, among the men of my generation under the twin influence of existentialism and Marxism, to emphasize the rootedness of the historian in his own time, his choices, or his determinations. If the rehashing of these obvious points was useful against the positivist illusion of objectivity, it risks indefinitely fueling professions of faith and crepuscular polemics."[32] If the twisting of Sartre's words is strong—Sartre never spoke of "rootedness" but of the need to draw insights for a reflective praxis in the present which is conscious of history in the present, praxis of a present situation to be analyzed—at least Furet recognizes the link between the position of the committed subject and the possibility of not believing that history can simply be positivistically objectivized.

But the recusal of committed history takes another turn, because on it asserts the gratuitousness of a new desire to know: "the gratuitous activity of knowing the past." This gratuitous activity, for François Furet starting in 1967, marks what he calls the end of ideologies and what I call depoliticization.

This gratuitous activity is of course opposed to politically invested activity, and hence if we follow the reasoning, is opposed to the ritual retribution inflicted on myth by historians of the revolutionary period,

---

32 Ibid., 24.

regardless of the scholarly advances produced in this area. Furet has very harsh words, citing intellectual "laziness" and referring to Georges Lefebvre at once as the greatest university historian of the French Revolution in the twentieth century, the most erudite, and yet incapable of proposing a new "synthetic vision of the immense event to which he dedicated his life."[33] Synthesis and myth go together; they are ultimately quasi-synonymous. Displacing the synthetic vision should have led to slaying the mythical dragon and proposing another vision. But according to Furet, erudition cannot kill the dragon because it is of a different nature than scientific knowledge. The question of detail as the possibility of returning, supported by new and pertinent tools to produce new theoretical proposals, a question dear to Sartre in the *Critique of Dialectical Reason*, is swept aside here.

First implicitly and then explicitly, François Furet returns to Lévi-Strauss while imitating (*pasticher*) the language of the revolution itself, which is admittedly quite funny. The first chain of phrases: "There will come a day when the political beliefs, which for two centuries have nourished the debates of our societies, will appear as surprising to men as the inexhaustible variety and endless violence of the religious conflicts in Europe between the 15th and 17th centuries."[34] Recall Saint-Just and company: "We will one day be astonished that in the 18th century we were less advanced than the time of Caesar—there the tyrant was massacred in the middle of the Senate, with no formalities except twenty-three stabs in the back and with no other law than the liberty of Rome."[35] Grégoire: "Posterity will be astonished that we were able to question whether a nation can judge its chief civil servant."[36] The man named Ichon, again during the king's trial: "We are astonished, and doubtless after us, posterity will be astonished that the French Republic saw from its dawn in the sanctuary of philosophy and laws disguised as a paradox."[37] It must be said that this art of projecting a future judgment is very revolutionary.[38] But where Lévi-Strauss sees a political event, Furet sees a religious war. If there is myth, for Furet, it is a fact of religion and an irrationality specific to religions. The historiographical debate is a debate between crepuscular believers who wage wars

---

33 Ibid.,
34 Ibid., 27.
35 Saint-Just, discours pour le procès du roi, November 13, 1792.
36 Grégoire, Convention, November 19, 1792.
37 Société des amis de la Liberté et de l'égalité, November 28, 1792.
38 On this point, see my article "L'inquiétude de la transmission," in *Histoire d'un trésor perdu, transmettre la Révolution* (Paris: Les Prairies ordinaires, 2013). The preceding citations are extracted from this work.

of religion instead of doing scholarly work, work that is at a distance, in Lévi-Strauss's terms.

Let us continue: "It is probably the modern political field itself, as constituted by the French Revolution, which will appear as an explanatory system and psychological investment of another age. But for this 'cooling' of the object 'French Revolution', to speak in Lévi-Straussian terms, it is not sufficient to wait for time to pass. We can define its conditions, and even identify its first elements, in our present."[39]

Thus, the cold or cooling, not to say, dead object, an object that has been deactivated, is indeed conceptualized via Lévi-Strauss, and hence refers to a cold history which aims to perpetuate the structure of societies indefinitely, to make them persevere in their being. Yet it is not this perseverance which, according to Furet, is arriving at a point exhaustion, but rather the "hot" political use of the history of the French Revolution, the belief that it is still possible to draw from it for the purposes of analysis of the contradictions that inhabit the democratic conflicts of the present. This is why he departs from Lévi-Strauss, who asserted that this cooling would come with the passing of time, and claims, through a Foucauldian "diagnosis the present," that it is already here. He assures us that this hot, mythical history is already dead. The French Revolution is over, and this indeed means that it no longer produces "hot" political effects. But like the characters of the twilight westerns, it has become a witness to an already outdated world. The political effects of the history of the French Revolution as a cold history lay in its enabling of Western societies to simply reproduce themselves without conflict.

We can therefore understand that this particular Revolution, framed in this way, might not interest Foucault. If it is a question of being interested in the Revolution in the manner of Furet, it is not because Furet illuminates the phenomenon of "insurrection" but because he analyzes an object of the past in a way that separates it from the present. As a result, Foucault can only grasp the discontinuities between the French Revolution and the Iranian Revolution, the dead revolution and the living revolution, and with the Iranian Revolution, can only diagnose a pure present.[40]

Furet then sketches two directions which in fact intersect and perhaps become three. The first concerns historical knowledge as such. Furet insists

---

39 Furet, *Penser la Révolution française*, 27. Translator's rendering

40 A pure present which in our opinion does not exist, just as there is a pure past. On this point Georges Didi-Huberman is particularly clarifying. Following Loraux and Rancière, he refuses to make history a pure science and he develops a theory and practice of anachronism. Georges Didi Huberman, *Devant le temps. Histoire de l'art et anachronisme des images* (Paris: Minuit, 2000).

again on the requirements of a "new history" which "ceases to be knowledge where the facts are supposed to speak for themselves, as long as they have been established according to the rules. It must state the problem it is trying to analyze, the data that it uses, the hypotheses on which it is working, and the conclusions it obtains."[41] The second concerns work on the French Revolution, which must emerge from its mythical historiography and align itself with these new standards of the profession, standards which effectively stem from the school of the *Annales* journal. "In effect, what this historiography of the French Revolution should announce is not its colors, but its concepts."[42] So, for Furet, the historiography of the French Revolution is all the more mythical as its concepts are those of a Marxist communism that has prevented it from inventing its own concepts, as it has done in the analysis of other historical fields. The third direction is what one could call a sort of paradoxical return to Marx, an anti-communist and anti-totalitarian Marx. If on the level of theory, this return might have ultimately been fairly close to Sartre's proposal to leave the vulgar Marxism behind, on the political level it leads, with a firm voluntarism, to another statement which, in our view, has deserved elucidation since it was introduced at the beginning of this work: "The French Revolution is the matrix of totalitarianisms."

"Today, the Gulag requires rethinking the Terror because of the identity of their project. The two revolutions remain linked. Half a century ago, they were systematically absolved, [. . .] today they stand accused of being consubstantial systems of meticulous constraint of bodies and of minds."[43] Thus, when Furet publishes *Interpreting the French Revolution* he paradoxically proposes adopting an approach to temporality that is close to Sartre's. History's present calls upon history's past. But how could one think that the revolutionary project of 1789, and even 1793, is identical with Stalinism? For those of my generation who committed to the study of Revolutionary texts and practices, there is a strong feeling that this is nonsense, that it is intellectual opacity, a misinterpretation focused on the figure of Robespierre-the-tyrant as an analogue of Hitler, Stalin, and Mao.

But if it is a question of understanding how such a statement could have been produced, we also seek to understand how it was received.

---

41 Furet, *Penser la Révolution française*, 30.
42 Ibid., 29.
43 Ibid.

12

"THE FRENCH REVOLUTION AS MATRIX OF TOTALITARIANISM"

The Enigma of a Bizarre Statement

ALIBI HISTORIOGRAPHY: A STATE OF POLITICAL AND IDEOLOGICAL BATTLE

When I began my studies on the French Revolution at the Sorbonne in 1985, the possibility of conceiving of the French Revolution as a "matrix of totalitarianism" was, for a number of young historians studying with Michel Vovelle, a bizarre intellectual enigma. We saw nothing but an ideological and political conflict disguised in preparations for the bicentenary, a banal historiographical struggle between the old and the new, the old Jacobin Marxists and Sorbonnards and the new critical historians of the EHESS. The latter claim to produce a knowledge of the French Revolution that is finally distanced from any civic or political perspective in the name of the true historical science. In close relation to the *Annales ESC* journal, they are interested in the revolutionary period while maintaining their privileged link with the Braudélienne long *durée*, and an invalidating version of short and mobile time.[1] The scansion of the object will lengthen more and more in this current, which some prefer to call "revisionist" rather than "critical." For those who are interested in history as the language of politics, there are two political camps that confront each other with two conceptions of historiography, certainly, but above all two different moral points of view on the revolutionary period.

The first camp continue to seek an understanding of the dynamics, the aporias, and the project of the Revolution in order to garner insights into the development of human societies as they were attempting to emancipate

---

1 On this point, see chapter 9.

themselves from feudal powers. The second, conversely, frame the event as a culmination of a juridico-political evolution which, according to scientific indicators, would have taken place even without a revolution. The revolution is thus framed as a "slip" (*dérapage*).

In the meantime, there are many of us who are spontaneously confident in the freedom and equality that is inaugurated during this foundational event. There is something incomprehensible about disqualifying the whole series of events, including the Declaration of the Rights of Man and the Citizen, the foundation, in our view, of past and future reciprocal freedom. Some, however, believe that 1793 submerged 1789. In Andrzej Wajda's film *Danton* (1983), the Declaration of the Rights of Man and the Citizen is learned like a catechism, under slaps, and said in a fragile voice by a scared little boy. It is a shock. The voice is lost in the dread of a contemporary soundtrack, as if the Declaration had been lost in the episode of the Terror. In the end, it had only been a false pretense camouflaged as a rectitude that would soon be called "Human Rightsism" (*droit de l'hommisme*), showing the horrors of all revolution, by definition violent and, even in this film, perverse in its ideals. Far from valorizing the event, the film commissioned for the bicentenary exploded it with arguments from the so-called critical movement centered around François Furet and Mona Ozouf. All of this appeared to me as an immense absurdity, given that I had committed to work on the revolutionary period as a counter-figure to the Vichy regime, and that, in my view, far from engendering totalitarianism, it had for the first time produced an emancipation based on this great text: the Declaration of the Rights of Man and Citizen.

The feeling that I had then was that the disgust for Stalinist totalitarianism, a theme so assiduously addressed by the great Polish director, had produced a retroactive effect on the imaginary of all revolution, which *as revolution* would be *a priori* suspected of totalitarianism.

It is, in fact, a very aggressive offensive not only against the French Revolution but also against the left-wing anti-totalitarian movement called "Socialism or Barbarism" (*Socialisme ou barbarie*), begun in 1948. The journal of the same name, founded by Cornélius Castoriadis and Claude Lefort, had presented autonomy and councilism as an anti-Stalinist and anti-bureaucratic horizon. In 1948, Socialism or Barbarism asserted an anti-totalitarian position that constitutes an authentic current which could be described as revolutionary–self-management. In it is a critique of Stalinism and various communisms, including Trotskyism. Freedom in a foundational conception of political being in the world is at the heart of a strongly democratic framework. At the end of the Second World War, this critique of totalitarianism was very present. But it was not an invention, either. The first anti-totalitarian critique, which accounts for the oppressive nature of both Bolshevism and Nazism, came from German left-critique in the faltering Weimer Republic.[2]

Nevertheless, the intellectual current closely tied to François Furet proceed as if this past did not exist, as if they are the first and only ones to produce a critique of Stalinism and totalitarianism. Killing two birds with one stone, they also effaced the critical force of the event of May 1968, which enabled a first experimentation with anti-totalitarian theses, as Jean-François Lyotard recalled in referring to the reaction of the members of Socialism or Barbarism at the time: "We found ourselves, each in his own way, more or less on the same level as the movement of '68, which appeared to us, in large part, as saying and doing what we had sketched in words and actions in miniature and as a premonition, and as inventing even more beautiful things that we had not thought of."[3]

But it remains the case that the anti-totalitarian position of that time did not make the French Revolution a "pre-totalitarian" period or a "matrix of totalitarianisms." We thus have a very serious reorientation of anti-totalitarian thought.

The work of Michael Scott Christofferson[4] claimed that the issue of totalitarianism as such, and the concern for others who lived under its yoke, was not François Furet's genuine concern but rather an alibi. As we have just mentioned, anti-totalitarianism did not wait for Solzhenitsyn and his *Gulag Archipelago*, which was published in France in 1974, to formulate a left anti-totalitarian position. Christofferson insists on this. The Solzhenitsyn effect is not the story of revelation but of an instrument. The anti-totalitarian constellation around Furet was not discovering totalitarianism, it only interested them belatedly.

This is how François Furet waged a battle that was indissociably historiographical, ideological, and political. According to Christofferson, Furet's ideological and political struggle in the media too precedence over the historiographical struggle. His aim, under the guise of the disqualification of the "revolutionary myth," was as much the disqualification of the unity of the left in 1972 as the elevation of what we will henceforth call the "second left." For Christofferson, "his argumentation remained neither at the level of historical science, nor even at the political level. He foregrounded his

---

2 See William David Jones, *The Lost Debate, German Socialist Intellectuals and Totalitarianism* (Urbana-Champagne: University of Illinois Press, 1999).
3 J.-F. Lyotard, *Dérive à partir de Marx et Freud* (Paris: Galilée, 1994), 16.
4 M. S. Christofferson, *Les Intellectuels contre la gauche* (Marseille: Agone, 2009).

memories as an ex-communist and praised the opening of the EHESS in relation to the university where Soboul held power. It was a total war"[5].

It is clear, however, that when François Furet makes the Jacobin "machine" the "matrix of totalitarianism," the statement finds a reception that extends beyond the range of the Furet constellation. When Reynald Secher, a student of Chaunu[6], titles his book on the Vendée *The Franco-French Genocide*, he appears to take the so-called critical school at its word. It is not only Stalinism which boomeranged from the French Revolution, according to this critique, but Nazism too. And it is then that the blurring of meaning becomes particularly intense around the figure of Robespierre, who is compared to Stalin, Mao, and Hitler.

Although Christofferson's argument is convincing with regard to the period he studies, it is insufficient. It reduces the historiographical stakes to issues of politics, ideology, and media institutions. Certainly, the problem exists on this level, and we know how the media can accelerate the effectiveness of a position in its quest for ideological hegemony. But this cannot be the only cause. We must therefore understand why the statement "the French Revolution is the matrix of totalitarianism," as absurd as it appears to be, was accepted and was receivable.

CONFUSION AND ANNEXATION: HANNAH ARENDT AND CLAUDE LEFORT

The two great thinkers of totalitarianism are Hannah Arendt and Claude Lefort, and even if they were regularly solicited and involved, with or without their consent, in this Furet constellation, they should not be confused with one another. Nevertheless, because of the confusion surrounding the singularity of their thought, their prestigious and important intellectual names were subjected to a kind of lateral annexation, playing a supporting role in this Furet constellation.

Totalitarianism, for Hannah Arendt, is a dehumanization:

> Men insofar as they are more than animal reaction and fulfillment of functions are entirely superfluous to totalitarian regimes. Totalitarianism strives not toward despotic rule over men, but toward a system in which

---

5 Michael Scott Christofferson, Jacques Guilhaumou, and Julien Louvrier, "Aux sources de la relecture de l'histoire de la Révolution française par François Furet," *Annales historiques de la Révolution française* 360 (2010): 227–38.

6 At the time of the bicentenary, Pierre Chaunu, although a non-specialist of the Revolutionary period, regularly intervened in the public space, in a counterrevolutionary vein.

men are superfluous. Total power can be achieved and safeguarded only in a world of conditioned reflexes, of marionettes without the slightest trace of spontaneity. Precisely because man's resources are so great, he can be fully dominated only when he becomes a specimen of the animal-species man.[7]

It is in this regard that it appears to be a fundamentally different regime from other forms of tyranny:

> Totalitarianism differs essentially from other forms of political oppression known to us such as despotism, tyranny and dictatorship. Wherever it rose to power, it developed entirely new political institutions and destroyed all social, legal and political traditions of the country. No matter what the specifically national tradition or the particular spiritual source of its ideology, totalitarian government always transformed classes into masses, supplanted the party system, not by one-party dictatorships, but by a mass movement, shifted the center of power from the army to the police, and established a foreign policy openly directed toward world domination.[8]

Admittedly, her criticism of human rights, and her ambivalences about the political interpretation of an event which, in her view, begins well but becomes disastrous, could lead to her being annexed into the Furet camp. But she never draws an equivalence between revolution as such and totalitarianism. Her critique is ultimately more banal, critiquing the power (*puissance*) of the revolutionary crowd and the apparent way that the indivisibility of sovereignty inherited from Jean Bodin prevented federative thought in France. In a general way, Hannah Arendt's book attests to a great misrecognition of the French Revolution. On the other hand, it does not take a strongly anti-revolutionary position, since it considers councilism to be a revolutionary form that allows for the freedom she defends. For her, this freedom is basically that of the ancients who lived their non-delegated political responsibilities every day, and not that of the "moderns" like Benjamin Constant, which François Furet defends as the good form of freedom. Finally, it should be remembered that from 1966 forward, Hannah Arendt had herself given up the concept of totalitarianism, not because she disavowed her analysis of it, but because she saw the dangers of too close an equivalence being drawn between Nazism and Stalinism.

---

7 Hannah Arendt, *Origins of Totalitarianism* (New York: Harcourt Brace, 1973), 457.
8 Ibid., 462.

Claude Lefort had gone, if not further, than elsewhere in his theoretical propositions on totalitarianism. For him, totalitarianism is in fact the other side of the democratic coin. Emerging from the history of Socialism or Barbarism, which he had left fairly early, in 1978 he wrote a book called *The Democratic Invention: The Limits of Totalitarian Domination*,[9] in which he demonstrates philosophically that totalitarianism is a reaction to democratic uncertainty. A process in which the division of the institution of the social, which precisely produces this uncertainty, is fantasmatically obliterated by the assertion of a unity without remainder, a one-people embodied in a site of power.

This book opens with an analysis of the Declaration of the Rights of Man and Citizen, the foundation of democracy and its principles. Lefort then shows that the specificity of this Declaration lies in asserting, for the first time in the history of humanity, in his view, an openness to indeterminacy, to the new, to the unknown, which henceforth gives meaning to the struggle against various forms of domination. At its very foundations, the Revolution had invented the anti-totalitarian tool par excellence, offering a point of support for the oppressed in their desire to regain their freedom. However, when he soberly analyzes the revolutionary Terror, noting aspects of the episode that might fall within the totalitarian schema, and sometimes posing projective questions like those raised by Françoise Brunel about the supposed strategic silence of Billaud Varenne, he immediately deconstructs it, in my view, by asserting: "Terror speaks." In effect, this amounts to saying that terror is anchored in complex democratic procedures. "The revolutionary Terror speaks. It implies its justification, a debate concerning its function, its ends, even its limits, and also implies its contestation—I mean among the men who took part."[10] Further on he adds: "Saint-Just perceived in a flash the contradiction of terror allied with freedom." He adds: "Generally speaking, those who share the responsibility for terrorist laws are for the most part inhabited by a contradiction." He then invokes not only the Montagnards, but also the Girondins and the Hébertists who all demanded and obtained laws of terror. Finally, he concludes: "Terror is revolutionary to the extent that it prohibits occupation of the place of power. In this sense, it has a democratic character." Thus, he does not reduce the terror to totalitarianism, but presents it as a

---

9 Claude Lefort, *L'Invention démocratique. Les limites de la domination totalitaire* (Paris: Fayard, 1981).

10 Claude Lefort, "La Terreur révolutionnaire," *Passé-Présent*, no. 2 (1983): 32. Text taken from Cl. Lefort, *Essais sur le politique* (Paris: Seuil, 1986). The citations which follow are drawn from this article.

democratic event. "Terror involves a mutual recognition of the terrorists as equal individuals before the law, the law of which the Terror is said to be the sword." Lefort finishes by ventriloquizing Saint-Just: "Our power, formidable as it is, is too hollow to be so terrible." In my view, Lefort ought to be reread and discussed today among historians, since like Hannah Arendt, he has a rather patchy understanding of events. His interpretation of the Cult of the Supreme Being as a new orthodoxy is in my opinion a gross misinterpretation.[11] But this is not what is at issue here. What should be retained is that for Claude Lefort, the Terror was not totalitarian because it remained democratic.

THE COUNTER-ARGUMENTS REMAIN INAUDIBLE: MICHEL FOUCAULT AND ÉTIENNE BALIBAR

Some, and there have been many, claimed that there were no counter-arguments made against François Furet. It seems important to us here to underscore that this is false. Responses were made on the political, ideological, and philosophical levels. They were weak on the strictly historiographical level because, it must be recognized, the "critical" current had almost always refused to debate with the historians at the Sorbonne, who chose not to directly respond but to simply pursue multiple other paths that they had opened. In any case, we must take stock of the fact that these responses were nevertheless infrequently relayed and were not immediate.

Five years after the publication of *Interpreting the French Revolution*, Michel Foucault, in his lecture on January 5, 1983, returns to Kant and his way of thinking the possibility of human progress. He then analyzes the answer that Kant can offer to the question "What is revolution?" in 1798, in his famous *Conflict of the Faculties*. Specifically, he focuses on the second essay, on the conflict between philosophy and law. This famous text deals with the possibility of progress and the necessity of thinking both the cause of its possible existence and above all its "evental" character (*son événementialité*). This is where the reference to the revolutionary period comes in for Kant as for Foucault. "It is not enough," writes Foucault, "to follow the teleological thread that makes progress possible; it is necessary to isolate,

---

11 The festival of the supreme being is far from being a theocracy; it is the invention of a conformist civil religion borrowed from the Shaftsbury model, which aims to avoid civil war while maintaining division (here religious) as constitutive of the social order. Floréal 18, the freedom of all religions is confirmed. Cf. Sophie Wahnich, "La fête de l'être suprême est ce seulement la faute à Rousseau?," in *Catalogue Rousseau et la Révolution française*, Bruno Bernardi (dir.), 138–56.

within history, an event which functions as a sign."¹² Yet for Kant, it is not the event of the French Revolution itself which signals progress, but the reaction of the public to it.

> The revolution of a gifted people which we have seen unfolding in our day may succeed or miscarry; it may be filled with misery and atrocities to the point that a sensible man, were he boldly to hope to execute it successfully the second time, would never resolve to make the experiment at such cost—this revolution, I say, nonetheless finds in the hearts of all spectators (who are not engaged in this game themselves) a wishful participation that borders closely on enthusiasm, the very expression of which is fraught with danger; this sympathy, therefore, can have no other cause than a moral predisposition in the human race.¹³

This moral disposition is what revolutionaries call the "feeling of humanity" (*sentiment d'humanité*). The experience of the Revolution, for Kant, is not the loss of the feeling of humanity but, to the contrary, it is the sign under the figure of enthusiasm. Now, this enthusiasm is, according to Kant, "the idea of the good accompanied by emotions," which are then called "sublime." This sublime is practical reason expressed in a feeling, a particularly heightened feeling: thinking the good and the universal appear inseparable from the desire for the good and the universal.

Kant thereby affirms a confidence in humankind. Foucault offers a lengthy citation of this text, and I will allow myself to do the same:

> Now I claim to be able to predict to the human race—even without prophetic insight—according to the aspects and omens of our day, the attainment of this goal. That is, I predict its progress toward the better which, from now on, turns out to be no longer completely retrogressive. For such a phenomenon in human history *is not to be forgotten*, because it has revealed a tendency and faculty in human nature for improvement such that no politician, affecting wisdom, might have conjured out of the course of things hitherto existing, and one which nature and freedom alone, united in the human race in conformity with inner principles of right, could have promised. But so far as time is concerned, it can promise this only indefinitely and as a contingent event. But even if the end viewed in connection with this event should not now be attained, even if the revolution or reform of a national constitution should finally miscarry, or, after some time had elapsed, everything

---

12 Michel Foucault, *Dits et Écrits*, t. IV, 683.
13 Immanuel Kant, *Conflict of the Faculties*, trans. Mary Gregor (New York: Abaris Books, 1979), 153.

"The French Revolution as Matrix of Totalitarianism"   185

should relapse into its former rut (as politicians now predict), that philosophical prophecy still would lose nothing of its force. For that event is too important, too much interwoven with the interest of humanity, and its influence too widely propagated in all areas of the world to not be recalled on any favorable occasion by the nations which would then be roused to a repetition of new efforts of this kind; because then, in an affair so important for humanity, the intended constitution, at a certain time, must finally attain that constancy which instruction by repeated experience suffices to establish in the minds of all men.[14]

In response to this passage, Foucault concludes in these terms: "I think this text is really extremely interesting, obviously not just within the system of Kantian thought, but for its presentation as a prediction, a prophetic text, about the meaning and value, not of the Revolution, which in any case always risks returning to the old ways, but of the Revolution as an event, as a sort of event whose content is unimportant, but whose existence in the past constitutes a permanent virtuality, the guarantee for future history of the non-forgetfulness and continuity of a movement towards progress."[15]

Also, faced with the discourse of the good and the bad Revolution proper to François Furet's disparaging of 1792, he asserts: "Here again the task of philosophy is not to determine what is the part of the Revolution which is worth preserving and valuing as a model. It is to know what to make of this will to revolution, of this 'enthusiasm' for the Revolution which is something other than the revolutionary enterprise itself."[16] As we saw with respect to the Iranian revolution and its political spiritualism, for Foucault this question of political emotions is fundamental, just as they are evidently fundamental for Kant.

Now, says Foucault, it is not the remains of the *Aufklärung* that must be retained; it is the very question of the event and its meaning (the question of the historicity of the thought of the universal) that must be kept present and held onto as something that must be thought. And Foucault proposes to do precisely that through an "ontology of the present," posing, not the question of an analytics of the truth, but the following question: "What is the current field of possible experiences?." He also calls this an "ontology of ourselves."

---

14 Ibid., 159.
15 Michel Foucault, *The Government of Self and Others*, trans. Graham Burchell, ed. Arnold Davidson (New York: Palgrave Macmillan, 2010), 19.
16 Michel Foucault, *Dits et Écrits*, t. IV, 687. Translator's rendering.

The Revolution is thus not a matrix or cause of this or that, but a virtuality which is always to be taken hold of again, reinterrogated by an "enthusiastic desire" in relation to our present.

A few years later, Étienne Balibar, a former student of Althusser, gave a lecture titled "The Proposition of Equaliberty," in which he tears apart the binary opposition between freedom and equality.[17] Here, it is once again the question of truth, of an analytics of truth, which is raised: "What interests me above all here is the truth of this proposition, which I will call the proposition of equaliberty, and on this basis the rupture it produces in the political field. But these are equally the reasons for its instability, the forms in which an incessant division has developed out of what had been produced as a unity of opposites."[18] Balibar analyzes the Declaration of the Rights of Man and Citizen of 1789, which is revolutionary in his view because it produces a double identification of man and citizen and freedom and equality. The rights of man are "exactly the same" as the rights of the citizen: "freedom, property, security, and resistance to oppression." These are the famous natural, inalienable rights of man. Along with article 1—"All men are born and remain free and equal in rights"—Balibar asserts that all the declared rights are political, that equality and freedom are two concepts which are indissociable and political. There is not political freedom on one side and social equality on the other. Hence the notion of equaliberty. For Balibar, "the (de facto) historical conditions of freedom are exactly the same as the (de facto) historical conditions of equality." And, he adds, "they are necessarily always contradicted together." This contradiction produces a gap between the Declaration as such and the politics it produces. Contradicting the politics of the rights of man means dissociating freedom and equality. Saint-Just thus declared in 1794: "We must cease believing that to be free is to declare oneself free to do wrong."[19] To be free is to produce, through the Declaration of rights, a reciprocal dependence which engenders freedom and equality as non-domination and as respect for the other as for oneself. However, for Balibar, the instability of this non-domination leads to finding terms of bonding, terms of mediation, played out in fraternity and property as self-ownership. Balibar then insists on the fact that it is not a question of Platonic, essentialized givens, but rather of historical practices.

Around the bicentenary, we thus see the emergence of a solid argument against crushing the French Revolution underneath the totalitarian

---

17 Étienne Balibar, *La Proposition de l'égaliberté* (Paris: PUF, 2010).
18 Étienne Balibar, "The Proposition of Equaliberty," *Equaliberty*, Trans. James Ingram, Durham: Duke University Press, 2014 36–37.
19 Saint-Just, 26 Germinal, Year 2.

imaginary. But these strong theoretical interventions have but a small echo. Doubtless in Foucault's case, it is because he is dying and cannot bear the brunt of the debate. He only witnesses the early stages of the bicentenary. And with respect to Balibar and the former Althusserians,[20] it is because each is inclined at the time to reinvent their position in isolation, and because the time for possible, visible convergences had not come.

Therefore, contrary to many received ideas, it is not for a lack of counter-arguments but perhaps thanks to what Foucault might have called the propitious, fertile ground of the theoretico-active that lends the famous statement[21] its efficacy. What is the theoretico-active which makes this statement possible and even obvious? And first of all, how should we interpret it?

THE THEORETICO-ACTIVE GROUND OF THE STATEMENT "THE FRENCH REVOLUTION IS THE MATRIX OF TOTALITARIANISMS"

To understand this theoretico-active ground, we must newly approach François Furet's claims in *Interpreting the French Revolution*. His demonstration takes up syncretic and contradictory elements of the available epistemologies for doing philosophy, history, and the human sciences. In his critique, Godechot captures this when he criticizes Furet's writing style as "jargon that is fashionable among Parisian snobs."[22]

Why syncretic? Because the very notion of "matrix" actually takes on several meanings that are constituted upstream as contradictory.

In a first hypothesis, the matrix of totalitarianism emerges from the boomerang effect: With "the issue of the Gulag [. . .] the Russian example was bound to turn around, like a boomerang, to strike its French 'origin.'"[23] For François Furet, the Jacobin discourse had instructed the Russian revolutionaries, who were repeating the French Revolution for the umpteenth time after 1830, 1848, 1871. The matrix is thus a sort of mold, a model. Hence, he asserts, "The Stalinist phenomenon [. . .] is rooted in the French intellectual left, in the Jacobin tradition."[24] He therefore claims that the ability to henceforth break away from this tradition is inaugural for the left.

---

20 Roger Establet, Pierre Machery, and Jacques Rancière in particular.
21 "The French Revolution is the matrix of totalitarianisms."
22 Jacques Godechot, *AHRF*, no. 235, 135–41.
23 François Furet, *Penser la Révolution française* (Paris: Gallimard, 1978), 29.
24 Ibid., 28.

"[A] left-wing culture, once it has made up its mind to think about the facts, namely the disastrous experience of twentieth-century communism, in terms of its own values, comes to take a critical view of its own ideology, interpretations, hopes and rationalizations. It is in left-wing culture that the sense of distance between history and the Revolution is taking root, precisely because it was the Left that believed that all of history was contained in the promises of the Revolution."[25] This is another way of denying that another left, different from the Stalinist left, once again existed from 1948 on: "The critique of Soviet totalitarianism is no longer the monopoly of the right."[26]

In this logic of a matrix as mold/model, it is indeed a question of putting into play, as a dialectic of situations, an analogical reflexivity of past/present where the notions of tradition-lineage dominate without discontinuity, if not that which scientific criticism would introduce in an ultimate way. Here we are quite close to a Marxist and Sartrean approach. The matrix of totalitarianism introduces a dialectic of times.

In a second hypothesis, the matrix would be another name for the nourishing soil, the épistèmê *à la Foucault, the theoretico-active, and I believe I have shown how these two temporal hypotheses of historicity were constructed one against the other.*

It would be the same conditions of possibility, in the form of a shared *épistèmê*, that would have produced both the Jacobin and the Stalinist-totalitarian projects, the same kind of revolutionary project which repeats its schemas. This does not make the French Revolution a model, but rather a case. The idea that the Gulag leads to a rethinking of the Terror because of an identity between the two projects respects Foucauldian discontinuity. There is no need for lineage, just a similar way of thinking. It is this framing that allows Furet to claim that the Terror belongs to the Revolutionary schema, that the Terror was inscribed in the process of the French Revolution as early as 1789. "The Terror was an integral part of the revolutionary ideology, which, just as it shaped action and politics of this era, over-invests the meaning of the circumstances it largely gave birth to."[27] The Revolution produces terror as the clouds announce a storm. It has become a theoretical law. Furet then takes the sensitive point of the purges to reinforce the identity of the two schemas. "Take for example the purges within the Revolutionary leadership, which constitutes a common characteristic of the two histories: Stalin, like Robespierre, liquidated his former companions in

---

25 Ibid.
26 Ibid., 27.
27 Ibid., 105.

the name of the struggle against the counter-revolution. From then on, the two 'spontaneous' interpretations of the purge—the French example coming to the rescue of the other—are reinforced and congealed around the idea that the counter-revolution is in the revolution, from which it must be flushed out."[28]

But because it is not simple to hold the dialectic of times in a filial tradition together with the diagnostic of the present, a mediation is needed. A mediation which interested all the protagonists of the epistemological debate of the 1950s to 1970s.

Still in the pages of *Interpreting the French Revolution*, the two revolutions which remain linked are accused of being consubstantially "systems of meticulous constraint on bodies and minds."[29]

This idea of "meticulous constraint on bodies and minds" points toward another horizon, that of Sade. The mediation which makes it possible to understand the fertile ground that existed at this time is the preoccupation with Sade from 1945 to 1975 and ultimately the hijacking he was subjected to.

I would like to demonstrate that this about-face with respect to Sade led to a double enunciative reversal. At first Sade, though a Thermidorian, became for a certain number of French writers the veritable revolutionary hero as against both Jacobin and bourgeois narrow-mindedness. Sade serves to disqualify the bourgeois revolution, allowing the Revolution to be held far from Sartre's *Critique*, from that of Georges Lefebvre and his invocation of peasant and popular-urban revolutions in this so-called bourgeois revolution, from that of the orthodox Marxist. And once Sade had been rehabilitated as a symbol of the Revolution, one can observe a new reversal that makes it possible to plunge the French Revolution into ignominy as a project that would eventually lead to acting with cruelty in the name of a future good.

Now, it is the rendering equivalent or quasi-equivalent of Kant and Sade which makes it possible to create this ignominy. Note that the authors we have just examined are distributed in these enunciative reversals.

Sartre is interested in Sade, however, he does not make him a revolutionary hero but an instance of aristocratic defense, defense of an aristocracy which knows that is has fallen, a thoroughly singular figure inside the revolutionary process. He explains this both in the *Critique of Dialectical Reason* and in the edition of *L'Arc* that was dedicated to him. This then applies to his supposed interlocutors, Lacan, Foucault, and Barthes, all of whom were

---

28 Ibid., 142.
29 Ibid., 29.

fascinated by Sade. He demonstrates the insufficiency of an archaeological approach and proposes a dialectical approach.

> Sade's work is part of a certain "archaeological" ensemble. There is the language of the time, there is also a type of dead thought that is deposited there. One of the essential themes of this ideology is nature. The bourgeois of the 18th century considers nature good. But Sade, for his part, is not bourgeois. He is an aristocrat who assists in the progressive decline of his class. He knows that privileges are in process of disappearing. In relation to others, therefore, he finds himself in the position of a man who theoretically has unlimited rights, and who at the same time can no longer exercise them, can no longer satisfy his individual desire as an aristocrat. This is the initial situation. To grasp its meaning, Sade will have to go beyond it, through a subjective synthesis, Sadism. Sadism is a theory of the relationship between men; what Sade seeks is communication. But in order to express his thoughts on this, he has to use the language given to him. A century later, Sadism will be defined as anti-physis. In the 18th century, this is not possible: Sade is obliged to pass through the idea of nature. He will therefore build a theory of nature similar to that of the bourgeois, with this single difference: instead of being good, nature is bad, it wants the death of man. Thus, Juliette ends with the image of a man jerking off in a volcano. What I am telling you here is very quick, to be sure. But you can see that there is a double relation: "nature" from Sade the meaning of his thought, but Sade himself steals the meaning of nature.[30]

What about Foucault? He was first fascinated by Sade as a figure of the outside in relation to the eighteenth-century *épistèmé*, the only figure capable of a real break that announces modernity. He then turned away from him at the time when Pasolini, in his film *Salo, or the 120 days of Sodom*, makes him into a fascist figure. Foucault describes him then as the "sergeant of sex."[31]

But here we must also summon another constellation of texts which will allow us to bring the figure of Lacan into our reflection. He himself reflects, in his 1959–1960 seminar *The Ethics of Psychoanalysis*, on the fact that Sade and his work had arrived "at such a point of promotion that we must regard it as bearing some confusion, if not of being excessive."[32]

---

30 "Jean Paul Sartre répond," *L'Arc*, no. 30, 1966, Jean-Paul Sartre, 91. Translator's rendering.
31 Michel Foucault, "Sade sergent du sexe," *Dits et Écrits*, t. I, 1686.
32 Jacques Lacan, *The Ethics of Psychoanalysis*, ed. Jacques-Alain Miller, trans. Dennis Porter, (New York: Norton, 1997).

To this extent, the work of Lacan—as a warning sign, given that it exerts, as we all know, very specific influence on psychoanalysis in France today which continues to leave traces in the public space[33]—makes it possible to see and to understand how Sade was able to become, in the different modes of his reception, the twentieth-century ethical and historical arbiter of the French Revolutionary event.

Sade versus Kant if Kant is in the shared imaginary, the theorist of a well-meaning bourgeois revolution to be suppressed. We find the surrealists, to whom we owe the everlasting image of the stature of a petrified Sade facing a Bastille in flames. But also all those who claimed him and went beyond him to make him a singular object that makes it possible to found modernity as such—Man Ray and his friends, René Char, Klossowski, Bataille, Blanchot, and Sollers—must be revisited.

Sade with Kant: if Kant is the theorist of apathy as the only ethical norm, but we already know that this is false thanks to the *Conflict of the Faculties*, and if Kant is simplified by reducing his thought to a single practical reason, there is no conceivable place for what I along with the Revolutionaries call "sensible reason," which is opposed precisely to this procedural or apathetic reason. Sade certainly valorized procedural reason at the expense of the sensible in the accomplishment of perversion until the point of death, but Kant valorizes the sensible as an *a priori* given of consciousness and values the enthusiasm of the spectators of the Revolution as a sign of progress. . . . But that does not stop the connection between the two from having some weight. We find it again in Adorno and Horkheimer in 1944, and then in the 1947 translation. But there is also a Sade who is completely opposed to Kant, precisely the Sade of Lacan, who also puts the *Critique of Practical Reason* and Sade in relation, but does not, for all that, make them equivalent.

All these thinkers took Sade seriously and at one time made him a hero of cruelty. Indeed, it is on this question of cruelty, its place and its effects, that it is necessary to think again in order to understand how the French Revolution was able to be recast in light of the Gulag, but also to allow us to rethink it in regard to its ability or inability to control cruelty.

We have examined two enunciative reversals: the one which makes Sade an exemplary hero of that which is genuinely novel in the French Revolution where he had only been a marginal figure, even an antihero; and, having rehabilitated Sade as a symbol of the Revolution, a second

---

33 Many psychoanalysts who are detractors of the Revolutionary period claim Lacan, and we will see that here too what occurs is an ideological annexation or projection, an abuse of his work.

reversal that makes it possible to plunge the French Revolution in ignominy as of a project which will ultimately have led to active cruelty in name of a future good. It would be appropriate today, in my view, to include a third reversal. Extricating the Revolution from this ignominy by demonstrating that it is indeed an event of sensible reason that unfolded upstream of the Kant of the *Conflict of the Faculties* and downstream of that of the *Critique of Practical Reason*. That the Revolution is neither Kantian, nor Sadian, nor mythical, but rather historical; and that it is one of the places where a new "faith in the impossible"[34] is invented, that is to say, a faith in humanization, to use of this term that Adorno reinvents in *Negative Dialectics* in what he calls the inconceivable, or the non-conceptualizable; that is to say, a sensible which, like music, opens, according to him, other procedures of humanization than are offered by the traditions of Western philosophy. *He* was working then with a misreading of this revolutionary sensible reason which is not the procedural reason of Sade, the sergeant of sex, nor that of unlimited liberalism, disregarding the other's life and their simple right to exist.

---

34 According to the expression of Edgar Quinet.

13

SADE AND THE ETHICAL FOLD OF THE FRENCH REVOLUTION

How did Sade become a revolutionary hero for numerous intellectuals from the beginning of the twentieth century to the 1970s? It would all start with Apollinaire, and then with surrealism and as a symptom, the famous 1937 image by Man Ray that we just evoked, the portrait of the Marquis de Sade facing a Bastille in flames—the hottest event of the Revolution and a petrified Sade. But the image becomes more complex: it is the stones of the Bastille that allow the statue to be built. We must untangle the skein made of several threads and unexpected knots without getting too far from the subject of the French Revolution because the enigma is indeed there for us. How was Sade, the one presented as the apogee of fascism in Pasolini's film *Salo, or the 120 Days of Sodom* (1975), able to be considered as its opposite at the end of the Second World War?

SADE: REVOLUTIONARY HERO?

The image of Sade produced by Man Ray in 1937 and published in the collection produced jointly with Paul Éluard, *Les Mains Libres*,[1] needed to fill a void at the moment when Maurice Heine wanted to publish Sade's unpublished works. What interests Man Ray in Sade is the political visionary. In an interview with Pierre Bourgeade, he alludes to his having read the novel *Aline et Valcourt*. This novel, he says, "is the most important, in my view, because of all the political questions it addresses and not because of the pornography. It is a bit boring to read, it is true, but I read it from

---

1 Paul Éluard and Man Ray, *Les Mains libres* (Paris: Gallimard, 1937). Translator's rendering.

cover to cover. In this book, Sade already speaks of making a United States of Europe! He solved all of our problems!"[2] Hence, Sade can function as a surface for the projection of utopia. It is in terms of a mirror, a mirror that denounces, that Man Ray apprehends Sade. "To be sure, I did not take Sade and everything he recounted at his word. He himself said: 'I held a mirror up to my time and am accused of all this!' He showed what we could do if we had power!"[3] Thus, for Man Ray, Sade makes it possible to denounce the cruelty of the powerful. But often with the surrealists, the fascination goes beyond a knowledge of the power of masters because it is also a question of Sade's power as a dismantler of the false pretenses of bourgeois society.

Many surrealists are in fact in the lineage of the Sade, who transgresses bourgeois values, even to the point of inventing the woman of the future, liberated from bourgeois control over the body. Sade represents, then, a moral exteriority, an absolute. Now, for René Char, this absolute that does not compromise is as much that of Sade as of Saint-Just.[4] According to him, their association goes through their common desire for the subversion of contractual or legislative power. It is evading the laws and guaranteeing oneself by the institution that opposes power. The questioning of the law as such thus unites them. For René Char, Sade and Saint-Just are both capable of thinking a required death that would not pass through the law, since for one as for the other, it would have no legitimacy.[5] In 1926, René Char explicitly brings them together in a poem which was published in the journal *La Révolution surréaliste*:

> Enclose the specter of freedom in your walls, I defy anyone to place their hands on my shoulder—since after Saint-Just we must believe that there can be no rest for a revolutionary but in the tomb—and with Sade flattering himself that he is disappearing from the memory of men.[6]

---

2 Extracted from Pierre Bourgeade, *Bonsoir, Man Ray*, 2nd ed. (Belfond. 1990,), 95.

3 Ibid., 97.

4 See the article d'Éric Marty, "René Char, Sade et Saint-Just," *French Review* 62, no. 6 (May 1989), printed in the US.

5 C'est évidemment aller trop vite du côté de Saint-Just, car s'il faut peu de lois et beaucoup d'institutions en démocratie, Saint-Just n'envisage pas un monde sans lois, mais plutôt un monde où il faudrait toujours interroger la légitimité et la validité de la loi. Je renvoie sur ce point à mon article intitulé "L'amour des lois," paru dans la revue *Jus politicum*, en ligne. This is evidently moving too quickly, for Saint-Just, since if democracy institutions and few laws, Saint-Just does not envision a world without laws but rather a world in which the legitimacy and validity of the law is ceaselessly interrogated.

6 *La Révolution surréaliste*, March 1926, republished in René Char, *Œuvres complètes* (Paris, Gallimard, Bibliothèque de la pléiade, 1983), 29. Translator's rendering.

Yet Sade is on the side of absolute arbitrariness, while Char and Saint-Just profess an anti-legalism (*antijuridisme*). When the crime is beyond the law, killing is not murder. But for Sade, killing one's victims is murder. However, this fundamental gap is erased by the confidence in Sade's caustic power. The French Revolution is thereby fetishized through the figure of the guillotine, in a lineage that runs from Rimbaud to Lautréamont. Meanwhile, Thermidor is still perceived by these surrealists as the failure of the Revolution and not as its victory. In October 1930, René Char, who never stops interrogating Sade, makes Sadian violence into purifying revolutionary violence.

> Sade, love finally saved from the sky's mud, hypocrisy passed through arms and eyes, this inheritance will suffice for men against famine, their beautiful strangling hands leaving their pockets.[7]

Cruel violence is, for the young man, a political weapon.

Robert Desnos also makes Sade a moral figure because, as he puts it, "de Sade is more of a moralist than any other. All of his heroes are haunted by their desire to match their outer life with their inner life, all of them have strong ideas about love and the chain of events. Virtue, far from appearing ridiculous under his pen, appears equally admirable as crime, but no more and no less."[8] Thus begins, in conjunction with the overvaluation of Sade, an equivalence of virtue and crime and not just the valorization of a divided subject who will no longer be duped by good feelings.

This ambivalence is more than eroded by the experience of the French Resistance to the Nazi occupation, which replays the revolutionary monument and more specifically the figure of Saint-Just. Aragon, Breton, and Dionys Mascolo (alias Jean Gratien) republish select pieces of Saint-Just, and the tracts are edited to emphasize the heroic figure of the young Saint-Just in order to incite young French people to resist the STO. As for René Char, himself a member of the Resistance, he makes Saint-Just an ethical model for his silence during Thermidor but keeps Sade in his home. Others at the time vehemently reject him as a harbinger of Nazism.

There is then a deaf struggle between the supporters of a Nazi Sade and those of a revolutionary Sade by the critical competence that he would continue to drive. Thus, Sade is still ambivalent, and he remains

---

7 René Char, *Le Surréalisme au service de la Révolution*, no. 2, 6—translator's rendering.
8 Robert Desnos, *L'Érotism*, (Paris: Cercle des Arts, 1953), 465.

so at the end of the war in Pierre Klossowski's *Sade mon prochain*[9] (1947), a decisive book for working on the link between Sade and the revolutionary hero.

Pierre Klossowski had been working on this troubling figure since the 1930s, at Battaille's Collège de sociologie. But with the Liberation, he returns to the misunderstood transmission of the history of the French Revolution. He also maintains that this transmission produced a myth for intellectuals of the left. This mythical narrative was based on a legend of the "People," and the values of freedom, equality, and fraternity of the republican motto, themselves legendary, a legend continued by the imaginary of a communist accomplishment consistent with Kojève's "integral man" and the citizen of the Hegelian universal State. He is already very close to the statements of François Furet when the latter explains that Stalinist intellectuals forged their specificity in France in the crucible of this French republican ideal. To this republican and communist narrative, Klossowski opposes the Sadian narrative. What is it?

Until then the ideology of God, of aristocratic name and rank, held the people in slavery, but at the dawn of the Revolution, the aristocratic master killed God. If one wants to dominate, one needs a slave who is an accomplice to in one's desire to dominate: a slave that would enjoy their submission to the lucidity of a libertine elite, both politically and sexually. It would thus be the limitless desire of the elites, that is to say excess, that would become the norm of social life, excess which actualizes itself in the riot, where the rioters are at the service of the elites, themselves an excess against bourgeois norms.

Now, if one hears correctly, such a Sadian hero actually manufactures the counterrevolutionary people allied with the Muscadins.

In any case, supposing there is an encounter between the rioters and the master, it is fleeting because the master in fact remains in solidarity with the values he transgresses (his enjoyment depends on it). To this end, Klossowski's analysis appears close to the one Sartre offers in the *Critique of Dialectical Reason*, where he refers to Simone de Beauvoir's *Must We Burn Sade?*: "'Sadism' is a blind attempt to reaffirm in violence his rights as a warrior, founding them on the subjective *quality* of his person [. . .] he finds himself face to face with the essential Idea: the Idea of Nature. He wants to show that the law of Nature is the law of the strongest, that massacres and tortures only reproduce natural destructions [. . .] the most heinous crimes

---

9 Pierre Klossowski, *Sade mon prochain* (Paris: Seuil, 1947).

are good and the finest virtues wicked [. . .] the only relation of person to person is that which binds the torturer his victim."¹⁰

Klossowski adds that this people does not want to be the accomplice of the Master against God, but rather to invent the so-called republican values. But the only equality which exists for Sade is complicity in murder. The rioter, the terrorist, and the Sadian Master are now made equivalent. However, Klossowski draws a distinction between the people and the populace. The alliance against the bourgeoisie is made between an aristocracy drunk on its omnipotence and a populace submitted to the Master's desire. Equality as reciprocity and religion of the supreme being as a religion of the virtue of duties cannot be encountered by Sade. Rather, he is inventing the desiring overman, opposed to the subman subjected to this desire which is none other than the desire to enjoy death in mastery.

This imaginary is then projected back onto the period of the Terror. The terrorists would experience this enjoyment of death that accompanies mastery. On the opposite side, the crowd is drunk and also inhabited by bloodthirsty desires, but it does not possess mastery. It remains that of the masters who manipulate them. The crowd described by Hyppolyte Taine is analogous here to the one described by Sade.¹¹ Either emancipatory hopes are disfigured in the desire for death and chaos, or they are nothing but the veil of chaos, the veneer of virtue shattering. As Éric Marty says, the revolutionary riot described by Sade¹² reminds one of a populist coup d'état with its surprise attack, rapes, pillages.¹³

In the face of this fascination with Sade, Albert Camus, Raymond Queneau, and Michel Leiris had serious reservations (as Foucault later would) about his importance.

Thus, Raymond Queneau writes, first in 1945 and then in *Bâtons, chiffres et lettres* (1950): "That Sade was not personally a terrorist, that his work has a profound human value, will not prevent all those who have more or less supported the theses of the Marquis from having to envisage, without hypocrisy, the reality of the extermination camps with their horrors no longer locked in a man's head, but practiced by thousands of fanatics. Mass graves complete philosophies, as unpleasant as this can be."¹⁴

---

10 Jean-Paul Sartre, *Search for a Method* (New York: Vintage, 1968), 114–15.
11 The year 1789 is qualified by Sade as a year of delirium and insanity, *Histoire de Juliette*, t. II, 3 e partie, 248.
12 *Histoire de Juliette*, t. III, 5 e partie, éd. cit., 95–96.
13 Éric Marty, *Pourquoi le XX siècle a-t-il pris Sade au sérieux?* op. cit., 47.
14 Raymond Queneau, *Bâtons, chiffres et lettres* (Paris: Gallimard, 1950), 152. Translator's rendering.

The question in 1945 concerning the relationship between Sade and the world, therefore, is evidently not only that of the formation of left-wing intellectuals or their rescue, but rather that of the possible passage from Sade's fantasy to reality. Sade is not associated by everyone with the Revolution, but is instead, as during the Resistance, associated with a prefiguration of the camps and death, where the Master executioner is the Gestapo. The latter had indeed subjected its victims to all the tortures.

But if Sade, beyond Klossowski's text, maintains a preeminent presence in the intellectual field despite this critical effort, it is because this historical association is discredited by Bataille and Blanchot. They explicitly take a position against Adorno and Horkheimer, who very explicitly assimilate Sade with Nazism, but we will return to this. For in the tangle, they also assimilate Kant and Sade, and this is another thread to unravel.

THE FABRICATION OF A PASSIONATE AND UNASSIMILABLE SADE

Georges Bataille and Maurice Blanchot published on Sade the same year as Pierre Klossowski. Bataille published a text on literature and evil in *Critique*, and presented at a conference on Sade and morality. Blanchot published "Meeting Sade" in *Les Temps Modernes*. Both consider Sade as the embodiment of radical subversion, who must ultimately remain impossible to assimilate. Impossible by consequence to assimilate with Nazism.

The argument that makes it possible to formulate the gap between Nazism and Sade appears in a somewhat fortuitous way. It emerges in Bataille's answer to a student after a talk on May 12, 1947. The question addressed the link between the cremation ovens and Sade. However, on this occasion, Bataille recognizes common images between the Sadian imaginary and the camps: "It is clear that, compared to the executions of the Terror that Sade envisioned in *Philosophy in the Boudoir*, the executions of the Nazis responded much more to the images, to the suggestions of Sade."[15] Thus Sade, from the imaginary point of view, would be closer to the Nazis than to the revolutionaries, and in fact Bataille marks a gap between the Terror and the experience of the Nazi concentration camp and extermination. But in marking the gap, he also renews the analogy. Let us continue: "But they also always responded to the fundamental objection that Sade made to the executions of the Terror, since from one end to the

---

15 Georges Bataille, *Œuvres complètes*, t. VII, 372–373.

other, the unleashing of passions which raged in Buchenwald or Auschwitz was under the government of reason."[16]

Bataille thus gives the impression that murder in Sade is not under the government of reason but under that of passions, emotions. But this is false. Sade does not object to terror because it results from cold and procedural reason, but because it creates judicial law. He is opposed to the law (which can be warm and protective, by the way), not to procedure, because he keeps inventing cold-thought procedures. It is thus not cold, bureaucratic reason which horrifies him, but the law as a limit and as a site of the State. Refusing the law and the State death penalty does not mean refusing rational procedure, and once again, everyone knows how Sade's scenarios are thought out before their execution, like the writing of evil to be put into action.

If in 1947 this defense was fortuitous, it returns in more a reflective way when Bataille testifies during the trial against Jean-Jacques Pauvert. The latter had decided to publish the complete works of an author about whom everyone was speaking, but whom nobody could read. In this trial, which opened on December 15, 1956, Bataille returns to the idea that morbid enjoyment is what leads people away from reason and hence away from morality:

> "Nobody had said it before [. . .] (the Marquis de Sade), [. . .] that man found a satisfaction in the admiration for death and pain. This can be regarded as reprehensible, and I feel that way too. I consider the admiration of death and pain perfectly condemnable; but if we take reality into account, we realize that however reprehensible that admiration is, it has always played a considerable role in history. I believe that from a moral point of view, it is extremely important for us to know, given that morality commands obedience to reason, what the possible causes are of disobedience to this rule. Now, Sade has represented an invaluable document for us, insofar as he knew how to develop and make sensible the deepest cause that we have for disobeying reason."[17]

On the one hand, Bataille here generalizes the enjoyment (*jouissance*) before death and pain, and on the other, he opposes reason and enjoyment, finally claiming that reading Sade is a matter of prevention.

If the drive for cruelty and destruction is generalizable, perversion is not identifiable with this drive; it is one of the directions this drive can take.

---

16 Ibid.
17 Georges Bataille, *L'Affaire Sade. Le procès, Œuvres complètes*, t. XII (Paris: Gallimard, 453. Translator's rendering.

Finally, Bataille acts as if reason were only on the side of restraint and could not be the sensible reason of the sensualists and the faculty of judging. Yet this sensible reason makes satisfaction and rationality inseparable; there is no opposition between moral satisfaction and this desiring reason. One can desire the law sensibly and rationally at the same time, and thus be satisfied with it. Reason is not something we obey as if under coercion, but rather the locus of a "calm passion," to borrow an expression from the eighteenth-century Scottish thinkers. There can be morality and reason without coercion. Ultimately, Bataille condemns the taste for pain and for death, but makes it an active invariant in history that we should come to know. Sade is then the site of this necessary knowledge. Once again, far from thwarting what we call perversion, Sade's writings aim at action. Nothing here comes to control the taste for death, since that would require morality in Bataille's sense, highly restrictive and instituted beforehand as a prerequisite. He thus adds: "I believe that for someone who wants to get to the bottom of what man means, reading Sade is not only commendable, but completely necessary."[18] Hence, Bataille naturalizes what could be called the taste for death, without making it a subjective or historical particularity. Although he makes no connection here with Nazism, but with what psychoanalysts call a drive for destruction and cruelty, he gives arguments and credibility to the idea, so widespread today, that a little Nazi lies dormant in each of us, and that it is good to know this—something that is of course more than questionable. Bataille wants to believe that when we tremble before Sade, we tremble before ourselves, and that we must read Sade to thwart our evil drives by being already aware of them. But for Sade, writing does not aim to prevent the crime by giving it an imaginary form. It aims instead at inciting to act, to dare to become this criminal who enjoys their cruel or perverse crime as mastery of death, in procedural reason and mastery.

Finally, Bataille opposes the Nazis who hide their crimes to Sade, who writes them. But reading the nomenclature of perversions does not purge anything, and if the Nazi executioners hid their crimes, this resembles Sade's desire not to leave any traces after his death, his belief that his texts would be published. To read Sade is therefore not to outsmart evil.

Jean Paulhan, following Bataille, refers to psychoanalysis as able to lend credence to the necessity of reading Sade. "It is certain that Sade came at a time when a kind of soft philosophy fully accepted that man was good and that it was enough to return him to his nature for all to go well. From there, Sade was led by contrast to demonstrate that man is wicked, and to

---

18 Ibid., 454.

demonstrate in great detail, the manifold ways that this wickedness stems primarily from sexuality, which Freud and others would later take up."[19]

Sade is thus in excess only to be misunderstood, but he is unassimilable because this drive/perversion is what humans do not want to know about themselves. Since this drive/perversion concerns everyone, according to Bataille, it cannot be connected to Nazism as a historical specificity. Since Bataille thinks the drives in opposition to reason, he cannot imagine Sade on the side of imaginative procedural reason plugged into this drive for destruction.

However, with Blanchot, another step is taken in granting Sade an ultimately emancipatory value. In effect, for Blanchot, the Pervert is the one who makes it possible to go beyond the impasse of humanism, that is to say beyond consciousness aligned with bourgeois ploys. The Pervert would be the one who is free from this false (good) consciousness, and could truly act and transform the world.

In *Literature and the Right to Death*, Blanchot depicts Sade as a writer who writes while proclaiming "I am the Revolution." Effectively, for Blanchot, the Revolution must see about Evil and must dialogue with it. If this dialogue is interrupted, "then the intellectual can cease to be and take his card to the communist party."[20] The communist party is thus, according to him, the place of good conscience and good sentiments, the place that turns its back on the necessity of thinking through evil. This is why the Revolution in Blanchot merges with sacrificial terror. Self-sacrifice and sacrifice of the other, which is in fact the assertion that there is no revolution unless the saving of life ceases. For Blanchot the revolutionary has already given their life, there is no more "right to life" but rather a "right to death": the right to inflict it on a traitor, and the right to receive it as one agrees to a decision.

It seems to me that the death that lurks in Sartre's pledged group, where everyone is under the gaze of those with whom he has taken an oath and who, if he betrays them, can kill him, is very close to the right of death in Blanchot. Sartre's pessimism about the instituted Revolution is closely linked with this Blanchot. Does not the latter say, "Death is the work of freedom in free men."[21] Here, too, the question of freedom is only determined at the expense of this death which lurks. The terrorists, for

---

19 The author does not cite.—Translator's note
20 Maurice Garçon, *L'Affaire Sade, témoignages de Georges Bataille, Jean Paulhan, André Breton et Jean Cocteau* (Paris: Jean-Jacques Pauvert, 1963).
21 Maurice Blanchot, *Ecrits politiques*, 1953–1993 (Paris: Gallimard, 2008), 310. Translator's rendering.

Blanchot, are those who "desire absolute freedom, and are fully conscious that this constitutes a desire for their own death, they are conscious of the freedom they affirm, as they are conscious of their death, which they realize, and consequently they behave during their life-times, not like people living among other living people, but like beings deprived of being, like universal thoughts, pure abstractions beyond history, judging and deciding in the name of all of history."[22] Abstraction is once again opposed to sensible embodiment and conspires with the de Maistrian critique of the French Revolution.

Foucault, following in the wake of this unassimilable Sade, speaks for his part of a discourse of "the outside." In *The Order of Things*, Sade occupies a threshold which separates the discourse of representation in the classical age and the modern *épistémê*. Even if Sade produces, in Foucault's terms, "a general grammar of perversions," violence, death, and sex explode order. Ultimately, Sade dwells in excess because he is in fact ironic, and nullifies the division between madness and reason, and in Foucault's words, he undermines "all the verbiage on man and nature."[23] Kant then occupies the other edge of the enlightenment, the one which leads to opening an *épistémê* where the transcendental and the empirical can no longer be united. In the 1960s, Sade, like Nietzsche, is a Foucauldian hero. It is only in 1975 that Foucault rejects Sade as the "sergeant of sex" who prevents life from inventing itself. It was almost ten years later that he published his work on Kant and Enlightenment. And in this work, it is not just a question of responding to his previous works but also of responding to Adorno and Horkheimer, who equated Kant and Sade and thus apparently pass a brutal judgment on the revolutionary experience and on Kant.

KANT AND SADE

For Adorno and Horkheimer, the formalism of pure reason and of being in Kant is an analogous procedure to Sadian nothingness. With Kant, they say, the law no longer depends on the good, but it is the Good which depends on the law. This is how the categorical imperative and its prescriptive character undermined the subject's creation of meaning. This is why, according to them, Sade and Nietzsche, far from turning their backs on the

---

22 Maurice Blanchot, *The Work of Fire*, trans. Charlotte Mandel (Stanford: Stanford University Press, 1995), 320.

23 Michel Foucault, *Histoire de la folie à l'âge classique*, Paris, Gallimard, 1961, réédition « Tel », 1972, 552. Translator's rendering.

work of the Enlightenment, accomplish it in the form of an instrumental and procedural rationality. Nazi extermination is the form of experience of this rationality which produces domination, destruction, and methodical cruelty. The affirmation of self, say the two Frankfurt school philosophers, leads to the destruction of others.

Now, let us say it straight away that what Adorno and Horkheimer denounce is very precisely what the French revolutionaries in 1789 called "domination," against which the most radical among them never cease struggling, since it creates a state of war and not a state of civility. The only revolutionary freedom that is valid according to the Declaration of the Rights of Man and Citizen is effectively reciprocal freedom, freedom as a non-domination that implies entering into a social contact with others and not destroying them. This does not prevent us from thinking the necessity of defensive war, which can deploy great cruelty but can also reassert right in the face of force. This war of defense is conceived as a right of resistance to oppression which itself is based on a sensualist knowledge, the only one capable of founding law, according to Sieyès in his reasoned exposition.[24] We know in our body if we are oppressed. It is not an intellectual reasoning that allows us to judge this, but sensation.[25] But if one is oppressed, the use of violence to resist oppression founds a right, whereas the violence of oppression founds nothing. With Terror, being the "the war of freedom against tyranny,"[26] the tyrant can effectively be an irreconcilable enemy to be destroyed. It is still necessary to say who the enemy-tyrant is, and why. Procedural tyranny is thus not that of the "terrorists" but that of Constituents like Le Chapelier and other supporters of an economic liberalism which puts the existence of others in danger. The Frankfurt school, seeing only this side of the Revolution, once again adheres to the idea of bourgeois revolution, which benefits the procedural bourgeois capitalists and can be reduced to that alone, without understanding that the struggle against precisely this was also unfolding.

If Adorno and Horkheimer are right to denounce a bourgeois formalist rationalism that leads to the reification of the human, they are absolutely wrong, in my view, to equate Kant and Sade, or at least it would

---

24 Abbé Sieyès, *Reconnaissance et exposition raisonnée des droits de l'homme et du citoyen*, comité de constitution, July 20 and 21, 1789 (http://gallica.bnf.fr/ark:/12148/).
25 Cf. my article "Individualité et subjectivation pendant la période révolutionnaire," in *L'Individu aujourd'hui, débats sociologiques et contrepoints philosophiques*, ed. Philippe Corcuff, Christian Le Bart, and François de Singly (Rennes: Presses universitaires de Rennes, 2010).
26 According to the Robespierre's expression on 17 Pluviose, Year II (February 5, 1794) "on the principles of political morality that should guide the National Convention in the internal administration of the Republic."

be necessary to say which Kant. Certainly not that of the *Conflict of the Faculties*.

Yet this equation has been emulated. Deleuze, in *Anti-Oedipus*, asserts that "it is not reason's dormancy that produces monsters but rather vigilant and insomniac rationality."[27] In *La Chinoise,* Godard constructs a sequence where, after having shown Foucault's *The Order of Things*, he asserts through images that Immanuel Kant is the Adolf Eichmann of western philosophy. Kant becomes responsible for Nazism. For Adorno and Horkheimer, Sade is the bridge between Kant and Auschwitz. They therefore denounce two procedural rationalities which made historically equivalent, and forget about sensible reason. They have therefore fabricated a terrible misunderstanding of what played out in the 18th century as a political struggle which is in fact the foundation of what they are calling for. By cutting off the sensualist and revolutionary filiation of the desire to re-found humanity on the inconceivable—another name for physical, sensible experience—Adorno and Horkheimer obstruct the transmission of the object "French Revolution," which was not fundamentally a site of apathy but rather enthusiasm. Flames rather than stones, and flames that do not lead inexorably to stones.

The one who really challenged this equivalence of Kant and Sade is Lacan in his seminar on ethics in 1959–1960. The movement of this creation crisis is also that of a transmutation of what he calls the "sentimental," or in Kant's terms, the "pathological object" (the object of a passion, of affection), the examination the meaning of "desiring."

The Kantian morality of the *Critique of Practical Reason* is indeed one of apathy, of the absence of passion evident in the famous formula "act is if the maxim of your action could be taken as a universal maxim," a formula translated by Lacan in this way: "Act so that the maxim of your will may always be taken as the principle of laws that are valid for all." [28] As Lacan had shown that this ethics linked to Newton's science, he questions how it would connect to the science of the 1950s: "Never act except in such a way that your action may be programmed."[29] The sovereign, submitted to scientific programming, that is to say a perfectly procedural reason, which would also be a law of nature, relieves the subject of any responsibility toward themselves or others. It is on this point that Lacan shows the

---

27 Gilles Deleuze and Félix Guattari, *L'Anti-Œdipe* (Paris: Minuit), 44.

28 Jacques Lacan, *The Ethics of Psychoanalysis, 1959-1969*, ed. Jacques-Alain Miller, Trans. Dennis Porter, New York: Norton, 1992. 77.

29 Ibid. Such programming exists now in a number of Asian cities, where each life is connected to a terminal which registers every action of daily life.

possible connection with Sade's text *Philosophy in the Boudoir*, and more specifically *Français encore un effort pour être républicain*.

He asserts that it is "Kantian criteria" that Sade's anti-morality advances when he defends incest, adultery, theft, calumny, in fact "all the laws of the Decalogue." This is translated by Lacan into a new formula: "Let us take as the universal maxim of our conduct the right to enjoy any other person whatsoever as the instrument of our pleasure."[30] This conception, Lacan says, "opens wide the flood gates that in imagination he proposes as the horizon of our desire; everyone is invited to pursue to the limit the demands of his lust, and to realize them."[31] Now, he says, our feelings lead us to find this repugnant, but if, like Kant, we eliminate all feeling from morality, then even if this society that he describes as "sadist" is a kind of obverse, it can correspond to Kantian ethics as elaborated in 1788 (or an ethics of the Enlightenment, but before the French Revolution). Another point of convergence is that when something resurfaces that has to do with feeling, it consists of "pain" in Kant as in Sade. And to conclude momentarily as Adorno and Horkheimer: "Kant is of the same opinion as Sade."[32]

But whether it is Kant's humiliation in front of the law or that of Sade, for Lacan, all peoples have in fact maintained something like a Decalogue as a religious and moral referent. And it is by commenting on the Ten Commandments, and specifically on "Thou shalt not lie," that "the intimate link between desire, in its structuring function, with the law is felt most tangibly. In truth, this commandment exists to make us feel the true function of the law."[33] For, he adds, the subject of the enunciation having been absent, in the precept "Thou shalt not lie" "is included the possibility of the lie as the most fundamental desire."[34] For all that, Lacan does not conclude with what he considers a facile position, which would be to say that "the respect of the human person involves the right to lie." Far from it, he claims that there is an "antinomic function between the law and desire, as conditioned by speech."[35] This is, in his view, "the human condition," and as such, as a cornerstone of the law, desire, and speech, it deserves to be "respected." Respect for the human person consists in giving them the responsibility for this antinomy of law and desire. It consists in the non-programmable, therefore. The sentimental is not the sentimental, but desire. But "the dialectical relationship between desire and the Law causes our desire to flare

---

30 Ibid., 79.
31 Ibid.
32 Ibid., 78
33 Ibid., 81–82.
34 Ibid.
35 Ibid.

up only in relation to the Law, through which it becomes the desire for death." "Transgressing the law to enjoy a right to death? Still Sade, then. But no. We will have to explore that which, over the centuries, human beings have succeeded in elaborating that transgresses the Law, puts them in a relationship to desire that transgresses interdiction, and introduces an erotics that is above morality."[36]

An erotics and not pathos, but nevertheless, affected bodies. Bodies affected by desire. A body which flares up like the flames of the Bastille, and like Sade does not flare up, as he invents, not an erotics but rather its reverse, not a sensual emancipation but a subjugation, as Foucault understands when he names him the "Sergeant of sex."

To advance on this question, Lacan takes the example of a reason capable of containing desire, to spare oneself death, of renouncing one's sexuality, because one would be punished with death—renouncing friendship by delivering a false testimony to save one's life. Now, Lacan tells us, the subject can hesitate, he can go there anyway, to this forbidden room, and can also refuse to bear this false testimony and thus renounce the saving of their life. And this is where ethics is precisely at stake, maintaining the power of love and friendship as a site of desire, against a reality principle. It is the power of desire which thus founds ethics in Lacan, and not procedure. The ethical act consists in following one's desire, provided that it is not under the blade of death either given or received as a principle of enjoyment, in short, that this desire is precisely not sadist, but erotic. So, the ethical act is not grounded in sentimental interests to be satisfied or honored, whether it is pity or interest properly understood, but rather in the satisfaction of desire on the side of life, the fact of acting from one's own desire, without ceding on it, satisfying the criteria of the Kantian ethical act. We can then say that "following one's own desire" comes back to "doing one's duty."

Very clearly, in the end, Lacan is with Kant and against Sade, having traversed that which brings them together, namely, the relation to pain and humiliation as an experience in truth of a certain enjoyment.

It is in this way that the desire for Revolution is not realized through the blade of death, in the enjoyment (*jouissance*) of death, but in the restraint of this deadly dimension—difficult, to be sure, to exile entirely—and can be a perfectly ethical desire.

This is why Slavoj Zizek says that, for Lacan, "Kant is not a covert Sadian, by contrast Sade is a covert Kantian." Zizek adds that "because

---

36 Ibid., 84.

of its political consequences, the difference is major: by considering the libidinal structure of totalitarian regimes as perverse (the totalitarian subject assumes the position of the object-instrument of the Other's enjoyment)," "Sade as the truth of Kant would signify that Kantian ethics harbors totalitarian potentialities within it; meanwhile, if one considers that Kantian ethics precisely prohibits the subject from assuming the position of the object-instrument of the Other's enjoyment, from invoking the latter in the assumption of the entire responsibility for what he proclaims to be his duty, then Kant is the anti-totalitarian par excellence."[37]

Nevertheless, this profuse fascination allowed for a strange gibberish of which the expression "French Revolution, matrix of totalitarianism," which appeared under Furet's pen, is a symptom. In a certain way, it would take a capacity to put the conflict of the faculties in play with sensible forms to thwart it. The finesse of a Peter Weiss, the radicality of a Pasolini, the anxious lucidity of a René Char attempted, in my opinion, to untie the world from the vile (*l'immonde*), without certainty.

UNTYING THE WORLD OF THE VILE

Peter Weiss warns of the trap which lies in drawing a too quick equivalence between the French Revolution and Sade, a socialism which is not living up to its promises and the French Revolution.

His play shown in 1964, *The Persecution and Assassination of Jean-Paul Marat, As Performed by the Inmates of the Asylum of Charenton under the Direction of the Marquis de Sade*, simplified by Peter Brook in *Marat/Sade*, places Sade face to face with Marat, with socialism as a subtext of Marat. In it, Peter Weiss mixes historical documentation (the assassination of Marat by Charlotte Corday on July 13, 1793), psychodrama (the performance given by the patients in 1808 at the instigation of Sade, in front of the director the asylum and Parisian public) and the philosophical dispute between Sade and Marat. As a playwright, he invents their fictional encounter, since the two men never met. This fiction makes it possible to stage two sides of the French Revolution. On one side, individualism pushed to the extreme embodied by Sade, where his Sadian fantasy and his writing are king. On the other, Marat, political and social upheaval and its pitfalls: powers constructed into systems in the name of the noble ideas of

---

37 Slavoj Zizek, "Kant avec (ou contre) Sade?," *Savoirs cliniques*, no. 4 (2004): 98. Translator's rendering.

free peoples. What is ultimately brought face to face are two follies: that of an absolute individualism, and that of an errant collective when the individual is forgotten. In this way, we return to the objectives of Sartre's *Situations II*: inventing a socialist revolution which would not cheat the individual and subjectivity.

If Peter Weiss's conclusions are bitter, they push toward the invention of a utopia which frees bodies and minds. Thus, the French Revolution as seen by Sade is certainly an opportunity to speak in subtext about the deviation of socialism, but like Socialism or Barbarism, without renouncing it. For Peter Weiss, and this is particularly legible in his novels, it is the anxieties linked to the bloody opacity of the world, wars, repressions, and destructions which push us toward this necessary utopia. And in this regard, Peter Weiss does not confuse Stalinism and Nazism.

When he speaks of Auschwitz, he evokes "a place to which I was destined and which I escaped." He attended the long trial (twenty months from December 20, 1963, to August 19, 1965) of twenty-two people responsible for the extermination camp at Auschwitz before the court of Frankfurt-am-Main. He then composed an oratorio in eleven songs based on his notes, the transcriptions of witnesses, and debates in the *Frankfurter Tageszeitung, L'Instruction*. On October 19, 1965, the play premiered simultaneously in sixteen theaters across East and West Germany.

But the sadistic and "meticulous constraint" on bodies and minds of which Furet speaks is staged ten years later by Pasolini in 1975, in *Salo, or the 120 Days of Sodom*, which places Sade in the context of the of the Republic of Salo. A "historian," that is, one of the subjugated and prostituted women who describe the procedure of cruel coercion which ultimately leads to death; she herself dies. Telling this story is fatal. Pasolini dies before the release of the film. The same year, René Char writes the poem *Aromates chasseurs*.[38] In it we find the nagging political question: how to escape capture by the State, which is constitutively totalitarian for Char.

"There are those who drank the water from Marat's bathtub and we who shivered on the horizon of Saint-Just and Lenin. But Stalin is perpetually imminent. Hitler's jaw is preserved with respect. [. . .] Subordination or terror then both at the same time, totalitarianism towards which everything converges: the wedding ring of the desert, sinister games, the punitive pause . . . Blind, do not piss on the glowing verse, along among everything he hastens."[39]

---

38 Char, *Œuvres complètes*, 517.
39 Ibid.

Drinking water from Marat's bath, which stages him as both a martyr and a simple body sick from his skin, is like an act of a saint. But René Char is not a saint, he shuddered between fear and enthusiasm, it is undecidable, when legality disappears in the face of the Revolution. But this Revolution can always be captured by an incarnation of the State apparatus; this is Stalin as a lurking danger. But we fetishize the executioner, the jaw of a man-eater, of a predator, why else talk about this jaw? Hitler is not Stalin. And terror comes as an alternative to subordination, so it is terror with equality, terror with the rights of man, or the terror of the rights of man. But when equality disappears in favor of this subordination, then there alone totalitarianism emerges. Not that of the Revolution, but that of its negation. Totalitarianism, for René Char, is not terror but its meaninglessness when it no longer guarantees the rights of man and the citizen. Ultimately, he speaks of a simple star shining, fragile, vulnerable, the blind can destroy it. This shining star is the Revolution.

Pasolini speaks at the same time of *Lucioli*, which Georges Didi-Hubermann[40] leads us to reread. A few months before his death, on February 1, 1975, Pier Paolo Pasolini publishes this article in *Corriere*. In choosing fireflies as a metaphor for a revolutionized society, he inverted the image of Dante where the small lights are those of the dreadful, whereas the great Light is that of Heaven. Thus, if the world can still be enlightened, it is with the final scintillations of a civilization, those of a culture which, across Europe, were going to be devoured by the apocalypse in De Martino's[41] sense. We should not give up protecting these last fireflies.

But René Char does not stop there. He does not stop questioning totalitarianism and untying it from the Revolution. In 1979, the collection *Fenêtres dormantes et porte sur le toit* appeared. In it we find a poem titled "The Bloody Utopias of the 20th Century." Here he cedes the word "utopia" to the adversary, but attempts to take it back using as his only tool the desire with which this book will finish.

> Ni la corne totalitaire ni le paralogisme ne se sont logés dans notre front.
> La notion du juste et de l'injuste dans les faits usuels a tenu en haleine la sympathie.
>
> L'hémophilie politique de gens qui se pensent émancipés.

---

40 Georges Didi-Hubermann, *Survivance des lucioles* (Paris: Minuit, 2009).
41 Ernesto De Martino, *La Fin du monde. Essai sur les apocalypses culturelles* (Paris: EHESS, 2016).

> Combien sont épris de l'humanité et non de l'homme! Pour élever la première, ils abaissent le second.
>
> L'égalité compose avec l'agresseur. C'est sa malédiction. Et notre figure s'en accommode. Comme on voudrait que la rédaction universelle ne fût pas, une seule nuit, interrompue, sinon par l'impulsion oblique d'un fanal amoureux! Ainsi devise le désir.

The rhinoceros is next to Sadian confusion. Faced with this, Kant's "sympathy of aspiration" remains under the figure of the feeling of right and wrong, of an ethical responsibility with no certitude. Loving spilled blood cannot be emancipatory, and Sade, whose name is no longer mentioned, is implicitly rejected. Peter Weiss, Sartre, Socialism or Barbarism, could be a subtext of this affirmation of a necessary convergence of love of humanity and of each of those who constitute it as one. Could universal writing be anything other than that of the Declaration of equality, corrupted by those who give way on their desire. Uninterrupted writing, uninterrupted inscription in history, the desire for equality as motto for the love of life.

The theoretico-active produced by the fascination for Sade will have been ultimately thwarted by poets.

CONCLUSION
Clearing Some Foggy Patches

This itinerary, from the Sartrean appropriation of the French Revolution in the *Critique of Dialectical Reason* up to the rejection of the statement "The Revolution is the matrix of totalitarianism," through to the ethics of desire in Lacan, seems to make a temporal loop. It does not aim, however, at what might appear as a dual return to Sartre and Lacan.

Rather, it hopes to have shed light on a factual given: the evolution of the place occupied by the French Revolution in the social imaginary owes less to historians than to the philosophical, scientific, or ideological discourses of the eras traversed, from which historians are themselves downstream.

It hopes to have elucidated where we stood with respect to the Revolution around the time of the bicentenary, and where we stand today. It remains for us to clarify what we wish to do with this "history of the French Revolution," knowing that this "we" cannot simply be that of the scientific community.

ARCHAEOLOGY OF A FINISHED/ INTERMINABLE REVOLUTION

These discourses, which since 1945 have organized the social imaginary, emanate from a series of refined disciplines. In Sartre's case, it is philosophy, of course existentialism. But for a host of Marxist traditions and critical traditions internal to Marxism, particularly in the 1960s, all philosophies soon qualified as humanist either because of their interest in Man with a capital *M* or simply because they do not reject it. In fact, Sartre, who juggles multiple disciplinary knowledges in the *Critique*, claims to have a set of aims that should be particularly interesting to anthropology: "In short, we are dealing with neither human history, nor sociology, nor ethnography. To parody a title of Kant's, we would claim, rather, to be laying the foundations for 'Prolegomena to any future anthropology.'"[1] Lévi-Strauss actually felt that this addressed him, as an anthropologist and as a Marxist. However, Sartre and Lévi-Strauss share neither the same conception of anthropology nor the same conception of Marxism.

Sartre postulates that this future anthropology will be based on a dialectical reason, which he develops by associating existentialism and dialectical materialism. He is fundamentally anti-naturalist. Lévi-Strauss, however, calls for a true science of man which will be based fundamentally on analytical reason and a more classical conception of dialectical reason. For Sartre, human reason is dialectical because each synthetic subject is in touch with the world as a whole. But before knowing the whole of the world, they know their own experiences as a subject, which allow them to develop totalizations, let us say partial syntheses. In this way, they disqualify a materialism given from the outside: "This external materialism lays down the dialectic as exteriority: the Nature of man lies outside him in an *a priori* law, in an extra-human nature, in a history that begins with the nebulae. For this universal dialectic, partial totalisations do not have even provisional value; they do not exist. Everything must always be referred to the totality of *natural history* of which human history is only a particular form."[2] Sartre then seeks, through totalizations, what he calls a Human Truth that passes through History, that is to say, according to him, humanity's art of taking charge of contradictions in order to evolve societies.

For Lévi-Strauss, totalization is already given before the analytical work of "dissolution." Far from wanting to seek the truth of Man through totalization, Lévi-Strauss claims to want to dissolve Man with a capital *M*. "To dissolve is to produce a reduction, but one must be ready to accept, as a consequence of each reduction, the total overturning of any preconceived idea concerning the level, whichever it may be, one is striving to attain. The idea of some general humanity to which ethnographic reduction leads, will bear no relation to any one may have formed in advance."[3] The dialectical effort is that of a leap of thought in which we recast totality after its dissolution. He speaks of "the leap it must make, to close the gap between the ever unforeseen complexity of this new object and the intellectual

---

[1] Jean-Paul Sartre, *Critique of Dialectical Reason* (London: Verso, 2004), 65–66.
[2] Ibid., 27.
[3] Claude Lévi-Strauss, *The Savage Mind* (London: Weidenfield and Nicolson, 1966), 427. Translation altered.

means at its disposal."⁴ The leap would be the invention of new intellectual or scientific tools. Lévi-Strauss, like Sartre, claims a "progressive-regressive" approach, but argues that "scientific explanation consists not in moving from the complex to the simple but in the replacement of a less intelligible complexity by one which is more so."⁵ "The real question," he writes, "is not whether our endeavour to understand involves a gain or a loss of meaning, but whether the meaning we preserve is of more value than that we have been judicious enough to relinquish."⁶ And he concludes: Marx and Freud "have taught us that man has meaning only on the condition that he view himself as meaningful. [. . .] But it must be added that *this meaning is never the right one*: superstructures are faulty acts which have 'made it' socially."⁷

This epistemological debate, which explicitly opposes a regime of meaning or truth to a regime of scientific practice and the real—specific to the natural sciences—takes history and more particularly the object "French Revolution" as sites of obstruction.

Claude Lévi-Strauss defends the idea that history is not a discipline with a different object than anthropology, but that it is a method, a method where comparisons and classifications are made by temporal category, what he calls "chronological coding." It distinguishes classes of dates according to the intervals of time it considers. He concludes by asserting that "[i]n fact history is tied neither to man nor to any particular object. It consists wholly in its method, [. . .] history may lead to anything, provided you get out of it."⁸ In Lévi-Strauss's hands, history thus becomes a scientific discipline auxiliary to anthropology and all other knowledge of the so-called human sciences. If history is this scientific method of the temporal variable, then the history called "History of the Revolution" is just as mythical as Lévi-Strauss's "cold history" of so-called savages. For Lévi-Strauss, history in Sartre is a "synchronic totality manifested in men's becoming." Sartre situates himself vis-à-vis history, like primitives vis-à-vis the eternal past. This is why for Lévi-Strauss, history in Sartre's system plays the role of a myth. This does not mean then that the event vanishes as such, but that its narrative has a particular social function, namely, to encourage one to assume a mode of being in the world and to act accordingly. To this extent, the narrative does not fall within what Lévi-Strauss calls science, but is rooted

---

4 Ibid., 253.
5 Ibid.
6 Ibid.
7 Ibid., 253–54.
8 Ibid., 262.

in a knowledge which resembles that which all human beings forge in order to be able to assume their condition as humans. It reminds one of what Nietzsche called a history that is "useful for life," which he contrasts with the "garden of knowledge" of the "idle, spoiled child."[9]

The effects of this debate over the history of the French revolution are manifold and, in part, indirect. Within the Marxist field, naturalism reconsolidates an orthodox use of historical materialism, and along with it the traditional modes of doing the history of the French Revolution that are generally criticized by Sartre, even if there are exceptions. Régine Robin thus reexamines the concept of the bourgeois Revolution in her dissertation on French society, and instead of rejecting it, she invents the notion of the "Ancien Régime's Bourgeoisie." She thereby takes seriously the conjuncture as lived but overdetermined (hence, far from Sartre), and the structure of language (thus assuming proximity to Lévi-Strauss and especially Saussure). Outside the Marxist field, Lévi-Strauss's critique disqualifies the object "French Revolution" as an object of knowledge which interests all of humanity, as Kant and Fichte conceived of it. Indeed, while it is of interest to the French, or even Westerners, this object is inappropriate for the rest of the world. With the French Revolution reassigned to one specific culture, reflection on the singular-universal of the event—including its dimension of inaugural democracy produced by the affirmation of the rights of man and citizen—becomes entirely unavailable.

And the unpredictable effects of this unavailability are noticeable up to today. "Postcolonial" or "Subaltern Studies" refuse to take into account the political conflictuality of the Revolutionary period. These fields fold the event into a discourse of pure imperialist ethnocentrism without any desire to grasp that the current fights were already those of the revolutionaries. In fact, if there is still a revolutionary myth, this hasty dismissal has left it to be taken over by the right as a liberal and Western myth.

It is on this point that Foucault's discourse in the public space played an important role. He made the French Revolution a detestable object, ethnocentric, Franco-French, let us say a little bit of disgusting Western good conscience. But beyond this moral disqualification, he was the first in the 1960s outside the terrain of Marxism to have radicalized Lévi-Strauss's critique and nullified the value of the object both politically and

---

9 Friedrich Nietzsche, *Untimely Meditations*, ed. Daniel Braezeale, trans. R. J. Hollingdale (Cambridge: Cambridge University Press, 2007), 205. "We need history, certainly, but we need it for reasons different from those for which the idler in the garden of knowledge needs it, even though he may look nobly down on our rough and charmless needs and requirements. We need it, that is to say, for the sake of life and action, not so as to turn comfortably away from life and action, let alone for the purpose of extenuating the self-seeking life and the base and cowardly action."

Conclusion   215

epistemologically. Adopting Lévi-Strauss's idea of cold history and choosing the regime of science over the regime of truth, he produces a new way of doing history that can completely dispense with the notion of the event, in the Sartrean sense of an event of freedom. The history of the French Revolution as such finds no place in this new way of doing a science of the past. It is then that a discursive formation begins which seeks to combat Marxism, history as humanism (Foucault wishes, like Lévi-Strauss, for the death of Man with a capital *M*), and the history of the French Revolution as a privileged site for what appeared henceforth as a bygone era. With Foucault, history is "revolutionized" as Paul Veyne[10] puts it, or rather it "disappears" as a type of narrative, as Sartre bitterly complains. For Sartre, Michel Foucault's *The Order of Things* embodies what he calls the "refusal of history."[11] In this respect, he ushers in what François Hartog observes in his book *Believing in History*,[12] at a moment when the message seems to have been heard: we no longer believe in it. History, more often than not, is no longer done with a view to its usefulness for life, and no longer allows one to project oneself into a desirable future.

The last step of the process is then driven by François Furet's artful synthesis. We must study the French Revolution, he maintains, but study it like we would any sequence in history: recognize that it belongs to a bygone era which no longer generates conflicts, that it produced cultural achievements to be inventoried, and that it indeed belongs to cold history, that of objects which do not create contradiction and conflicts but must nevertheless be studied. In other words, the Revolution is "over."

Things got complicated, however, because Foucault did not stop there. In 1983, when the development of a certain science-history might have made one believe that the account of the Revolution was settled, he sets another discourse in motion, that of an interminable revolution. It is interminable not because of how it materially persists, but because of what it perpetually attests to: an "enthusiasm" for the Revolution, always virtually reborn.

In the time separating this moment from his earlier dismissal of the Revolution, there were two notable developments: his intellectual reporting on the Iranian revolution and counterrevolution, and his declaration that Sade is but a "sergeant of sex." And in fact, the question of enthusiasm, which is Kant's question, intersects at that time with the question, within psychoanalysis, of Sade. While Foucault always keeps psychoanalysis at a

---

10 Paul Veyne, *Comment on écrit l'histoire suivi de Foucault révolutionne l'histoire* (Paris: 1971).
11 "Jean Paul Sartre répond," *L'Arc*, no. 30 (1966): 87.
12 François Hartog, *Croire en l'histoire* (Paris: Flammarion, 2013).

distance, he shares with it an interest in Pasolini's identification of Sade with fascism.

Yet the disqualification of the Revolutionary period then took another turn. It is no longer just reproached for being Western-centric, but for being the proto-totalitarian matrix of totalitarianism. Yet Foucault, when he underscores the persistence of enthusiasm for the Revolution, does not do so in the sense of enthusiasm for totalitarianism, but the opposite.

So it was necessary to reject two intertwined discourses: one that made Sade a revolutionary hero, starting with the surrealists in the literary field and another that equated Kant and Sade (beginning with Adorno and Horkheimer), obscuring the role of enthusiasm and the emotions—of the inconceivable or the conceptually non-reducible—in Kant. This last thread made the Kantian law an apparatus of cruelty analogous to the laws of the Marquis de Sade. In 1960, Lacan undid this confusion. Against an apathy that he locates in Sade and the Kant of the *Critique of Practical Reason*, he demonstrates the moral force of the art of "desiring," and therefore of the art of not being apathetic, and connects this art of desiring to the question of the law. It would appear to me, however, that this has not been understood in the field of psychoanalysis. It is also striking that this art of desiring well, with Kant and against Sade, did not immediately reverberate in the judgment of the revolutionary moment, that the link was not made between the later Foucault and the Lacan of *The Ethics of Psychoanalysis*.

Proof of this oversight can be found Jacques Derrida's text "Psychoanalysis Searches the States of Its Soul: The Impossible Beyond of a Sovereign Cruelty,"[13] in which he highlights the proximity of the birth of law and the historical experience of the "worst cruelties." In the course of such reasoning, the French Revolution and the Shoah end up on the same plane of cruelty. He thus evokes

> An enormous, bottomless memory where the worst cruelty, the cruelty of a paregicide[14] that still remains to be thought, the cruelty of the Terror, the cruelty of the death penalty on a massive scale, the cruelty of all the tortures and executions in the aftermath of the 1917 revolution, the still open list of the most relentless cruelties, Shoah, genocides, mass deportations, and so forth, go side by side indissociably, as if the two processes were inseparable, with the invention of human rights, the foundation of the grounds of modern international law undergoing

---

13 Jacques Derrida, "Psychoanalysis Searches the States of Its Soul: The Impossible Beyond of a Sovereign Cruelty," in *Without Alibi*, ed. and trans., Peggy Kamuf (Stanford: Stanford University Press, 2002).

14 Derrida shortens "patri-regicide."

transformation, from which derives the condemnation of crimes against humanity (imprescriptible in France since 1964), the condemnation of genocide, as well as the promise, beginning on 4 Brumaire of year IV, made by the Convention, to abolish the death penalty in the French Republic.[15]

Suggesting proximities without specifying them lends itself to confusion. Psychoanalysis, he tells us, has not worked on them, but he does not take stock of Lacan's work on ethics, which is situated precisely between the law, cruelty, and apathy. Moreover, he makes no historical or philosophical distinctions within these apparent proximities, which are singular and cannot be collapsed. It was not the Nazis who invented international laws prohibiting crimes against humanity, but rather their enemies, who did so by retrieving the crime of *lèse-humanité* from the Revolutionaries themselves. And it is these revolutionaries who invented the rights of man and citizen and had to wage a cruel battle against those who refused them, including this "father-king." If there is indeed "a" cruelty of psychoanalysis, there are nevertheless "cruelties" in history, which are differentiated precisely by the mode of proximity or contradiction maintained with the Law and not with jurists. Once again, how can "paregicide" and the Shoah be placed on the same list? How can the quest for the rights of man and the desire for the capacity to restrain violence before it is experienced as a necessity simply neighbor their negation by the Third Reich?[16]

The damage done to the thought of this revolutionary invention by the claim that it is the "matrix of totalitarianisms" has yet to be fully appreciated, but the most worrisome effect is a relativism that awaits anyone with the audacity to reference the universality of revolutionary right (*droit révolutionnaire*).

Conceptions of the Revolution that are emancipated from this utterance have been, as we have shown, available for some time, but the discursive formation that it inaugurated at the end of the 1970s continues to create a strange patch of fog.[17]

During the years of the bicentenary, if the conflict was thunderous, its ins and outs were veiled to a novice researcher like me. I would now like to return to this veiling and to what made it possible, not in order to unveil this fantom history—so much had Sartrean philosophy become unavailable—but to get out of the prisons of a scientism which had become, and

---

15 Derrida, "Psychoanalysis Searches the States of Its Soul, 266.
16 Paul-Laurent Assoun's final book, *Tuer le mort*, also suggests this filiation, with the same confusion of epochs and stakes.
17 "une drôle de nappe de brouillard."

still seems to me to be the current "good conscience" of history in general and of the history of the Revolutionary period in particular.

BEING MODERN AT THE SORBONNE

Starting out (in 1986) as a young historian of the Revolutionary period in the bicentenary years plunged me into a battlefield where I knew little of the protagonists or the contours. I felt it, but only very imperfectly knew it. For my undergraduate degree, I had chosen a renowned history faculty on the left, and for my master's degree I discovered a place—The Institute for the History of the French Revolution—that was piloting the scientific project of the bicentenary, with Michel Vovelle as its head and with a focus on a way of doing history using a distinctly French kind of discourse analysis. This methodology was then supported institutionally by the Saint-Cloud laboratory. But Jacques Guilhaumou, whom Françoise Brunel had advised me to contact, encouraged me above all to read Régine Robin's book *History and Linguistics*, as well as the works he had coauthored with Robin and Denise Maldidier. Another trio—Jacques Guilhaumou, Françoise Brunel, and Florence Gauthier—held a seminar, "Philosophy and Revolution," at the European Research University, which I also frequently attended.

This seminar functioned as a kind of dissent from the Sorbonne, an institution inherited from the Soboul period and which brought together various historians, from the most classic to the most critical of the so-called Jacobin tendency, as well as Michel Vovelle's many students. While attending the major seminar, this dissent took the form of advocating a return to the texts, to discourse analysis, and placed significant emphasis on the confrontation of the revolutionary event and the philosophical arguments drawn from the Revolution itself and from its immediate contemporaneity. Robespierre, Locke, Mably, Kant, and Fichte. The rift between the old guard and the moderns thus found another form. It sometimes led to what struck me as opposing places. Jacques Guilhaumou, in an article published in *Espaces Temps* in 1992,[18] was able to assert that "the most fruitful advance has been made by François Furet, Marcel Gauchet, and Mona Ozouf,"[19] referring then to the *Critical Dictionary of the French Revolution*. And yet he would deplore that the latter were only interested in the "speech of the assembly," excluding the "spokesperson" "for the crime of excessive

---

18 Jacques Guilhaumou, "L'argument philosophique en histoire. Le laboratoire Révolution française," *Espaces Temps* 49, no. 1 (1992): 150–61.
19 Ibid., 154.

activism."[20] I understood very late that there was in fact a methodological alliance between supposed moderns.

In each of these milieus, my generation of historians found something to nourish a solid historiographical, methodological, and theoretical reflection. But there were also lacunae that we did not suspect. Above all, it seemed to me that our discussions carefully avoided being confronted with what had in fact bothered me most: the effective disqualification that the French Revolution was undergoing in the public sphere in the midst of the bicentenary. When I expressed concern about it, I was told, "It will pass." Today, when I seek to understand those years, more often than not I am told, "It's over." Was the bicentenary a trial without a subject? With regard to the historiographical and political process which led to either the disqualification or to the banalization of the object "French Revolution," did it really occur with thinking and opining subjects, even though the television and radio sets never emptied? The notion of the "system" which outstrips the individual made it possible to relinquish all responsibility except scientific responsibility, with science considered as a practice requiring a distance bordering on desubjectivation, a practice requiring intelligence and accumulated knowledge, but not the consciousness of the historian.

It was extremely strange for me, especially since—for the study of the Revolutionary period—the philosophical reflexivity of the actual actors and the analysis of their spoken interactions entailed the valorization of each thinking subject as creating their own interpretation of the event, producing viewpoints and desires. With regard to history, there did exist at the time a valorization of intersubjective communication in the manner of Habermas. But understanding revolutionary actors was assumed to be incapable of producing any schemas of action in the present. The scholar had to stay out of the fray. The watchword was distancing oneself in relation to the situation, "as is the role of the man of science," Lévi-Strauss would say, and "modern" masters would repeat.

After listening for a long time to such prescriptions with confusion, I told myself that perhaps I did not have the disposition of a true scientific historian. If science necessitated such a withdrawal, then I would write books for the public arena and not scholarly articles. I was a teacher, I would teach, and I would write. This is where I was when I was saved by three new intellectual interventions, three readings which answered my questions and relieved me of these torments.

---

20 Ibid.

RÉGINE ROBIN, JACQUES RANCIÈRE, NICOLE LORAUX: THREE READINGS

The first reading is that of Régine Robin in *Le Roman mémorial*.[21] This book reflected on the contemporary purpose of history in its supposedly dangerous connections with memory. Her aim in this regard was twofold: to show that memory and history could not be separated so simply, and that history is a specific part of social memory. But it was also to refuse the creation of well-marked identities, the weight of the symbolic, rationalizing legitimations, comfortable identifications. She offered it to me before I left for Montreal, where I would join her at a laboratory of discourse analysis and socio-criticism of texts that she had just created with Marc Angenot. But if she had helped me in this desire for a change of scene, she had also told me that she no longer worked on discourse analysis, and that what interested her now was the writing of history. What was at play in this shift of interests was what she called the very impossibility of history, because no matter what we do, the real resists all interpretation. The past is never what one believes it to be. Writing history is the fabrication of retrospective order and always distorts the true, because the latter is unknowable. There was thus a reconceptualization of the division which opposed regimes of meaning to regimes of scientificity, in favor of an interrogation of the order of narratives, whether or not they are capable of glimpsing this inaccessible real. What is required to do history is "the historian's imaginative slippage," which allows her to in fact assume her incompleteness, to affirm this while refusing to maintain a clear position which distinguishes the archival referent from what the scholar does with it. The scholar should recognize that she is able to pose good questions, but not always able to answer them.

Régine Robin had also called for working toward a certain deconstruction of the subject, either complete or completely absent for the historian, against what she called a "shameful positivism." Fiction, she claimed, can be more rigorous than history. To work in this way is not to abandon the rationality of knowledge, but to change the historian's approach with regard to the archive, the constitution of bodies of work, methodologies and analyses to be implemented, with a view to the textual productions which would flow from this work. In fact, she hoped for the historian to become a critical and committed intellectual (*intellectual engagé*) through this reflection on writing. She wished for an ironic, uneasy historian, who would give the critical function a genuine existence in society without

---

21 Régine Robin, *Le Roman mémoriel* (Montréal: Le Préambule, 1989).

taking themselves to be a social spokesperson. By accepting discomfort, uncertainty, even intellectual torment, the historian would be confronted with their ethics, and would not allow themselves to use a compass given in advance. They would be "out of place" and have to construct their bearing with what I now call "sensible reason." Similar to that of revolutionaries, it is a reflexivity tied to a sensible experience of the world, to a position in the world.

This reading permitted all questions and made it possible for commitment to occupy an important place, at least on the critical side, far from the illusions of a true science. It had a freeing effect on me, which made me want to continue my training, since I had started by reading the Régine Robin of 1973; and now the Régine Robin of 1989 was encouraging me to break certain ties. It was exciting yet reassuring.

This question of writing of and of deconstruction was shared at the time by the whole current of post-structuralism, notably by Derrida in philosophy and Clifford Geertz in anthropology. But with Régine Robin, we were not doing "French Theory," but engaged in an inextricably intellectual and personal quest in which the mourning for a generalized theory of the world and for a certain use of Marxism made it necessary to attempt partial configurations (*bricolages partiels*) and all sorts of critical experimentations—in a rigorous way. And all of this took place in the field of history. It was rare and remains so.

The second transformative reading was Jacques Rancière's *The Names of History*. He defended the idea of the historian's triple contract: scientific, political, and poetic. The objective was to reconnect with the tradition of an ambitious historical discourse, one that is reconciled with itself as an art of narrative, open toward the world and with the hope of acting on it. These were close to Régine Robin's concerns. Historical science should neither be made to renounce the tricks of literature, nor made to reject the historian's political contract. As for science, it had to be seized anew, with a regime of truth and meaning which would be constituted by literature itself. Far from statistical tools, information technology, and the laws of large numbers and anonymity, we should be concerned with literary procedures, narrativizing, metaphor, the operation of translating archives through the author's writing. Therein lies the historian's science. The historian should assume the burden, one could even say the command, of making the archive and its mute testaments speak. To this end, Jacques Rancière had analyzed Michelet's recounting of the Festival of the Federation on July 14, 1790, and showed that it is not always useful to reproduce the words in the archive. The invention of federations is legible in the materiality of preserved documents, ribbons, and embellished writings giving meaning to the "dull accounts of federation festivals." According to Rancière, Michelet does not mislead the reader through his narrative, since he announces that he is speaking about what he has seen and not what he has read. He speaks from his gaze, and that gaze has seen "love in fraternization." Michelet designates this effective historical operation: it is staging (*mise en scène*). The historian, through an invented but typical story, transmits the meaning of the federation festivals.

For Rancière, these questions were absolutely connected with the historiography of the Revolutionary period. He showed that the refusal of meta language, that is to say, the refusal to use non-reflexive interpretive categories, leads to a revisionist conception of history. According to Rancière, the desire in Alfred Cobban's work to liquidate words and notions deemed improper for interpreting the French Revolution entails the denial of the of the event itself.

I was relieved and critical at the same time. The notion of contract implied contracting parties. As a contract of enunciation, the narrative contract assumed, on the one hand, the subjective assumption of the position of the historian—an author who would explicitly assume their position is substituted for the quasi-anonymous scientist who hides behind their apparatus (*dispositif*). On the other hand, it presupposes a subject-reader, a reader ready to take on non-answers, non-knowledges, and non-places, a reader who would no longer be the consumer of a lesson or a body of knowledge, but the historian's interlocutor. I felt that there was a great risk of seeing an impoverished interpretation of the narrative contract substituted for any poetic ambition, that it might lead to a simple return to storytelling.

I was also stunned. Should taking an interest in the question of the historian's languages lead once again to forgetting the languages of the archive as an object of historical work? The discrepancy between "the dull stories of federations" and the love attested to by the materials seemed to me to be the historical object of today. To do this history, the history of silent or stuttering testaments, the archive should not be stored in a cabinet. The excess of words is badly apportioned (*mal partagée*) speech, undivided speech. To take the place of these voiceless social formations was, it seemed to me, to redouble this lack of apportionment. How can we ensure that the invention which goes through words belongs one day to the voiceless? What civic political speech can do without invention? It was also necessary to acknowledge that the invention of the world could go through other modes of representation, and to analyze the conflicts between these different modes of representation. It seemed important to me to try to understand how a society or social formation is informed and formed by languages and gestures, and in this way avoid placing the archives in a cabinet.

The historian could not once again become the great magical translator of lost or fragile voices. What gives force to these voices is the timeliness of what they transmit, even in their absence. I thought that there were no other possibilities, today, than simply agreeing to speak of absence, of incompatibility or loss, as one accepts to bring the contemporaneity of our fissures to bear on the work of subjectivation. Finally, if the genuine curiosity of the historian continues to lead to the precipices of time and death, to reach these edges and lead his interlocutors to them, the historian must first walk along safer paths, those of the representable and of partial descriptions, multiplied beams and discontinuity of light. Along these paths, there was still much to absorb and to learn, because in order to assume the precipices of time and of death, assuming the political contract, it was worth it to arrive there with the audacity of one who knows that they must now confront the void, with the innocence of recklessness.

What would ground the value of historical discourse today, in my view, was not only the explicit assumption of a subject position, but a demanding search for an adequacy between the regimes of truth adopted, the objects and questions dealt with, the sources used, the doubts accepted but limited, and above all, the aim of the project. If history could be flawed from the point of view of the political contract, it is undoubtedly because of its inability to say for whom and for what it is speaking, its having lost itself in the obviousness of an institution and comfort in the foundering description instead of circling the problem it sought to solve.

These questions would be posed in a masterly way by Nicole Loraux a few months later in the spring of 1993, in her great article "The Praise of Anachronism in History."[22]

I was advised to read this by a colleague who found that I lacked prudence in desiring to bring up the war in the former Yugoslavia in a chapter on revolutionary fraternity. However, far from leading me to be more cautious, as my interlocutor had hoped, she enabled me to take on what Nicole Loraux called "the audacity of being a historian." Up to this time, that audacity had not altogether avoided fueling concern. The historical real, if the historian accepts hearing it, signals what cannot be transposed from one era to the next without remainder. The worry would not go away, but thanks to this encounter, would be quieter.

---

22 Nicole Loraux, "Éloge de l'anachronisme en histoire, " *Le Genre humain*, Paris, Seuil, 1993.

After an extremely precise work of discourse analysis thematizing the foreigner in Year II, work which had made me taste the joys of radical historicism, a single statement had come to interrupt an approach that was too self-assured. It came from article 7 of the law of August 3, 1793, on foreigners: "Those who obtain a certificate of hospitality will be required to wear a tricolor ribbon on their left arm, on which the word 'hospitality' will be written, along with the name of the nation in which they were born."[23] Certainly, it was about hospitality and perhaps even honor, since the distinctive marker was associated with the three colors, but foreigners could not avoid it and were required to show their identity in social space. And as for those who had not obtained hospitality certificates, they had to leave the territory . . . . And then this identity linked to place of birth, the impossibility of dispensing with this contingency of birth in favor of the subjective appropriation of the event of the French Revolution . . . . Reading this article of law in the course of perusing the large volumes of the *Parliamentary Archives* imposed new necessities on the historian of the French Revolution that I was. Continuing to work on the history of the notion of the foreigner during the French Revolution meant taking the risk of mourning, mourning for a historical out-of-place (*hors-lieu historique*) embodied by this Revolution, mourning for a perfect model that would only have been betrayed, for a time when it would have been enough simply to dip into it so as to invent a better politics in the present, a present politics made up of charters, undocumented migrants, and confusion.

Henceforth, I carried out my work by taking seriously the gap between the emotional reactions that certain Revolutionary statements would elicit today—reactions of indignation, even disappointment and incomprehension among those who had been fascinated by this Revolutionary period—and the insistent feeling that it was doubtless not necessary to get ahead of ourselves. Consider the project announced by Saint-Just, the project of founding a city (*cité*) that is "one people, in friendship, with hospitality and fraternity." It would be taken as a merely ideological and manipulative statement and would have led to renouncing the work that was only just beginning. It was necessary to control this disavowal, to control the anachronism of the sensible in politics, without masking the difficulties with the object to be studied.

Nicole Loraux's article put my methodological intuitions into words, intuitions which had imposed themselves on me as necessities

---

23 See my book: Wahnich, *L'Impossible citoyen, l'étranger dans le discours de la Révolution française* (Paris: Albin Michel, 1997), reprinted in the collection "Évolution de l'humanité." 2010.

that were difficult to think and which presented themselves, so to speak, "all reflected" in the first-person narration of the singular journey of a renowned historian. As a result of it, I was able to resume the narration of the delights of this reading, in which "the present is the most effective motor of the drive to understand" for certain historians. It is an effective motor for reasons that are not all institutional, but have to do with "psychic and intellectual structure." Thus, my emotions in front of article 7 of the law on foreigners were no longer something to hide but something to explicitly assume, something present in my relation to the present, at least to my present as affected by a proximate past: the past of the Second World War in France. These historians, continued Nicole Loraux, "perhaps addressed themselves to the most distant past only to better guarantee the possibility of a good distance between their object and their affects."[24]

Emphasizing the role of these affects as "question shifters" (*embrayeurs de questions*) was not without consequence on the general discipline. If it was not a question of asserting that only this relation to affects as a relation to the present made it possible to develop the field of historical studies, it was indeed a question of pluralizing the ways of doing history, of constructing its objects and inscribing them in the social and political field. Anachronism as a relationship to the present and to affects proposed to offer a new place for the past and could profoundly transform the challenges of the discipline and the choices of objects that could be constituted there.

How can we think the connection between distinct desires for knowledge that came to clash and collide with one another?

What I had understood from this "work in a regime of anachronism" proposed by Nicole Loraux seemed to me to engage not only those famous historians of antiquity but the whole of their historical field and the function they wished either to claim or refuse in society, including in its dimension of political society. Indeed, the questions and affects of ancient historians that Nicole Loraux evoked were political affects, provoked by political positions: Jean-Pierre Vernant, confronted with the Community Party of the 1960s, working on the question of "debate and the free confrontation of opposing ideas"; Pierre Vidal-Naquet investigating the question of the citizen army through the Athenian hoplite after the experience of the Algerian war; Nicole Loraux who, faced with the amnesty of Paul Touvier and the ostensibly provocative interview with Darquier de Pellepoix, former commissioner "for Jewish questions," analyzes the amnesty

---

24 Loraux, "Éloge de l'anachronisme en histoire."

from the Thirty Tyrants of Athens carried out "by the victorious democratic resistance fighters."

In 1993, the end of grand, organizing narratives was hailed by many as a relief. Few would allow themselves to admit that there is also loss in this manner of settling accounts over the politicization of the discipline of history. To say that major works are born out of a committed relation to politics was therefore far from trivial. It clearly meant going against the tide and offering a new way of thinking the politicization of historical objects, because this relationship to the present not only poses questions which invest the past with meaning in view of the present, but also guarantees a return toward the present "ballasted" with new knowledge from of the past. "Everything is not absolutely possible when one applies questions of the present to the past, but we can nevertheless experiment with anything on the condition of always being conscious of the angle of attack and the intended object. The fact remains that, working in the regime of anachronism, there is undoubtedly more to be learned from the approach which consists in returning to the present ballasted by problems from the past."[25] Anachronism entails "doing history tied to the present." Historicism would be but one tool for presenting the present. This claim is not entirely new, and Nicole Loraux cites Marc Bloch. In another register, we could also reference Henri Irénée Marrou or Georges Duby as progenitors of this tendency. The carving out of historical objects is almost always partly tied to the historian's present, but most often reluctantly, forcing us to later reconstruct the *Zeitgeist* that led them to produce their work. What Nicole Loraux proposed was to take this constraint seriously and elucidate it through this approach of "controlled anachronism." However, this approach is not simply a first step, but a reflexive to-and-fro which requires a very precise knowledge of the period of which one is a specialist, so as to make it an effective mirror of the present. We could also call it an effective reserve of "analagons" to be analyzed and deepened in the search for new questions to pose to the present.

This way of carving out historical objects is antipodal to work based on a commemorative calendar, and to an academic division of time which is not marked by salient events which remain current but organizes itself through a "wise" periodization by century with one following the other in homogenous and empty time. With controlled anachronism, it is no longer collective memory that organizes the work, but rather the present insofar as it produces affects in the historian.

---

25 Ibid.

The present is vague. How should it be sorted? How does one grasp a pertinent object? This choice is no longer guaranteed by the institution but is the fruit of a lived subjective interrogation. It might be that of the historian described by Walter Benjamin, for whom "knowledge of the past [. . .] would resemble the act by which a memory is seized at the moment of sudden danger, a memory which saves him."[26] At this precise point, that of the "present of history," the encounter between history and politics becomes acute and determinative. If "the only time of politics is the present," history should not be "a hypostatized and ventriloqual knowledge, a positive automaton," but should once again become "material for a political knowledge." It is this material that the historian could have the ambition of providing. It is therefore less a question of establishing genealogies than of grasping analogous phenomena in their discontinuous modes of actualization. This would involve moving away from continuist (*continuiste*) and historicist narratives. It would mean giving up "establishing lineages, which presupposes self-sustaining phenomena, to reconstitute the precedents that each moment reactivates."[27]

The thesis was soon completed and had found, *in extremis*, an inscription in the field of historians as it was constituted. But it was still controversial, because if anachronism and the historian's affects had acquired a rightful place thanks to Nicole Loraux's courageous article, it remained in the fringes of the discipline. History as a discipline had been shaken by the "critical turn,"[28] by the debates which had pitted Jacques Rancière and his *The Names of History* against the many guardians of the temple. Historians reaffirmed, against the "linguistic turn," the persistent need for a scholarly and neutral language which did not risk leaking the news that historians are endowed not only with reason but with sensibility, with one just as much as the other determining their work. Finally, we will have understood that the price of this subjective politicization passes through two radical challenges to the historian's most established procedures and discourse.

The first radical challenge: the ambition of an imaginary totalization of historical works, whose summation would make it possible to account for the whole of a society's past, is replaced by an imaginary of the democratic prism. This prism is constituted by the multiplicity of viewpoints which are so many historiographical statements at the intersection of scholarship

---

26 Walter Benjamin, *Sur le concept d'histoire. Œuvres completes*. 435–36. Translator's rendering.
27 Bernard Lepetit, *Les Formes de l'expérience* (Paris: Albin Michel, 1995), 19. Translator's rendering.
28 *Annales, Économies, sociétés, civilisations. Histoire et sciences sociales, un tournant critique*. December, 1989.

and subjectivized social traditions. There is no longer a cumulative effect of knowledges but effects of shadow and light depending on the multiplicity of ways of making history play out in History. If the "drive to understand," so dear to Nicole Loraux but also to Georges Duby,[29] is always individual, it must find a network—implicit or explicit—among contemporaries, a space of expression and reception.

The second radical challenge: the division of historical time can no longer obey the sole rule of linear chronology. Analogical work leads to constructing relations between past and present, but also to confronting different pasts. It introduces a mode of reflection in which comparison pertains not just to space but to time. Of course, one cannot compare what does not present any intersection of political stakes, but we must, as Nicole Loraux says, postulate an "other time" which for Loraux is the time of the "passions" in their relation to power (*pouvoir*), or recurring time, the time of "the repetitive." It is a question, in her own terms, "of establishing the repetitive in the interstices of official historical time, in its returns, reversals, suspensions which give conflict its temporality." The historian's recognition of the value of the affects leads them to restore the passions to their function as a link between times. This link can be called "human nature," the "repetitive," or the "island of stillness"—it is time which "negates history" and which makes "the time of history." The temporal thread of narrative can no longer obey the same wise and linear rules. The return of narrativizing is then confronted with the question "How to recount this particular story?" To restore discontinuity and nonlinear causality, it is necessary to move away from the narrative regime specific to the novels of the nineteenth century and to privilege that of twentieth-century literature which rejects the "sticky paste capable of putting together meaning from any ruins."[30]

FANTOMS MAKE THEIR NESTS IN THE FRACTURES OF HISTORY: SARTRE AND MARX

Putting together meaning from any ruins[31]; that is where we are. How does one write the history of ruins? The ruins of certitudes, the ruin of totalizations, and of completeness. This is where we have to clear a path. But

---

29 Georges Duby, *L'histoire continue* (Paris: Fayard, 1989), and Guy Lardreau and Georges Duby, *Dialogues* (Paris: Flammarion, 1986).
30 Claude Simon, cited by Jacques Rancière, *Les Noms de l'histoire*, Paris, Seuil, 1992.202.
31 "*Bricoler du sens avec toute ruine.*"

before attempting to do so, I must come back to what now figures for me—and only recently, since I had not been familiar with it—as a missing, or repressed, or fantom object: the *Critique of Dialectical Reason*. Without this missing piece, it would not have been possible, in my view, to "rediscover" this subject of incompleteness, this time of controlled anachronism, this precariousness or discomfort of the critical position, composed of uncertainties. As for the mourning of totalizations, perhaps it should remain melancholic, that is to say, not be done completely. Régine Robin has often told me that "history in tatters is not history deconstructed." For her, the debacle of Marxism of her generation did not mean that there would not be the construction of a new edifice, but one could not yet identify its forms. And this edifice in Sartre's work was precisely not an edifice, because the totalization was as fluid as the situation, unfolding like lightning, a "beautiful risk" in the words of Robert Castel. This was the latter's title for the article he published in *L'Arc*, in the issue devoted to Sartre in 1966. For Robert Castel, with the *Critique of Dialectical Reason*, it was a question of "determining oneself in relation to a choice that engages the future of research."[32] If we did not want to let all positive knowledge scatter into multiple and heterogeneous knowledges, it was first necessary to try to think synthesis, and this is where the "beautiful risk" theorized by Sartre in the *Critique* lies: initiating a thought of syntheses without certitudes, but as a way of envisioning free thought which would seek by this effort to escape its own conditioning. For the subject of this effort was no longer that of Cartesian thought. The Sartrean subject of the *Critique* is incomplete because they are governed by the material they produce, the famous practico-inert, and by counter-praxis, the work of the unforeseeable, of the negative, even when their acts are "emancipated"—that is to say, even when they are no longer a simple element of a series, but a member of a fused or pledged group. The Sartrean subject is not the all-powerful subject of nineteenth-century transcendental metaphysics. This is a false accusation that has been brought against him, and many commentaries on this remain to come.

Yet the Sartrean subject did not possess this precarious, decentered, initiating freedom—which is freedom nonetheless—as a simple individual. The reconquest of this freedom could only take place in the rare moments when a collectivity of people, serialized by the inertia of the practico-inert, was transformed into a group-in-fusion, described at length in the *Critique* through the example of the storming of the Bastille. Freedom cannot be reconquered except through the collective act of freeing oneself. It is an

---

32 Robert Castel, "Le beau risqué," *L'Arc*, no. 30 (1966): 26.

effort, but the situation is unstable, and to maintain this effort, the effort itself must be alienated in an oath, thereby producing a pledged group, bound by an Oath to remain free. Then, through a "free praxis" and not through an external action exerted on the fused group, exigency is born. Free praxis is maintained under the condition of this collective where each is the guarantor of freedom vis-à-vis the other, and thus historically responsible for the possibility of remaining free. Freedom would therefore only ever be revolutionary. And this is why the history of the French Revolution is so important in the reflection. To do this history is always already to produce a partial totalization of major significance for anyone interested by freedom in history.

Would Nicole Loraux have needed the concept of controlled anachronism, or would she have thought in terms of the dialectic of times if this mode of temporalization, far from the eternal arrow of linear progress, had been taken into account as early as the 1960s? Is Sartre's dialectical time so different from controlled anachronism when Sartre takes up the fundamental critique of capitalist time as homogenous and empty? Is it a coincidence that the examples chosen by Nicole Loraux take place in the configuration of the 1960s and 1970s when she is writing in 1993? Vernant, 1962, Vidal-Naquet, 1968, and for Nicole Loraux herself, the Paul Touvier affair in 1972. Is her historicism really something other than Sartre's imperative to analyze situational details? Or, conversely, is not Sartre's demand, when he evokes the dialectical leap, to allow questions from the present drive the work, to work with the greatest rigor and intensity on materials from the past and to return to the present through this dialectical leap, a demand for the "risky bet." Is Nicole Loraux's famous "audacity" audacity as a historian but also indissociably civic and political audacity, perhaps the dialectical leap? Does Sartre not declare that all scholarly knowledge of situations, like the practical knowledge of situations, is in fact impossible to achieve perfectly and in a stabilized way? Does this observed movement not resemble the work of history in the democratic age, made of "multiple paths with unforeseen intersections" in Rancière's words, and Régine Robin's wager that fictional writing might catch sight of the real?

Certainly, the incomplete subject for Régine Robin, as for Nicole Loraux, is the one brought to light by psychoanalysis and not only the practico-inert and counter-praxis. Doubtless, this critique of linear time in Nicole Loraux does not owe its power solely to the critique of progress but to the discovery of the functioning of the time of the unconscious. Yet along this path, what returns are social modalities of being in the world, which for Sartre would fall under the practico-inert. "Fields of immobile times" could be another name for the "indissoluble past in the present," even if the question of the denial of conflict in Nicole Loraux offers this indissoluble character a strong and specific explanation. But this ultimately ties in with Sartrean concerns: What could not be dialectized by the subject or by the collective remains immobile, unsubmitted to the work of developing contradictions. The fields of immobile times would offer another explanation of "cold" or stagnant history, without the subjects of history having to take charge of it.

Of course, I am well aware that perhaps I, in turn, am inventing a "sticky paste" to hold things together after a period of dejection. But the ways of rethinking the production of knowledge, far from the institutional fortresses of scholarly and scientific "good conscience" in the 1990s, seem to me to be returning to the path abandoned because of the so-called structuralist critique, the path of the Sartrean proposition to renew the "unsurpassable philosophy of our time"—Marxism. This is evident in Régine Robin, who never denied the joy that reading Althusser had given her. She had, moreover, written an article with Jacques Guilhaumou, in an issue of *Dialectiques* devoted to Althusser, titled "Identity Rediscovered," in which they explained that Althusser had in fact made it possible to better live incompleteness and the division of the subject, to discover the right to make mistakes, end self-censorship and reunite with the taste for writing.

Michel Vovelle has always battled with ideology in his work on representations of death, the role of the festival, and on de-Christianization. In 1986 he gathered his reflections in a volume titled *Ideologies and Mentalities*, in which he pleaded for a "study of complex, dialectical mediations between men's real lives and their collective imaginary which aims, beyond the discourses and the religiosity of the elites, at the knowledge of the anonymous masses."[33] He then affirmed the need for a conceptualized history. Jacques Rancière had participated with Althusser in the theoretical enterprise of *Reading Capital*, published in 1965. In his chapter, "The Concept of Critique and the Critique of Political Economy from the '1844 Manuscripts' to 'Capital,'" at least two subheadings signal what was to come: "Critical Discourse and Scientific Discourse," and "The Enchanted World." Finally, Nicole Loraux, too, is nourished by this question of ideology, and it is in fact the basis of her dissertation, defended in 1977.[34] Loraux had focused on the notion of ideology and false consciousness in order to apply it to the ancient world through the analysis of a very particular literary

---

33 Michel Vovelle, *Idéologies et mentalités*, 36.
34 Nicole Loraux, *L'Invention d'Athènes. Histoire de l'oraison funèbre dans la "cité classique"* (Paris: EHESS, 1981; Payot, 1993).

genre: funeral oration. Unlike Moses Finley, she did not believe that Athens was immune from all forms of alienation. The direct democracy of the *polis* does not prevent false consciousness. The critical tools that Marx had used to develop a critique of *The German Ideology* could therefore be used by historians to undermine the image that historiography had constructed of the oldest democracy.

It may sound strange to me now, but it took me a while to realize that far from being agnostic toward Marxism (*a-Marxist*), I was in fact a contraband Marxist. Orthodox Marxism was moribund around the time of the bicentenary, but if one of Sartre's prescriptions had finally succeeded, it was his insistence on the need to reinvent Marxism, or more precisely to invent other paths to its rediscovery.

Was Sartre necessary? Perhaps not in general for Marxism, or for history, even less for anthropology. But despite everything, on the history of the revolutionary period, I hope I have been able to show in these pages that he was not only a theoretical pioneer, but also able to provide real advances in the interpretation and understanding of events and actors, the comprehension of situations and what configures them. I believe in particular that on this subject, he opened the way to Marxist work on the sacred and the emotions, on the materiality of the conditions of the sacred, on what animates the passage from seriality to fusion. Finally, he invited us to work on this edge of death, when the institution of the pledge comes to immobilize the fused group.

I did not know when I set out to work on the emotions that the work would lead me to the sacred, and ultimately to the institution of the social and the political by civil institutions. Jean-Paul Sartre occupied, for me and no doubt for others, the place of a fantom. What had been evacuated with the repression of *The Critique of Dialectical Reason* would have to be found differently, but found nonetheless.

But it was both on the question of the writing of history and this precise point of revolutionary emotions that my disagreement (*différend*) with discourse analysis, which now seemed to me very scientific, widened. Not all Marxists were ready to consent to what Régine Robin, Jacques Rancière, and Nicole Loraux had invented, nor even to recognize them as avatars of Marxism in its contemporary development. As for those who no longer wanted to hear about Marxism at all, whatever forms it took, they watered down, simplified, and marginalized these strong ideas.

The shields produced against these were not then fundamentally different from those which had led to the foreclosure of Sartre and the object 'French Revolution' along with him. This is why it was important for me to go through the modalities of this repression, because they also produce repetition in Loraux's sense. This repetition takes the form of a historiographical apathy. Under the pretext not having a global theoretical model, theory itself is rejected; under the pretext of not doing militant history, the historian's point of view is evacuated, and the historical object is constructed in an arbitrary inventory. It is too often merely the sources, and the commemorative calendar, that guide the historian in their choice of subject, rather than the questions that torment them. The audacity of the historian exists, but only covertly because it has not been consolidated as a value in the profession. The scientific credit freely offered by Nicole Loraux's effort seems in part wasted. As for the writing, it is most often absent, bland and lacking intonation, a sort of transparent, desubjectivized enunciative absence. Roland Barthes, in *Writing Degree Zero* (1953), sees in it a style that denies literature, an "a-literary" writing, "an ideal absence of style." The historian thus declares that they absent, far from the questions asked by Régine Robin and Jacques Rancière.

CLEARING A PATH: AN APPEAL FOR ANOTHER HISTORY OF THE FRENCH REVOLUTION

Before closing this inquiry, I would, despite everything, like to state that these debates, so lively and conflictual, can today be grasped as laboratories having delivered tools forged precisely in this moment of crisis. They make it possible, today, to renew the field of history of the French Revolution, to reinvent this object 'French Revolution,' which I for my part am attempting to do.

In criticizing "vulgar Marxist" historiography, Jean-Paul Sartre invents a different perspective on revolutionary uncertainty. He helps us focus attention on the unpredictable moments when everything changes, and thus allows us to give new meaning to the event as such. This is the first important achievement which can be used in the analysis of current revolutions. Sartre helps us not give up on or reject the revolutionary character of an event too quickly because of its always uncertain character.[35]

It is then, at the moment when he grasps this uncertainty, that he reemphasizes the question of the sacred in politics, the religious-political link in what it allows and what it prohibits. Foucault would only pose this question when it came to the Iranian Revolution, but both allow us to

---

35 See our article, titled "Incertitude du temps révolutionnaire," *Socio*, no. 2, Paris (2013).

understand that the sacred is not simply a metaphor but is highly active in the revolutionary situation, and that the historian can assign themselves the task of grasping how the sacred and the emotions become continuous and fashion the revolutionary dynamic.[36]

Finally, by rediscovering the critique of capitalist time, Sartre makes the revolutionary object, as an object of history, a singular-universal that is always current because always actualizable (*actualisable*), provided our situation calls for it. Claiming the emancipatory force of the universal has always made it possible to forge a political ideal capable of mobilizing toward a utopian beyond. Far from being an empty and deadly abstraction, on the contrary, it allows futures which are yet to emerge in the present.

It is paradoxically by criticizing the mythical history of the French Revolution, and by making history a pure method without object, that Claude Lévi-Strauss ultimately invites us to reflect not only on the function of mythical thought in history but also on a certain poetics of thinking history. He thus leads us to question the modes of inter-articulation of the scientific method and myth and reluctantly opens up thoroughly interesting perspectives so that history does not become a politically dead knowledge. Once again, controlled anachronism reconciles scientific history and mythical history.

But it is also by criticizing an ethnocentric conception of history that he in fact invites us to no longer place the French Revolution at the center of universal history, nor even at the center of Western history. By forcing us to decenter both the Revolution and what he calls "hot" history in favor of the multiplicity of histories of all civilizations—equal in human dignity— he obliges us to account for "cold" history at the heart of revolutionary history, to seek to understand how French Revolutionary society avoids overheating and preservers in its project by creating a rituality (*ritualité*) of the irreversible.[37] With Claude Lévi-Strauss, the French Revolution risks becoming an object like any other, an object which would no longer be the necessary object to understand the history of Man with a capital *M*. But if he rejects the possibility of redeeming the transcendental illusion of collective freedom, he nevertheless flags the need to think the singularity of the affirmation of this desire for freedom. To this end, he helps re-singularize the object 'Revolution' on the side of this historical affirmation of freedom

---

36 These are important points that founded the work both in the work titled *La Liberté ou la mort. Essai sur Terror et le terrorisme* (Paris: La Fabrique, 2003), and in *La Longue Patience du peuple, 1792, naissance de la République* (Paris: Payot, 2008).

37 We have recently reexamined this ritual of appeasement in *Réfléchir les rituels dans la Révolution française*, ethnographiques.org, 2017.

which never stops re-virtualizing itself. He thus invites us, like the Foucault of 1983, to account for a singular-universal which is not an imperial universal that offers models to simply be emulated.

Finally, let us recognize that it is from having refused interest in the French Revolution that Foucault arrives at the Iranian Revolution without prejudice, and that he can grasp the fleeting event of insurrectional political spiritualism. He discovers what is, for him, a non-statist mode of thinking the revolutionary process, which interests us in our attempt to understand the political spiritualism of the French Revolution. It also allows him to rediscover Kantian enthusiasm, and to leave us a testament to infinite revolutionary virtuality.

As for the psychoanalysts, by questioning what is at play in cruelty, they have in fact allowed us to account for the psychic economy and the economy of drives proper to revolutionaries. They also invite historians to take the question of emptions within revolutionary phenomena seriously, as Sartre had done both in the *Critique* and in the unpublished texts on the French Revolution that preceded it. They too have therefore solicited us to renew historical investigations of the lived experience of revolutionaries. Their mode of critique affirms at least one thing: we must listen to the actors, know how to lend them another ear, provide them with another hearing, know how to re-subjectivize the analytical reception of revolutionary languages. But I believe that beyond this good advice, we should take their questions seriously, even and especially if we do not agree with their answers.[38]

It is a question of clearly understanding that the questions of emotions, affects, and aesthetics are not just thematic but epistemological questions. This is precisely what is at stake with Sartre and his awareness of the sacred inscribed in the materiality of situations, his awareness of emotions lived either individually or collectively, of the consciousness of death; with Foucault and Kantian enthusiasm; with Freud and Lacan; with Nicole Loraux and his strong work on the affects of historians and historical actors alike; with Régine Robin and Jacques Rancière and the question of committed writing. If there are thematic issues, they are those of cruelty, apathy, emotional dynamics, the borders of the sacred and holy civilities. Neuroscience tells us nothing about this, and the current alliance between the history of emotions and the history of the sciences appears to me as naturalistic

---

38 This is what I attempted to do in my article "La Révolution française au regard de 'Totem et Tabou,'" published in the electronic journal *Recherches en psychanalyse*, where I discuss Jacques André's book, *La Révolution fratricide*, which deconstructs the representation of a frigid and disembodied revolution.

wandering which will explain nothing about the way this supposed physiology—physis—manifests itself in history.

Thus, we have neither to return to Sartre nor to Lacan, neither to Foucault nor to anyone else. The movement of research does not take place through returns but through loops, misunderstandings, deliberate or unfortunate deformations, and by reappropriations which are always inventions and not returns.

If the bicentenary had fabricated a sober object, our political present had required reconstituting the French Revolution as a 'hot' object in Lévi-Strauss's sense, one which could be revisited in order to analyze current contradictions and furnish new tools, analyzers of the social and political situation in this moment when history for the purposes of life presupposes a "troubling history," as Régine Robin called it. As for methods and tools, some of them are a legacy of this sequence from 1960 to 1989 that was so critical of the object 'revolution,' while others are inherited from the sequence that followed, it too often overlooked.

It would then be a different revolution that would appear at the intersection of method and myth. Doubtless we could then take the measure of a legacy that is impossible to fix in place, forestalling the impulse of cold history to declare the end of history.

For the French Revolution is decidedly not a myth, it did exist. Contrary to what Georges Lefebvre told us in response to Cobban, it does not need to be mobilized the way Sorel's myth of the general strike does. It needs to educate and give courage, through a good critical history which looks at its impasses, and a good monumental history which reminds us that, yes, men have been free and that therefore, no doubt, they are able to be free once more. It must give courage in these times of dread when there is a desire to erase even the idea of reciprocal freedom, universality, and equality.

The Revolution is no longer a myth as Levi-Struass understood it, since it is now most often ignored, and where it is known, it no longer offers everyone schemas of action so that they might act from it without even thinking of it. Heroism has no model, Saint-Just would say. Let us say that today there are no longer any such models, and that is without doubt a good thing. However, this does not prevent us from making, with Aguste Balnqui and Walter Benjamin after him, the "tiger's leap" into the past, and from knowing that when we "pick up the scent of the present in the jungle of the past," it is imaginative reinventions that are at work and not caricatural reproductions. We can return, ballasted by good questions to pose and to put to work in the present, and thus question at the same time the revolutionary problems of our moment, what the Revolution has delivered to us as repetitive, unthought, denied, but also its chances in our own contexts—and what the self-reflection of past revolutions can offer to us as we continue the open path of emancipation.

Finally, no, the Revolution is not a myth in the sense that it would allow us to thoughtlessly maintain the model of representative Western democracy. Even if today this model is brittle, and if it may be the case that "revolutions are the act by which humanity, travelling on a train, pulls the emergency break,"[39] as Walter Benjamin thinks, we still have to know how to pull this break, how to become dissatisfied with merely noting that the legacy has become hardened. We must pore over this legacy in its minute details.

Histories of the French Revolution as pluralized, political, historical, and scholarly laboratories for our time will not be written with insipid writing but with pressing political and ethical questions in view, along with everyone's emotions, in touch with their time.

And who can claim to be in charge of this?

---

39 Walter Benjamin, *Notes préparatoires sur les thèses sur le concept d'histoire*, trans. M. de Gandillac (Paris: Denoël, 1971), 190. Translator's rendering.